SOCIAL SECURITY FOR THE OLD

About the Author

Professor A.B. Bose obtained his Master's and doctoral degrees in Social Work from the University of Lucknow. He worked as Director in the Ministry of Social Welfare, Government of India; Adviser, Social Development and Women's Programmes, Planning Commission; and Director, National Institute of Public Cooperation and Child Development. His last assignment was as Professor and Director in the Indira Gandhi National Open University. Professor Bose has been associated with ageing issues for about two and half decades, and has participated in a number of seminars and conferences in India and abroad. Also, he has worked as United Nations Adviser/Consultant on social development, including ageing issues, in developing countries.

Social Security for the Old

Myth and Reality

A.B. Bose

Published for
Centre for Public Policy & Governance
Institute of Applied Manpower Research
by
CONCEPT PUBLISHING COMPANY, NEW DELHI-110 059

Cataloging in Publication Data—DK
Courtesy: D.K. Agencies (P) Ltd. <docinfo@dkagencies.com>

Bose, A. B. (Anil Baran)
Social security for the old : myth and reality / A.B. Bose.
p. cm.
In Indian context.
Includes bibliographical references (p.   )
Includes index.
ISBN 8180692779

1. Social security—India. 2. Older people—Services for—India.
I. Title.

DDC 362.954   22

ISBN 81-8069-277-9

First Published 2006

© A.B. Bose

Published and Printed by
Ashok Kumar Mittal
Concept Publishing Company
A/15-16, Commercial Block, Mohan Garden
New Delhi-110 059 (INDIA)

Phones : 25351460, 25351794
Fax : 091-11-25357103
Email : publishing@conceptpub.com

Foreword

Demographic ageing, and its social and economic ramifications, have now become an important area of social concern. People are living longer. This trend is far more visible in the developed countries. It is now becoming more evident in the developing countries, too. Demographers have become more active in projecting the trends and the financial and social implications of social security measures under different assumptions. Policy makers who were more concerned with the problems of children and youth have now become busy diagnosing and analyzing the social services needs of the elderly population whose requirements are quite different. Since the problem of demographic ageing varies in different countries, policy measures carved to address their concerns are also of a different kind. Sustainability of social security measures and the means of financing them are an immediate cause of anxiety, particularly for the low income groups.

In 2001, India had a population of about 77 million persons of age 60 years and above which is projected to reach about 308 million in 2050. The percentage of population of age 60 years and above is expected to rise from 7.5 per cent in 2001 to 20.1 per cent in 2050. For developing countries like India this would mean a massive input of services by the State, the market, non-governmental organizations and other institutions of civil society. India is thus facing the twin problems of developing a large young human resource, and also provide for the ageing members of society. The changing composition of the ageing in the years to come will imply a much higher level of education and different aspirations in the post-retirement stage. They will look for a far more participatory approach in their governance.

Professor A.B. Bose, a Consultant with the Centre for

Public Policy and Governance was asked to make a study of the ageing of population in India based on secondary data and micro studies published in journals and reports. He has made a detailed demographic analysis of the ageing of population in India and in other regions, and given the trends in their demographic characteristics. He has studied the issues in financial security in old age among different segments of the population. He has emphasized that an increasingly large number of workers have to start early in life to save and invest for returns in old age, more so because of the changing structure of the family which makes it difficult for earning family members to bear the entire burden of looking after older persons, and that, too, for a far longer period. Measures currently undertaken by the State to provide financial security have been analyzed and discussed. New instruments of policy are necessary to make the measures more viable. The state alone cannot support the massive amounts needed for social security for all segments of the population.

India has made gains in ushering latest technology in health and medical care but this reaches only those who can pay the costs. Public health services have not been able to reach out to the poor, particularly older persons living in rural areas. Advances in medical care can become notional when the bulk of older persons are unable to access and utilize them. There is thus a challenging need in which the public and the private sector have to develop complementary roles. Institutions like cooperatives and subsidized health insurance need to be developed.

While health and income security are vital needs of old age, there are other areas, too, which are more of an abstract nature but provide important succour and support to the old. Family is the best institution for the care of the old. However, family support in the case of an increasingly large number of old persons is showing a decline due to the changing structure of the family. It is important that new forms of care are set up. Coping mechanisms of the family to take care of the old are also necessary through establishing a wide range of welfare services.

The Government of India announced a national policy on older persons in 1999. It has outlined the principal areas of intervention and action by various agencies including the individual, the family, the State, private sector, and institutions of civil society. It is important that the policy is implemented. The first ten years after age 60 years are a resource which the nation must find ways to utilize. It is in the later years that the dependency syndrome progressively increases.

Work on the project started when my predecessor Dr. H. Ramachandran was the Director of the Institute. I am thankful to him for choosing a subject of contemporary social interest. Now that the study has been completed, it is important that the issues raised in the book are widely disseminated for discussion and debate on an emerging problem.

(Shailendra Sharma)
Director
Institute of Applied Manpower Research

New Delhi

Preface

Demographic change has influenced all countries of the globe. The latter half of the twentieth century brought a visible increase in life expectancy. The twenty-first century will carry the transition further. The trends are visible in India, too. The post-60 phase of a person's life will cover a life span of self and spouse for about 15 to 20 years. Security for this period is a basic need. The challenge now is not only to add years to life but also life to the added years.

Population aged 60 years and above in India in 2001 was about 77 million. According to projections by the United Nations, India will have 20 per cent of its population aged 60 years and above in 2050. In numbers, it will mean over 308 million persons. India will need to cope with social security arrangements for these persons. Income, health, housing, family care, welfare and other needs have to be met. Early planning for security in old age has become an urgent need.

Developed countries, as their population was greying, were able to generate resources which helped the state to finance social security needs of the elderly. They also comprised an educated and articulate component of the electorate, and were able to convince the government that their social security needs must get due recognition. India has to face the challenge of arriving at a satisfactory mix of allocation of resources for development and for social security in old age. The myth that the family on its own can take full care of older persons is no longer true. Participation by individuals, families, the community, employers, the state, the market and institutions of civil society will be necessary to arrive at a sustainable system of social security for the aged. Lobbying on behalf of older persons, who comprise 13 per cent of the electorate, will be an important mode to convince all political parties that families are unable to cope with the financial, health and other needs of the elderly, and the state must step in with sizeable investment for social security of older persons.. The gross inequalities promoted by state policy in the care of the elderly, whereby only a small segment of government/quasi government employees get all the benefits, has to be substituted by a more just and humane policy covering the entire population. The National Policy on Older Persons, 1999 assured older persons that "their concerns are national concerns, and that they will not be unprotected, ignored or marginalized." Unfortunately, not much has happened because the bulk of older persons are illiterate, unorganized, dispersed and largely poor with no voice to pressurise political parties and the state.

The present study is based on secondary data collected from research reports, journals and official publications. Absence of good quality data on social security among different segments of the population, the gaps, and on the coping mechanisms of families have been a major problem. Most data collection systems in India, including official agencies, have shown little interest in generating data on social security needs, a vital necessity for planning and programming.

The study has five chapters . Chapter I gives demographic trends in the ageing of population and the magnitude. It examines the rates of growth in different age segments, the dependency ratios, and the gender dimensions. Comparisons have been made between the global scenario and India. Social characteristics of the aged population have also been discussed. Chapter II analyses the issues relating to financial security of different segments of the population. Public assistance provided in old age, capacity of persons in different economic categories to save for old age security, retirement benefits, pension plans and role of private sector have been analyzed . Chapter III discusses life expectancy trends in old age, and analyses incidence of mortality, morbidity and disability in old age. It indicates the roles of different providers of healthcare, viz., the state, the market, co-operatives and non-governmental organizations. Issues relating to health security needs of the aged have also been considered. Chapter IV describes the trends in security provided by family care, living arrangements of the elderly, the availability of shelter, protection of life and property, and the emerging problems of abuse of older persons. Chapter V analyses the evolution of the national policy on older persons. It gives a critique of its contents, problems faced in its implementation, and the steps that need to be taken to activate it.

I am grateful to Professor H. Ramachandran, Director, IAMR and the Centre for Public Policy and Governance for giving me the opportunity to carry out the study. He has provided valuable intellectual support. Discussions with him have given fresh insights. I am thankful to Dr. Shailendra Sharma who took over as Director from Prof. Ramachandran for giving the final clearance for publication of the study. I have benefited from interaction with a number of professional colleagues, prominent among them being Shri R.G. Mitra, Shri S.K. Sinha and Shri G.B. Panda. Shri Varun Kumar provided assistance for a brief period in collecting information from various offices and libraries. Shri S.P. Singh has painstakingly undertaken computer processing of data and typed the manuscript.

The views expressed are those of the author. It is hoped that the study will open up discussion and debate on social security needs of a growing segment of the population, particularly persons from lower income groups.

A.B. Bose

Contents

Foreword by **Shailendra Sharma**   v

Preface   ix
List of Tables   xiv
List of Figures   xix

1. Demography of Ageing   1

2. Financial Security in Old Age   48

3. Health Security   138

4. Security of Family Care and Shelter   202

5. Policy for Older Persons   233

   References   253

   Index   259

List of Tables

1.1 Population in more developed and less developed regions, 1950 to 2050   3

1.2 Expectation of life at birth in more developed and less developed regions, 1950-55 to 2045-50   5

1.3 Median age in more developed and less developed regions, 1950 to 2050   7

1.4 Percentage distribution of population by age groups in more developed and less developed regions, 1950 to 2050   8

1.5 Decadal increase in population in broad age groups in more developed and less developed regions, 1950-60 to 2040-50   9

1.6 Age distribution of population aged 60 years and above in more developed and less developed regions, 1950 to 2050   11

1.7 Dependency ratio in more developed and less developed regions, 1950 to 2050   13

1.8 Sex ratio (no. of females per thousand males) in the age group 60 years and above in more developed and less developed regions, 1950 to 2050   14

1.9 Percentage of population aged 60 years and above in India, China, Japan, Asia and the world, 2000 to 2050   16

1.10 Number and percentage of persons aged 60 years and above, India, 1901 to 2050   18

1.11 Expectation of life at birth, India, 1951-60 to 2045-50   20

1.12 Percentage of population in age groups 0-14 years, 15-34 years, 35-59 years, 60 years and above, India, 1951 to 2050   24

1.13 Decadal increase in population in different age groups, India, 1951 to 2050   26

1.14 Age distribution of persons aged 60 years and
above, India, 1961 to 2050   27
1.15 Dependency ratios, India, 1951-2050   29
1.16 Sex ratio in the older age groups, India,
1901 to 2050   30
1.17 Percentage distribution of rural and urban
population aged 60 years and above, India,
1961 to 2001   31
1.18 Percentage distribution of persons aged 60 years
and above by sex and marital status in rural and
urban areas, India, 1961 to 2001   32
1.19 Percentage distribution by age, sex and marital
status of persons aged 60-69 years, 70-79 years,
and 80 years and above, India, 1961 to 2001   35
1.20 Percentage distribution of persons aged 60 years
and above by sex and level of education, India
and states, 2001   39
1.21 Percentage of persons aged 60 years and above
in states, 2001   43
2.1 Distribution per 1000 of aged persons by state
of economic independence, India, 1986-87
and 1995-96   49
2.2 Work participation rate in the age group 15-59
years, and in age group 60 years and above by
sex in rural and urban areas, India, 2001   52
2.3 Work participation rate (main + marginal) in the
age group 15-59 years in states, 2001   55
2.4 Work participation rate in the age group 60
years and above (main + marginal) in states,
by sex, all areas, 2001   56
2.5 Work participation rate (main + marginal) in the
age group 60-69 years, 70-79 years, and 80 years
and above in rural and urban areas by sex,
India, 2001   57
2.6 Percentage distribution of main workers, 15-59
years, and 60 years and above, by industrial
category and sex in rural and urban areas,
India 1991   60

2.7   Percentage distribution of workers by status of
      employment, India, 1972-73 to 1999-2000   62
2.8   Total employment and employment in the
      organized sector, India, 1983 to 1999-2000   63
2.9. Percentage of population below the poverty line,
      India, 1973-74 to 2007   64
2.10 Unemployment rate and percentage of population
      below the poverty line, India, 1987-88 to 1999-2000 66
2.11 Allocation, expenditure and beneficiaries under
      NOAP, India, 1995-96 to 2001-02   76
2.12 Industries/classes of establishments covered
      by EPF, 2003-04   95
2.13 Number of establishments covered by EPF and
      number of members, 1995 to 2004   96
2.14 Provident Fund contributions received, 1991-92
      to 2003-04   98
2.15 Number of pension beneficiaries, 1999-2000
      to 2001-02   104
2.16 Number of central government pensioners,
      1990-91 to 1994-95   115
2.17 Trends in central government expenditure on
      pensions, 1990-91 to 2001-02   116
2.18 Annual growth rate of pensions of states   119
3.1   Expectation of life at age 60 years and age 70
      years by sex, India, 1901-11 to 1995-99   139
3.2   Expectation of life at age 60 years and age 70
      years in rural and urban areas, India 1970-75
      to 1995-99   141
3.3   Expectation of life at age 60 years in 1970-75 and
      1995-99 in states   142
3.4   Extent of increase in life expectancy at age 60
      years in each state between 1970-75 and 1991-95   144
3.5   Expectation of life at age 60 years in states by sex,
      1995-99   144
3.6   Expectation of life at age 70 years in states by sex,
      1995-99   145
3.7   Expectation of life at age 60 years in rural and
      urban areas in states, 1995-99   146

3.8 Percentage distribution of deaths by broad age groups, India, 1991 to 2001   147

3.9 Deaths of persons aged 60 years and above as a percentage of total deaths by sex in states, 2000   148

3.10 Age specific death rate, India, 1970 to 2000   150

3.11 Age specific death rate of older persons by sex and rural urban residence, India, 1970 and 2000   151

3.12 Age specific death rate of persons aged 60 years and above by sex in states, 2000   152

3.13 Age specific death rate of persons aged 60 years and above by residence in states, 2000   153

3.14 Percentage distribution of deaths in age group 60 years and above in rural areas by probable cause of death, India, 1997 and 1998   155

3.15 Percentage of persons reporting ailments during the last 15 days by age, sex and type of ailment in rural and urban areas, India, 1995-96   160

3.16 Prevalence of long duration (chronic) ailment per 100,000 by age and sex in rural and urban areas, India, 1995-96   161

3.17 Percentage of persons aged 60 years and above reporting chronic disease by type, sex and residence, 1995-96   162

3.18 Per 1000 distribution of out-patient treatments during last 15 days by age and sex in rural and urban areas, India, 1995-96   162

3.19 Number of persons hospitalized during the last 365 days per 1000 persons by age and sex in rural and urban areas, India, 1995-96   163

3.20 Percentage of persons aged 60 years and above having disability by type, sex and residence, 1995-96   164

3.21 Percentage of persons aged 60 years and above with any disability in rural and urban areas in states, 1995-96   165

4.1 Number of care receivers (persons aged 65 years and above/persons aged 70 years and above) per 1000 care givers (females aged 15-49 years), India, 1961 to 2050   204

4.2   Per 1000 distribution of persons aged 60 years and
       above by type of living arrangements in rural
       and urban areas, India, 1995-96   208
4.3   Per 1000 distribution of persons aged 60 years and
       above living either alone or with only spouse
       in rural and urban areas in states, 1995-96   211
4.4   Per 1000 distribution of persons aged 60 years
       and above by surviving children, India, 1995-96   212
4.5   Distribution per 1000 households by tenure status,
       India, 1961 to 2001   213
4.6   Number of rooms per household, India, 2001   214
4.7   Number of accidental deaths by unnatural causes
       among persons aged 60 years and above,
       India, 2000   225
4.8   Number of suicides of persons aged 60 years and
       above by sex, India, 1996 to 2000   226

List of Figures

1.1 Percentage of persons aged 60 years and above in more developed and less developed regions, 1950 to 2050   4

1.2 Expectation of life at birth in more developed and less developed regions, 1950-55 to 2045-50   6

1.3 Median age in more developed and less developed regions, 1950 to 2050   7

1.4 Percentage of population aged 80 years and above among persons aged 60 years and above in more developed and less developed regions, 1950 to 2050   12

1.5 Percentage of population aged 60 years and above in Asia, Japan, China, India and the world, 2000 to 2050   17

1.6 Number of persons aged 60 years and above, India, 1901 to 2050   19

1.7 Median age, India, 1950 to 2050   21

1.8 Median age in states, 2001   22

1.9 Age and sex distribution of population, India, 1950, 2000, 2050   23

1.10 Age distribution, India, 1951 to 2050   25

1.11 Percentage of population of children and older persons, India, 1951 to 2050   25

1.12 Percentage distribution of persons aged 60-69 years, aged 70-79 years, and aged 80 years and above, India, 1961 to 2050   28

1.13 Percentage of married and widowed males and females aged 60 years and above, India, 1961 to 1991   33

1.14 Percentage of widowed females aged 60 years and above in states, 1991   37

1.15 Percentage of persons aged 60 years and above in
      states with level of education middle and
      above by sex, 2001   41
1.16 Number of persons aged 60 years and above in
      states, 2001   42
1.17 Percentage of persons aged 60 years and above
      in the electorate, India, 1941 to 2001   44
1.18 Percentage of persons aged 60 years and above
      in the electorate in states, 2001   45
2.1   Work participation rate (main + marginal workers)
      in rural and urban areas by age and sex, India, 2001   52
2.2   Work participation rate in age groups 15-59 years,
      and 60 years and above, by sex in rural and urban
      areas, India, 2001   54
2.3   Percentage distribution of workers by status of
      employment, 1972-73 to 1999-2000   62
2.4   Percentage of population below poverty line in
      rural and urban areas, India, 1973- 74 to 2006-07   65
2.5   Trends in central government expenditure on
      pensions, 1990-91 to 2001-02   116
3.1   Expectation of life at age 60 years and age 70
      years by sex, India, 1901-1910 to 1995-99   140
3.2   Expectation of life at age 60 years in states, 1995-99 143
3.3   Deaths of persons aged 60 years and above as a
      percentage of total number of deaths in states, 2000 149
4.1   Number of care receivers (persons aged 65+/70+
      per 1000 care givers (females aged 15-49 years),
      India, 1961 to 2050   205

1

Demography of Ageing

A remarkable gift of the twentieth century is the increase in
life expectancy among virtually all income segments in
different parts of the world. Major demographic transforma-
tions are taking place along with other social, economic and
political reforms. The enhancement of life span has become
possible due to improved systems of healthcare, both public
and private; better medical and diagnostic facilities; better
spread of education, particularly of women; improved
knowledge of preventive and curative healthcare; a higher level
of urbanization with better standards of medical care; a higher
standard of living of people with improved housing and
sanitation facilities; higher levels of earnings which give
the economic means to secure preventive, curative and
rehabilitative healthcare; new financing systems of healthcare;
an improved public health management and delivery system;
and greater awareness and knowledge of healthcare.
Simultaneously, the fertility rate has been going down. This
has been the outcome of several factors: higher age at marriage,
better child survival, availability of technological choices to
select a family size, improved levels of education, women's
own efforts at seeking economic independence, and improved
social security standards. Depending on equations of fertility
decline, decrease of mortality and the higher expectation of
life at birth, the proportion of persons aged 60 years and above
has been increasing throughout the world, even though to some
extent this has been offset by better child survival standards.

Before we look at the demographic situation in India, it
is important to look at the emerging trends in the greying of
populations in other parts of the world. This would give an

idea of the demographic transformation India could face in the coming decades, and the magnitude of efforts needed to resolve the implications of such a transition.

World Demographic Projections on Ageing

The United Nations has given demographic projections up to 2050. It gives the changing demographic scenario between the more developed and the less developed countries. The less developed countries are projected to increase their share of the total global population. For instance, in 1950, 32.3 per cent of the total population (all ages) lived in the more developed regions and 66.7 per cent in the less developed regions (Table 1.1). In 2000, the percentages were 19.7 and 80.3 respectively. In 2050, the projected percentage would be 13.7 in the more developed regions and 86.3 in the less developed regions. Between 1950 and 2050, the total population (all ages) is projected to increase in the more developed regions by 50.1 per cent, while in the less developed regions it would increase by 351 per cent.

The most populous region in the world would increasingly be the less developed region. Table 1.1 also shows that out of the total population aged 60 years and above in the world in 1950, 46.4 per cent were in the more developed regions and 53.6 per cent in the less developed regions. In 2000, the percentages were 38.2 and 61.8 respectively. In 2050, the projected percentage would be 20.6 in the more developed regions and 79.4 in the less developed regions, which would be about four times the number in more developed regions. Putting it differently, in the more developed regions, between 1950 and 2050, the population aged 60 years and above is projected to increase by a factor of 4.13 times, and in the less developed regions by a factor of 13.76 times.

Another interesting feature is the trend in the gap between the percentage of persons aged 60 years and above in more developed regions and in less developed regions (Figure 1.1). In 1950, the gap was 5.3. In 2000, it increased to 11.7. In 2050, the projected gap is 12.6.

Table 1.1: Population in more developed and less developed
regions, 1950 to 2050

Number/ Percentage	Year	More developed regions	Less developed regions	World
Number (all ages) (in '000)	1950	812,771 (32.3)	1,705,858 (66.7)	2,518,629 (100.0)
	1960	915,298 (30.3)	2,106,177 (69.7)	3,021,475 (100.0)
	1970	1,007,479 (27.3)	2,685,013 (72.7)	3,692,492 (100.0)
	1975	1,047,475 (25.7)	3,020,634 (74.3)	4,068,109 (100.0)
	1980	1,082,989 (24.4)	3,351,693 (75.6)	4,434,682 (100.0)
	1990	1,148,917 (21.8)	4,114,675 (78.2)	5,263,593 (100.0)
	2000	1,193,872 (19.7)	4,876,709 (80.3)	6,070,581 (100.0)
	2010	1,220,855 (17.9)	5,609,428 (82.1)	6,830,283 (100.0)
	2020	1,237,398 (16.4)	6,302,839 (83.6)	7,540,237 (100.0)
	2025	1,241,370 (15.8)	6,610,079 (84.2)	7,851,455 (100.0)
	2030	1,242,278 (15.3)	6,887,870 (84.7)	8,130,149 (100.0)
	2040	1,235,384 (14.4)	7,358,208 (85.6)	8,593,592 (100.0)
	2050	1,219,662 (13.7)	7,699,061 (86.3)	8,918,724 (100.0)
Number 60+ (in '000)	1950	95,349 (46.4)	109,986 (53.6)	205,337 (100.0)
	1960	115,648 (47.0)	130,431 (53.0)	246,080 (100.0)
	1970	146,471 (47.4)	164,903 (52.6)	311,377 (100.0)
	1975	161,541 (46.3)	187,515 (53.7)	349,056 (100.0)
	1980	167,955 (43.8)	213,577 (56.2)	381,531 (100.0)
	1990	202,728 (41.8)	282,542 (58.2)	485,269 (100.0)
	2000	231,793 (38.2)	374,632 (61.8)	606,425 (100.0)
	2010	266,217 (35.1)	492,534 (64.9)	758,751 (100.0)
	2020	318,683 (31.2)	703,292 (68.8)	1,021,976 (100.0)
	2025	343,568 (29.1)	836,369 (70.9)	1,179,937 (100.0)
	2030	361,421 (26.8)	986,874 (73.2)	1,348,294 (100.0)
	2040	383,412 (23.5)	1,247,477 (76.5)	1,630,891 (100.0)
	2050	393,737 (20.6)	1,513,515 (79.4)	1,907,252 (100.0)
Percentage 60+	1950	11.7	6.4	8.2
	1960	12.6	6.2	8.1
	1970	14.5	6.1	8.4
	1975	15.4	6.2	8.6
	1980	15.5	6.4	8.6
	1990	17.6	6.9	9.2
	2000	19.4	7.7	10.0
	2010	21.8	8.8	11.1
	2020	25.8	11.2	13.6
	2025	27.7	12.7	15.0
	2030	29.1	14.3	16.6
	2040	31.0	17.0	19.0
	2050	32.3	19.7	21.4

Source: Based on *World Population Prospects: The 2002 Revision.*

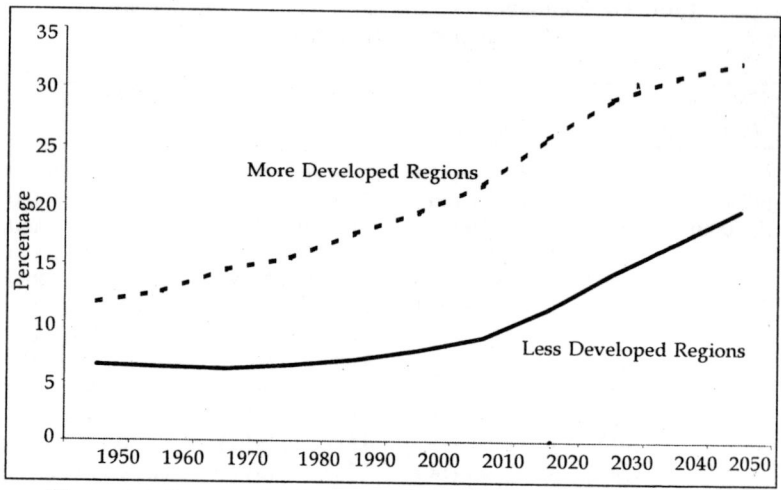

Figure 1.1: Percentage of persons aged 60 years and above in more
developed and less developed regions, 1950 to 2050

In both the more developed and the less developed
regions, ageing is universal and appears to be irreversible.
However, the less developed regions are ageing faster than
the more developed regions. This will be evident from the
percentage of population aged 60 years and above. In the less
developed regions, the percentage aged 60 years and above is
projected to increase from 7.7 per cent in 2000 to 19.7 per cent
in 2050, a factor of 2.6. In the more developed regions, it is
projected to increase from 19.4 per cent in 2000 to 32.3 per cent
in 2050, a factor of 1.7. The less developed countries will thus
have to face a far more difficult situation in having to cope
with the fast demographic ageing of populations, specially with
little or no social security systems for a very large percentage
in countries such as South Asia and Africa. More significant
than the percentages are the numbers involved. In 2000, the
number of persons aged 60 years and above was 375 million
in the less developed regions. In 2050, it is projected to increase
to 1513 million, four times the number.

Expectation of life at birth is increasing at a much faster
rate in the less developed regions where it was quite low and
thus had more scope to reduce mortality, particularly in the

earlier age groups. Data in Table 1.2 shows that between 1950–55 and 2045–50, the projected increase in expectation of life at birth in more developed regions is 15.5 years, and in the less developed regions 32.1 years.

Table 1.2: Expectation of life at birth in more developed and less developed regions, 1950–55 to 2045–50

Region	1950–1955	1960–1965	1970–1975	1980–1985	1990–1995	2000–2005	2010–2015	2020–2025	2030–2035	2040–2045	2045–2050
More developed regions	66.1	69.7	71.4	72.9	74.0	75.8	77.3	78.7	79.9	81.1	81.6
Less developed regions	41.0	47.7	54.7	58.5	61.5	63.4	65.3	67.3	69.8	72.1	73.1
World	46.5	52.4	58.0	61.3	63.8	65.4	67.2	69.1	71.3	73.4	74.3
Difference between more developed regions and less developed regions	25.1	22.0	16.7	14.4	12.5	12.4	12.0	11.4	10.1	9.0	8.5

Source: Based on *World Population Prospects: The 2002 Revision*

If we take the first fifty years of this period (1950–55 to 2000–05), the expectation of life at birth increased in the more developed regions by 9.7 years. In the less developed region it increased by 22.4 years, primarily because the population in this region began to have access to better healthcare and was able to reduce mortality, particularly in the earlier age groups. In the subsequent period (2000–05 to 2045–50), the expectation of life at birth in the more developed regions is projected to increase by 5.8 years and in the less developed regions by 9.7 years. The difference in expectation of life at birth has reduced between more developed regions and less developed regions. The difference is 25.1 years in 1950–55, 12.4 years in 2000–05 and 8.5 years in 2045–50. Figure 1.2 gives the trend in graphic form.

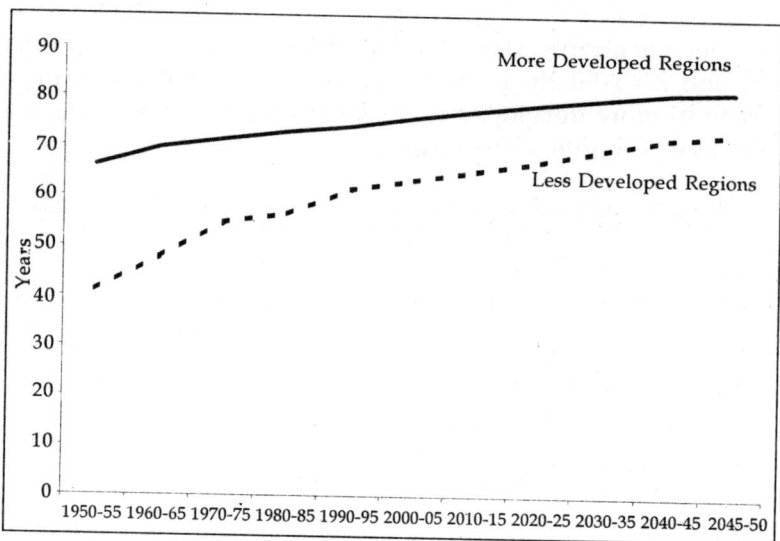

Figure 1.2: Expectation of life at birth in more developed and less developed regions, 1950–55 to 2045–50

The demographic ageing of population is also indicated by trends in median age, that is the age at which half the population is older and the other half younger. Table 1.3 gives the trends in the more developed and the less developed regions. In 1950, the less developed regions had a median age of 21.3 years, which increased to 24.1 years in 2000, a difference of only 2.8 years. The projected median age in 2050 is 35.7 years, a difference of 11.6 years. In the more developed regions, the median age in 1950 was 28.6 years which increased to 37.3 years in 2000, a difference of 8.7 years, which was 3 times the difference in less developed regions. An interesting feature is that in the less developed regions, between 1950 and 1990, there was a modest decline followed by a rise of only 0.7 years. In the more developed regions, on the other hand, the median age continued to rise, showing an increase of 5.8 years. Between 2000 and 2050, the median age in the more developed regions is projected to increase from 37.3 years to 45.2 years, a difference of 7.9 years, which is lower than the projected increase (11.6 years) in the case of less developed regions. For the world as a whole, the median age increased from 23.6 years to 26.4 years

Table 1.3: Median age in more developed and less developed
regions, 1950 to 2050

Year	More developed regions	Less developed regions	World	Difference between more developed regions and less developed regions
1950	28.6	21.3	23.6	7.3
1960	29.6	20.1	22.8	9.5
1970	30.6	19.0	21.7	11.6
1980	31.9	20.1	22.7	11.8
1990	34.4	22.0	24.3	12.4
2000	37.3	24.1	26.4	13.2
2010	40.0	26.3	28.4	13.7
2020	42.3	28.8	30.7	13.5
2030	44.2	31.2	33.0	13.0
2040	45.4	33.5	34.9	11.9
2050	45.2	35.7	36.8	9.5

Source: Based on *World Population Prospects: The 2002 Revision.*

between 1950 and 2000, a difference of 2.8 years. It is projected
to increase to 36.8 years in 2050, a difference of 10.4 years.
Figure 1.3 gives the trend in the two regions. The gap between
median age in more developed regions and less developed
regions tends to increase between 1950 and 2010; it tends to
decline thereafter.

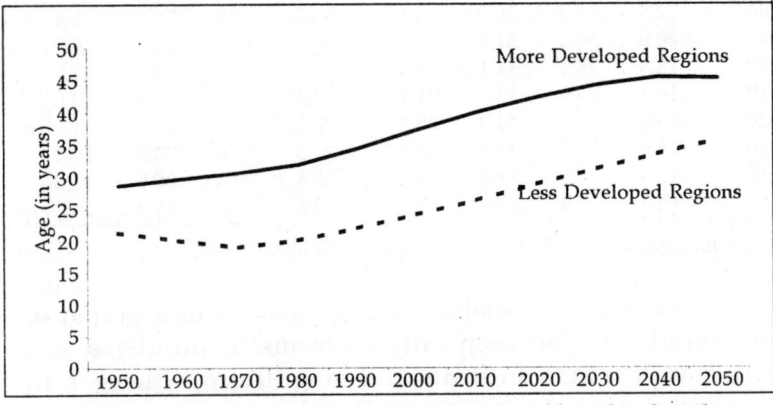

Figure 1.3: Median age in more developed and less developed
regions, 1950 to 2050

With demographic transition, the age composition of the population also undergoes a change as will be evident from Table 1.4 which gives the percentage of population in the age groups 0–14 years, 15–34 years, 35–59 years, and 60 years and above from 1950 to 2050. The data show that the percentage of population less than 15 years has been coming down, while the percentage of population aged 60 years and above has been increasing in both the regions. The percentage aged 60 years and above in the less developed regions projected for 2050 approximates that of the more developed regions in 2000. The population aged less than 15 years in the less developed regions projected for 2050 approximates that in the more developed regions in 1990. Also, in the more developed regions, the percentage aged 60 years and above in 2050 is projected to be twice the percentage in the age group 0–14 years. In the less developed regions, the projected percentages in the age group 0–14 years and 60 years and above will be about the same.

Table 1.4: Percentage distribution of population by age groups in more developed and less developed regions, 1950 to 2050

Year	More developed regions				Less developed regions			
	0–14	15–34	35–59	60+	0–14	15–34	35–59	60+
1950	27.4	31.0	29.9	11.7	37.6	33.2	22.8	6.4
1960	28.1	30.1	29.2	12.6	40.6	31.7	21.5	6.2
1970	26.0	30.3	29.2	8.4	41.6	31.5	20.8	6.1
1980	22.4	31.2	29.9	15.5	39.2	33.9	20.5	6.4
1990	20.5	30.4	31.4	17.6	35.7	35.7	21.7	6.9
2000	18.3	28.2	34.1	19.4	33.0	34.9	24.4	7.7
2010	16.3	26.6	35.3	21.8	29.4	34.0	27.8	8.8
2020	15.8	24.3	34.2	25.8	27.0	32.7	29.1	11.2
2030	15.5	22.5	32.9	29.1	24.5	31.0	30.2	14.3
2040	15.5	22.3	31.2	31.0	22.4	29.8	30.9	17.0
2050	15.7	22.4	29.6	32.3	20.8	28.2	31.3	19.7

Source: Based on *World Population Prospects: The 2002 Revision.*

Changes in composition of population over a period of time should not be seen only in terms of numbers and percentages which indicate the magnitude. Changes in characteristics are also important. Populations currently in the younger age groups, when they cross 60 years of age, will have more diverse socio-economic characteristics. They will have better education, more diverse employment experience, a better standard of living and resources, and different expectations of life in old age. They will look forward to active roles in different spheres for a more creative, productive and satisfactory life. Their aspirations for the post–60 stage of the life cycle will be different from those of the current generation.

Another indicator of demographic ageing is the comparative rate of growth in different segments of the population. Data in Table 1.5 on decadal increase from 1950–60 to 2040–50 shows that in the more developed regions, the

Table1.5: Decadal increase in population in broad age groups in more developed and less developed regions, 1950–60 to 2040–50

Decade	More developed regions					Less developed regions				
	0–14	15–34	35–59	60+	Total	0–14	15–34	35–59	60+	Total
1950–60	15.7	9.2	9.9	21.3	12.6	33.4	18.0	16.4	18.6	23.5
1960–70	1.8	10.8	10.0	26.7	10.1	30.6	26.6	23.2	26.4	27.5
1970–80	–7.2	14.2	10.0	14.7	7.5	17.7	34.5	23.2	29.5	24.8
1980–90	–2.9	0.3	11.5	20.7	6.1	11.8	29.2	30.1	32.3	22.8
1990–2000	–7.3	–3.8	12.9	14.3	3.9	9.5	15.9	33.2	32.6	18.5
2000–10	–9.3	–3.3	5.9	14.9	2.3	2.4	12.1	31.0	31.5	15.0
2010–20	–1.7	–7.7	–1.8	19.7	1.4	3.4	8.1	17.4	42.8	12.4
2020–30	–1.5	–6.8	–3.4	13.4	0.4	–0.9	3.5	13.4	40.3	9.3
2030–40	–0.4	–1.6	–5.8	6.1	–0.6	–2.5	2.7	9.4	26.4	6.8
2040–50	0.2	–1.0	–6.1	2.7	–1.3	–2.7	–0.8	6.1	21.3	4.6

Source: Based on *World Population Prospects: The 2002 Revision.*

segment aged 60 years and above represents the fastest growing age group in the population, overtaking decadal increases in the younger age groups. In the less developed regions, the trend becomes visible from 1970–80. The rate of decadal increase in the segment aged 60 years and above is far higher in the less developed regions than in the more developed regions. Percentage decadal increase of children begins to fall, far earlier in the more developed regions. A negative increase of children began in the decade 1970–80, and of young persons aged 15–34 years from 1990–2000. In the less developed regions, a negative increase is projected for children from 2020–30, and of young persons aged 15–34 years from 2040–50.

In the segment aged 60 years and above, decadal increase shows a fluctuating trend in the more developed regions between 1950–60 and 2010–20, after which it begins to fall. In the less developed regions, the segment aged 60 years and above shows a rise in percentage of decadal increase from 1950–60, reaching a peak in 2010–20 (43 per cent decadal increase), after which it begins to fall. Even then, the percentage decadal increase in population aged 60 years and above in the less developed regions in 2040–50 is projected to be about eight times that in the more developed regions, indicating a continued faster rate of growth. In numbers, this would mean an increase of about 10 million persons aged 60 years and above between 2040 and 2050 in the more developed regions, as compared to about 266 million persons in the same age group in the less developed regions.

The population aged 60 years and above is not a homogenous group. Demographers often classify them into three age groups (60–69 years, 70–79 years, and 80 years & above), depending on their expected capacity for active ageing. The data in Table 1.6 shows that in the more developed regions, the percentage in the age group 60–69 years has decreased from 59.3 in 1950 to 48.7 in 2000. It is expected to decline further to 38.7 per cent in 2050. In the age group 80 years and above, it has increased from 8.9 per cent in 1950 to 15.8 per cent in 2000, and is projected to be 28.6 per cent in 2050. In the less developed regions, too, the percentage in the age group 60–69 years has decreased from 67.7 in 1950 to 60.5 in 2000, and is projected to decline to 49.8 per cent in 2050. In the age group 80 years and above, it has increased from 4.8 per cent in 1950 to 8.6 per cent in 2000 and is projected to rise to 17.5 per cent in 2050. There is a much higher percentage of persons aged 80 years and above in the more developed regions compared to the less developed regions. In both the more developed and the less developed regions, the percentage in the age group 80 years and above is projected to be about twice that in 2000. In figures, the numbers are quite staggering. In the more developed regions, the projected number for 2050 is 113 million as compared to 37 million in 2000. In the less developed regions, the number of persons aged 80 years and above is projected to increase to about 265 million persons as compared to 32 million in 2000, indicating a heavy load on family finances and the need for tertiary healthcare and welfare services, both institutional and non-institutional.

Table 1.6: Age distribution of population aged 60 years and above in more developed and less developed regions, 1950 to 2050

Year	More developed regions				Less developed regions			
	60–69	70–79	80+	Total	60–69	70–79	80+	Total
1950	59.3	31.7	8.9	100.0	67.7	27.5	4.8	100.0
1960	57.6	32.2	10.1	100.0	64.8	29.7	5.5	100.0
1970	57.9	31.2	10.9	100.0	64.9	28.6	6.5	100.0
1980	50.9	36.0	13.1	100.0	63.2	30.3	6.5	100.0
1990	53.4	31.4	15.2	100.0	62.7	29.6	7.7	100.0
2000	48.7	35.4	15.8	100.0	60.5	30.8	8.6	100.0
2010	47.6	33.0	19.5	100.0	58.3	31.4	10.4	100.0
2020	48.2	32.2	19.7	100.0	60.2	29.1	10.7	100.0
2030	43.5	34.7	21.8	100.0	57.2	31.7	11.1	100.0
2040	39.7	34.1	26.2	100.0	51.2	34.5	14.3	100.0
2050	38.7	32.6	28.6	100.0	49.8	32.7	17.5	100.0

Source: Based on *World Population Prospects: The 2002 Revision.*

The relative percentages of persons aged 80 years and above residing in the more developed regions and the less developed regions show a variation between 1950 and 2050. In 1950, of the total persons aged 80 years and above in the world, 61.8 per cent were in the more developed regions and 38.2 per cent in the less developed regions. In 2000, the percentages were 53.1 and 46.9 respectively. The percentage living in the more developed regions declined further, and in 2050, the projected percentage in the more developed regions is 29.9 per cent, and in the less developed regions 70.1. Figure 1.4 gives the data in graphic form. In the more developed regions, the upward surge starts quite early, while in the less developed regions, the upward trend begins from 2030. The social services have to gear themselves to meet the needs of an estimated 1907 million persons aged 60 years and above in the world in 2050, of which about 20 per cent would be in the frail category. Viewed in terms of the total population (all ages), in the more developed regions the percentage aged 80 years and above increased from 1.0 in 1950 to 3.1 in 2000; it is projected to increase to 9.2 in 2050. In the less developed regions, the respective percentages are 0.3, 0.7 and 3.4.

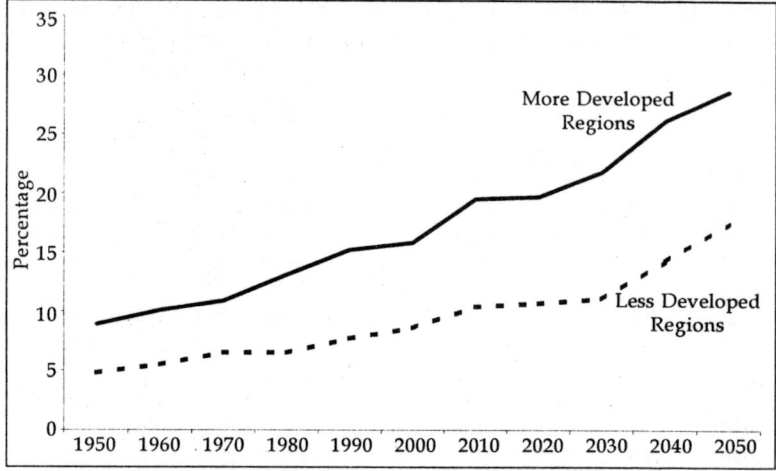

Figure 1.4: Percentage of population aged 80 years and above among persons aged 60 years and above in the more developed and less developed regions, 1950 to 2050

Dependency Ratio

The population of children and the old gives the dependency ratios vis-a-vis the working age population 15–59 years. The figures are of the nature of a crude ratio since not all males and females 15–59 years are workers, nor are all persons aged 60 years and above dependents. The age group 15–59 years is also not a homogeneous category.

Table 1.7 indicates that in the more developed regions, child dependency ratio (number of children aged 0–14 years per 1000 persons aged 15–59 years) is likely to decline from 449 in 1950 to 263 in 2010 and then rise to 303 in 2050; however, old age dependency ratio (number of persons aged 60 years and above per 1000 persons aged 15–59 years) is likely to increase from 193 in 1950 to 621 in 2050. If both the dependency ratios are added, the total dependency ratio would show a rising trend from 2000. In 2050, the total dependency ratio is projected to increase to 923, that is more than nine-tenths of the working age group. In the less developed regions, child dependency ratio is likely to decrease after an increase between 1950 and 1970. It is projected at 349 in 2050. Old age dependency ratio is likely to increase from 115 in 1950 to 330 in 2050, a rise of 187 per cent. If the two dependency ratios are added, the data would show a rising trend from 2010, after an up and down movement between 1950 and 2000. In 2050, the total dependency ratio would rise to 680, that is more than two-thirds of the population in the working age group.

Table 1.7: Dependency ratio in more developed and less developed regions, 1950 to 2050

Region	Dependency ratio	1950	1960	1970	1980	1990	2000	2010	2020	2030	2040	2050
More developed regions	(0–14)/ (15–59)	449	474	438	362	332	295	263	270	279	290	303
	(60+)/ 15–59)	193	213	245	250	286	312	352	440	525	581	621
	(60+)/ (0–14)	429	450	559	691	859	1059	1341	1633	1880	2002	2053
	(0–14)+ (60+/ (15–59)	642	687	682	612	618	606	615	710	804	871	923
Less developed regions	(0–14)/ (15–59)	672	764	797	727	622	556	475	438	401	369	349
	(60+)/ (15–59)	115	117	118	117	120	130	142	181	234	279	330
	(60+)/ (0–14)	171	152	148	161	192	233	299	413	584	758	945
	(0–14)+ (60+)/ (15–59)	788	881	914	844	742	686	617	618	635	648	680

Note: Ratio indicates the number per 1000 of the denominator.
Source: Based on *World Population Prospects, 2002 Revision*.

Changing Sex Ratio

A global phenomenon is the increase in number of women in the older age groups, as women tend to outlive men. This is true for both the more developed regions and the less developed regions. An important reason has been the stronger biological strength of women to survive. Also, a larger number of women are surviving the risks of maternal mortality. They are also less susceptible to the lifestyle risk factors characterizing the male population. Table 1.8 gives the number of females per 1000 males in the more developed and less developed regions from 1950 to 2050 in the general population

Table 1.8: Sex ratio (no. of females per 1000 males) in the age group 60 years and above in more developed and less developed regions, 1950 to 2050

Year	More developed regions					Less developed regions				
	All ages	60+	60–69	70–79	80+	All ages	60+	60–69	70–79	80+
1950	1099	1356	1281	1411	1739	962	1164	1104	1274	1469
1960	1084	1416	1320	1497	1782	966	1114	1059	1191	1420
1970	1075	1463	1317	1606	1995	965	1126	1084	1179	1335
1980	1069	1538	1357	1615	2241	964	1120	1050	1211	1465
1990	1063	1485	1271	1610	2241	965	1111	1040	1188	1488
2000	1059	1408	1178	1494	2209	971	1130	1054	1191	1540
2010	1059	1355	1139	1373	2069	975	1148	1062	1202	1555
2020	1059	1318	1140	1297	1968	981	1145	1058	1201	1584
2030	1060	1301	1106	1290	1853	988	1157	1068	1196	1594
2040	1061	1297	1083	1238	1837	995	1172	1061	1200	1594
2050	1057	1282	1064	1205	1790	1001	1172	1041	1188	1617

Source: Based on *World Population Prospects, 2002 Revision.*

(all ages) and in population aged 60 years and above. In the more developed regions, the sex ratio is adverse to males in both the general population and in the age group 60 years and above. It becomes, more adverse in the population aged 80 years and above. In the less developed regions, however, in the general population, the sex ratio is adverse to females but in the population aged 60 years and above it is adverse to males.

Here, too, it becomes more adverse to males at the higher age levels. Sex ratio in the age group 60 years and above, which is adverse to males in the developed regions, is on a steady decline even though it is still much higher than in the general population. This may be because of narrowing of the gap in mortality rates between males and females.

Ageing in Selected Countries

In the previous pages, countries have been classified on the basis of more developed and less developed regions to indicate the trends in the ageing of populations. We now give the demographic trends for some countries in both these groups. The data given in Table 1.9 shows that by 2050, most countries in both the regions are projected to have more than 20 per cent of persons aged 60 years and above in the total population. In the world as a whole, almost one-third of the population is projected to be 60 years of age and above in 2050. Among different continents, Africa will have the lowest percentage (10.1 per cent) and Europe the highest percentage (35.1) in 2050, which is almost three and a half times. Asia is projected to have 23 per cent of persons aged 60 years and above in 2050. Japan, Korea, Thailand and Singapore are projected to have more than 37 per cent persons aged 60 years and above. In 2050, Japan will rank the highest (42.4 per cent), followed by Italy (40.6 per cent). India is projected to have one-fifth of the population aged 60 years and above in 2050. This will be lower than the percentage in Japan in 1995.

Among different continents, Asia will occupy the centrestage in providing residence to more than half the global population aged 60 years and above. In 2000, Asia had 53.1 per cent of the world's total population aged 60 years and above. In 2050, it is projected to have 62.4 per cent of the global population.

In 2000, India had 12.7 per cent of the world's population aged 60 years and above. Projections for 2050 indicate that India is likely to have 16.2 per cent of the world's population aged 60 years and above. China, in 2000, had 21.2 per cent of the world's population aged 60 years and above. Projections for 2050 indicate that China will be inhabited by 21.9 per cent of the global population aged 60 years and above. These two countries, together, in 2050, are projected to have 38.1 per cent of the global population aged 60 years and above. In numbers it will mean about 1.84 times the population aged 60 years and above in the more developed regions. Figure 1.5 gives the relative situation in India, China, Japan, Asia and the world.

Table 1.9: Percentage of population aged 60 years and above in India, China, Japan, Asia and the world, 2000 to 2050

Region/Country	2000	2010	2020	2025	2030	2040	2050
World	19.4	21.8	25.8	27.7	29.1	31.0	32.3
Europe	20.2	22.1	26.2	28.4	30.2	33.0	35.1
North America	16.2	18.3	22.4	24.1	25.0	25.4	26.1
South America	8.3	9.9	13.0	14.9	16.7	20.4	24.1
Asia	8.8	10.1	12.9	14.7	16.8	19.9	22.8
Africa	5.0	5.3	6.0	6.4	6.7	8.0	10.1
Japan	23.3	30.2	34.0	35.5	37.3	41.6	42.4
Italy	24.1	27.2	30.8	33.7	36.9	41.0	40.6
Korea	11.0	14.7	21.1	25.0	28.8	34.5	38.9
Thailand	8.4	10.6	14.7	17.2	19.8	24.6	37.6
Singapore	10.5	15.7	26.0	31.1	34.7	36.8	37.4
Germany	23.2	25.7	28.3	32.1	34.5	34.4	34.5
Sweden	22.3	26.3	28.9	30.4	31.9	32.9	33.6
France	20.5	22.8	26.6	28.4	29.9	31.6	32.3
Canada	16.7	20.4	26.0	28.7	30.1	31.4	32.2
Denmark	20.0	23.8	27.2	29.0	30.7	31.7	30.6
Bangladesh	5.0	5.5	7.3	8.5	9.8	12.7	16.6
China	10.1	12.3	16.8	19.8	23.6	27.6	30.0
Australia	16.4	19.4	23.5	25.4	26.7	28.7	29.9
UK	20.7	22.5	24.5	26.2	27.6	28.8	29.8
Sri Lanka	9.8	12.1	16.3	18.9	21.2	25.3	29.3
USA	16.1	18.1	22.0	23.6	24.4	24.8	25.5
Indonesia	7.8	8.8	11.2	12.8	14.9	19.2	23.1
Malaysia	6.5	8.1	11.5	13.2	14.8	17.9	21.1
India	7.5	8.6	10.8	12.2	13.8	16.7	20.1
Philippines	5.5	6.7	8.9	10.2	11.8	15.4	19.8
Pakistan	5.7	5.9	6.8	7.3	7.8	9.5	12.6

Note: For countries, a descending order has been followed as per the projected percentage in 2050

Source: World Population Prospects: The 2002 Revision.

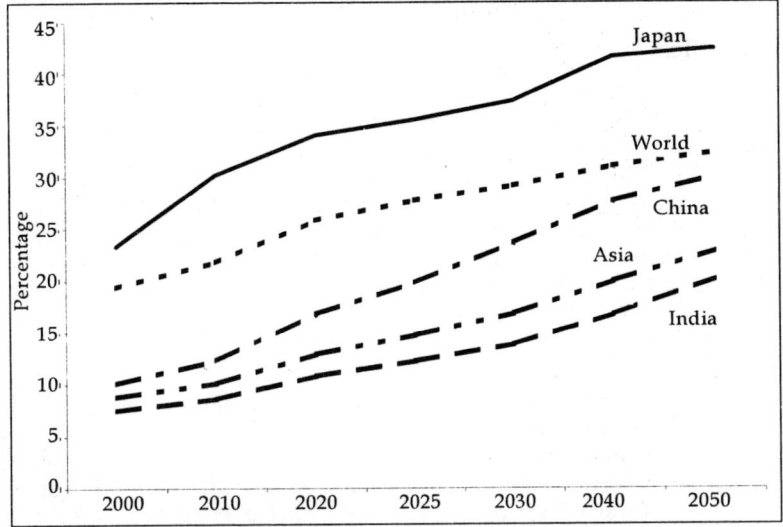

Figure 1.5: Percentage of population aged 60 years and above in Asia,
Japan, China, India and the world, 2000 to 2050

Demographic Projections on Ageing in India

Along with the rest of the world, the population of India is
also ageing. Table 1.10 gives the number of persons aged 60
years and above during the period 1901 to 2050, and the
percentage of population in this age group. From 1901 to 2001,
census figures have been used. Revised population projections
from 2006 to 2026 are not yet available from the office of the
Registrar General. The earlier projections from 1996 to 2016
on the basis of recommendations of the Technical Group on
Population Projections are no longer relevant. Population
projections from 2010 to 2050 given by the United Nations (2002
Revision) have been utilized. The data shows that demographic
ageing was at a low key in India in the twentieth century. In
1901, there were only 12.060 million persons aged 60 years and
above. In 1951, the number rose to 19.612 million, an increase
of 62.6 per cent. In the next 50 years, i.e. in 2001, the population
in this age group increased further to 76.622 million, an increase
of 290.7 per cent. Thus the increase in the second half of the

Table 1.10: Number and percentage of persons aged 60 years
and above, India, 1901 to 2050

Year	No. (in million)	%	Year	No. (in million)	%	Year	No. (in million)	%
1901	12.060	5.08	1961	24.712	5.63	2020	141.779	10.80
1911	13.169	5.24	1971	32.700	5.97	2030	194.795	13.75
1921	13.485	5.38	1981	44.348	6.49	2040	247.979	16.69
1931	14.208	5.11	1991	57.554	6.80	2050	308.463	20.14
1941	18.040	5.69	2001	76.622	7.47			
1951	19.612	5.50	2010	101.232	8.62			

Note: Figures for 1981 have included interpolated figures of Assam, and
           for 1991 interpolated figures of Jammu and Kashmir as Census could
           not be undertaken.

Source: (i) Figures for 1901 to 1951 have been taken from SB Mukhopa-
                dhyaya, *The Age Distribution of the Indian Population*, East West
                Centre.
           (ii) Figures for 1961 to 2001 have been taken from census reports.
                Figures for 2010 to 2050 have been taken from United Nations,
                World Population Prospects, The 2002 Revision.

twentieth century was 7.6 times the increase in the first half of
the twentieth century. In the first half of the twenty-first
century, the population aged 60 years and above is projected
at 308.463 million in 2050, an increase of 231.841 million from
2001, that is an increase of 302.6 per cent. The percentage of
population aged 60 years and above was in the range of 5 per
cent in the first seven decades of the twentieth century. In the
next two decades, it was in the range of 6 per cent. The
percentage began to rise from 2001. In 2020, it is projected to
reach a double digit figure. Thereafter, in the next 30 years, it
shows a much larger increase. The decadal increase in the
period 2040–50 is projected to be larger than the total
population aged 60 years and above in 1991. Figure 1.6 gives
the trend in graphic form.

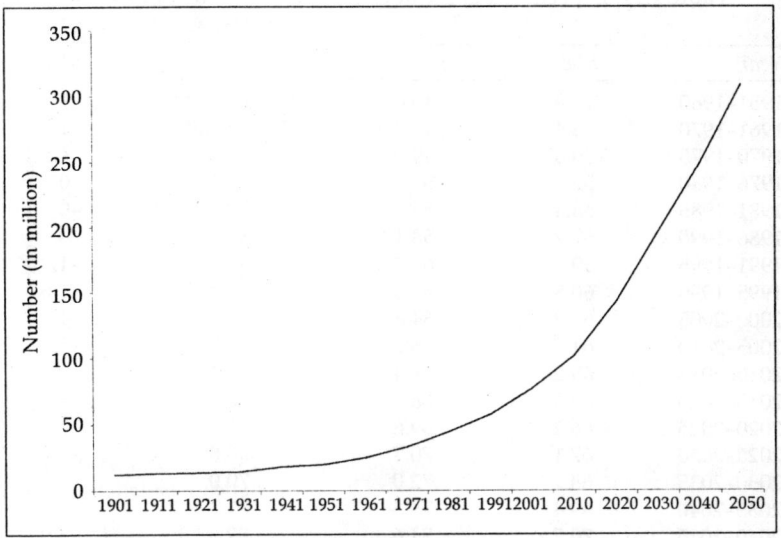

Figure 1.6: Number of persons aged 60 years and above,
India, 1901 to 2050

Increase in expectation of life at birth due to fall in mortality rate, particularly in the earlier stages of the life cycle, has led to an increase in number of persons aged 60 years and above. Table 1.11, which gives the expectation of life at birth from 1951–60 to 2045–50, shows that up to 1991–95 in the case of males, and up to 1986–90 in the case of females, expectation of life at birth was less than 60 years. In the 1950s, 1960s and 1970s, male expectation of life at birth was higher. From 1981–85, the position has reversed. Female life expectancy became higher and is projected to be the trend in the first half of this century. The difference between male and female expectation of life at birth from 2030–35 is expected to be about four years as compared to less than a year in the 1980s.

Table 1.11: Expectation of life at birth, India, 1951–60 to 2045–50

Year	Male	Female	Total	M-F
1951–1960	41.9	40.6	Not available	1.3
1961–1970	46.4	44.7	Not available	1.7
1970–1975	50.5	49.0	49.7	1.5
1976–1980	52.5	52.1	52.3	0.4
1981–1985	55.4	55.7	55.4	–0.3
1986–1990	57.7	58.1	57.7	–0.4
1991–1995	59.7	60.9	60.3	–1.2
1995–1999	60.8	62.5	61.7	–1.6
2000–2005	63.2	64.6	63.9	–1.4
2005–2010	64.5	66.2	65.3	–1.7
2010–2015	65.2	67.4	66.3	–2.2
2015–2020	65.5	68.5	66.9	–3.0
2020–2025	66.2	69.6	67.8	–3.4
2025–2030	67.1	70.7	68.8	–3.6
2030–2035	68.2	72.0	70.0	–3.8
2035–2040	69.4	73.3	71.3	–3.9
2040–2045	70.7	74.6	72.6	–3.9
2045–2050	71.9	75.8	73.8	–3.9

Source: (i) Figures for 1951–60 and 1961–1970 have been taken from Registrar General. (ii) Figures from 1970–75 to 1995–99 have been taken from SRS Abdridged Life Tables, Registrar General, India. (iii) Figures from 2000–2005 to 2045–2050 have been taken from United Nations, *World Population Prospects, The 2002 Revision.*

The median age of the population of India at different points of time gives an indication of the pace of ageing. The United Nations World Population Prospects (The 2002 Revision) has given the median age for India from 1950 to 2050 at 5 year intervals. Between 1950 and 1975, the median age remained stable at about 20 years. Between 1975 and 2000, it increased from 20 years to 23.4 years, that is by 3.4 years; between 2000 and 2025 years it increased from 23.4 years to 30.3 years that is by 6.9 years, and between 2025 and 2050 it increased from 30.3 years to 37.9 years, that is by 7.6 years. Placing the difference in a wider time span, the median age between 1950 and 2000 increased by 3 years; between 2000 and 2050 it is projected to increase by 14.5 years. Figure 1.7 gives the trend in rise of median age in India.

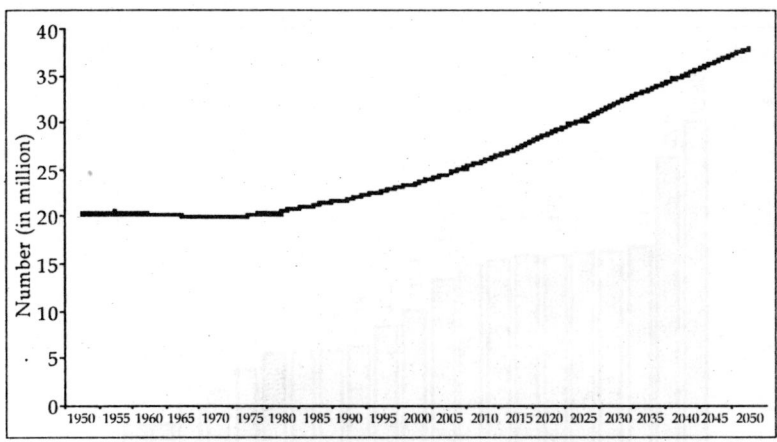

Figure 1.7: Median age, India, 1950 to 2050

The 2001 Census of India has provided the median age for India and the states. For India, it has given the median age as 22.7 years. The United Nations World Population Prospects gave a figure of 23.4 years in 2000, a slightly higher figure. Data on median age in 2001 for the 20 bigger states indicates that both Bihar and Uttar Pradesh had a median age below 20 years. At the other extreme, Kerala had the highest median age (27.95 years), followed by Tamil Nadu. Figure 1.8 gives the median age of states arranged in descending order.

The ageing of population in India can also be visually expressed through the age and sex pyramid of the population in 1950, 2000 and 2050. It is based on the age and sex distribution at five year intervals given by the United Nations World Population Prospects which provides a hundred-year time span. The pyramid given in Figure 1.9(a) shows a wide base in 1950, indicating a young population. Figure 1.9(b) shows that with demographic transformation, the lower portion of the pyramid begins to shrink, and the middle portion begins to expand. Figure 1.9(c) indicates that as the population ages further, the lower portion shrinks still more, and the proportion in the older age groups begins to expand, giving it the shape of an uneven structure with a bulging middle layer.

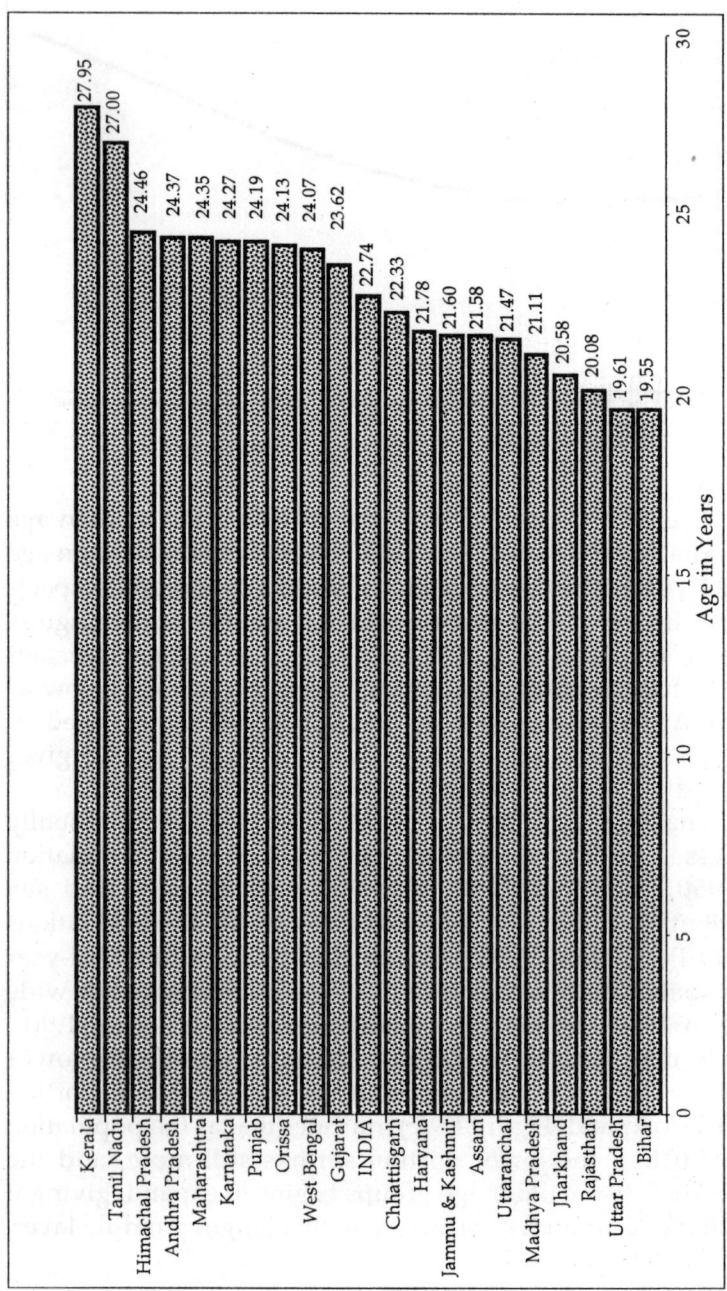

Figure 1.8: Median age in states, 2001

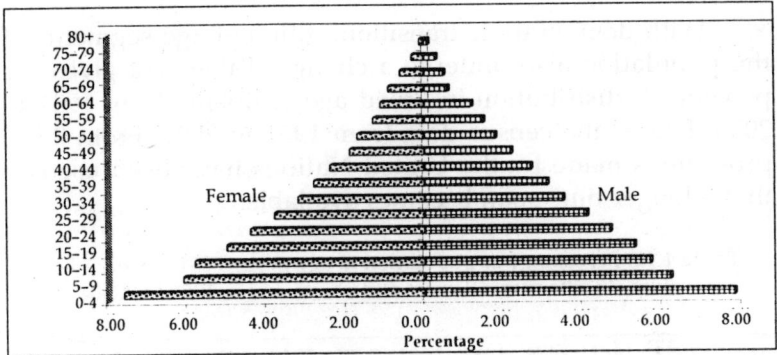

Figure 1.9 (a): Age and sex distribution of population, India, 1950.

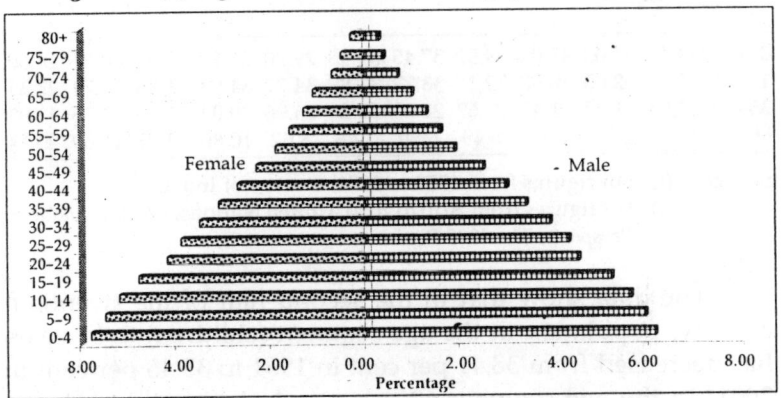

Figure 1.9 (b): Age and sex distribution of population, India, 2000

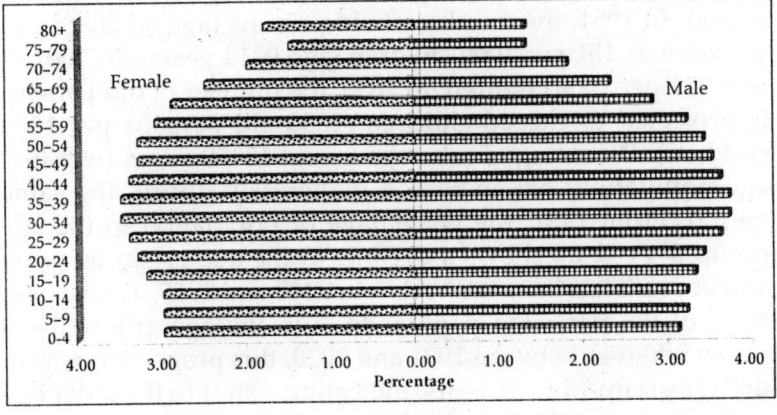

Figure 1.9 (c): Age and sex distribution of population, India, 2050

With demographic transition, different age segments of the population also undergo a change. Table 1.12 gives the percentage distribution in broad age segments from 1951 to 2050. It uses the census data from 1951 to 2001. From 2010, projections made by the United Nations have been used so that a longer time span becomes available.

Table 1.12: Percentage of population in age groups 0–14 years, 15–34 years, 35–59 years, 60 years and above, India, 1951 to 2050

Age (in years)	1951	1961	1971	1981	1991	2001	2010	2020	2030	2040	2050
0–14	38.41	41.05	42.02	39.57	37.45	35.45	29.70	26.14	23.06	20.21	18.60
15–34	33.15	32.05	30.58	32.27	33.72	33.89	34.72	34.03	31.80	29.74	27.34
35–59	22.94	21.27	21.43	21.67	22.03	23.20	26.96	29.03	31.39	33.36	33.92
60+	5.50	5.63	5.97	6.49	6.80	7.46	8.62	10.80	13.75	16.69	20.14

Source: (i) For figures from 1951 to 2001, Census of India.
          (ii) For figures from 2010 to 2050, United Nations, *World Population Prospects, The 2002 Revision.*

The data show that in the second half of the twentieth century, population in the age segment (children) 0–14 years has decreased from 38.41 per cent in 1951 to 35.45 per cent in 2001. In the age segment 60 years and above (old age), the percentage has increased from 5.50 in 1951 to 7.46 in the same period. In 1951, the number of old persons (age 60 years and above) was 151 per 1000 children (age 0–14 years). In 2001, it was 211 per 1000 children. In 2050, the number of old persons is projected to exceed children (1083 old persons per 1000 children). Percentage in the age group 15–59 years (working age population) has increased moderately during the same period. From 1981, the percentage of population in the age group 0–14 years shows a decline. In the age group 60 years and above it has increased. Also, in 2040 and 2050, almost one-third of the projected population is in the age group 35–59 years, whereas between 1991 and 2020, this proportion was in the age group 15 to 34 years, indicating a shift to the older age segment. Figure 1.10 shows the trend in graphic form.

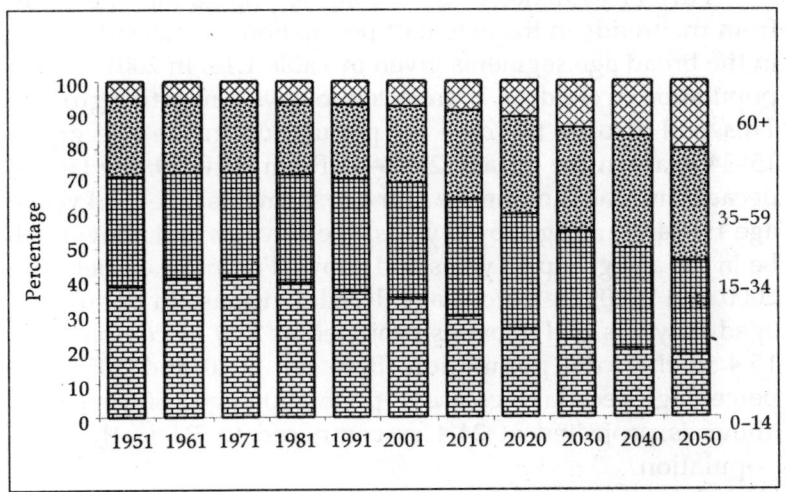

Figure 1.10: Age distribution, India, 1951 to 2050

Comparison of the percentage distribution in age segments 0–14 years (children) and 60 years and above (older persons) shows that in 1951, the percentage of children was seven times the percentage of older persons. In 2001, the ratio was 4.75 times. In 2050, the percentage of older persons is projected to be more than the percentage of children. Figure 1.11 gives the trend.

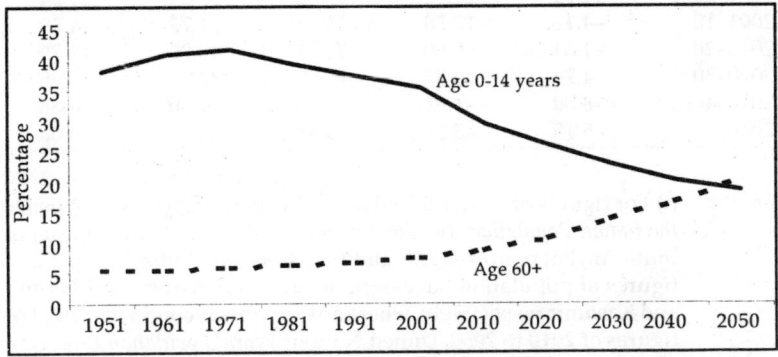

Figure 1.11: Percentage of population of children (aged 0–14 years) and older persons (aged 60 years and above), India, 1951 to 2050.

Further evidence of the ageing of population is evident from the trends in the extent of population increase/decrease in the broad age segments given in Table 1.13. In 2001–10, the population of children is projected to have a negative growth. This will also be the case for population in the age group 15–34 years in the decade 2030–40. From 2010–20, the largest decadal increase among the four age segments (age 0–14 years, age 15–34 years, age 35–59 years, age 60 years and above) will be in the age group 60 years and above. For instance, between 2000 and 2010, the percentage decadal increase in population aged 60 years and above is projected at 31.9 as compared to 15.4 in the total population. Between 2040 and 2050, the percentage decadal increase in population aged 60 years and above is projected at 24.4 as compared to 3.1 in the total population.

Table 1.13: Decadal increase in population in different age groups, India, 1951 to 2050

Decade	0–14 Years	15–34 Years	35–59 Years	60+ Years	Total
	% Increase/ Decrease	*% Increase/ Decrease*	*% Increase/ Decrease*	*% Increase/ Decrease*	*% Increase/ Decrease*
1951–61	31.39	18.92	14.03	26.00	22.98
1961–71	27.90	19.15	25.83	32.32	24.91
1971–81	17.39	31.59	26.10	35.62	24.69
1981–91	17.23	29.43	25.92	29.78	23.86
1991–2001	14.74	21.82	27.62	33.54	21.24
2001–10	–4.16	17.20	33.01	31.72	14.39
2010–20	–1.61	9.60	20.34	40.05	11.79
2020–30	–4.76	0.87	16.75	37.39	7.95
2030–40	–8.08	–1.91	11.46	27.30	4.88
2040–50	–5.15	–5.24	4.81	24.39	3.08

Source: (i) For figures of 1951, SB Mukhopadhyaya, *The Age Distribution of the Indian Population.* (ii) For figures of 1961 and 1971, Census of India. (iii) For figures of 1981 and 1991, Census of India. Interpolated figures of population have been included for Assam, and Jammu and Kashmir respectively, where no Census was conducted.(iv) For figures of 2010 to 2050, United Nations *World Population Prospects, The 2002 Revision.*

Persons aged 60 years and above are not a homogeneous group. It would be necessary to disaggregate this age group into three categories, viz. age 60–69 years, age 70–79 years, and age 80 years and above as the physical capacity for active ageing declines with age. Also, the higher age groups generate greater demands on family, community and state resources, both institutional and non-institutional. The needs for tertiary healthcare and welfare services are far higher in the older age groups. Globally, there has been a rise in the percentage of people aged 80 years and above due to the presence of more favourable factors which increase life expectancy after age 60 years. In India, however, there has been only a small increase in the percentage of persons between 1961 and 2001 as indicated by the data in Table 1.14. The percentage tends to rise from 2020. The small rate of increase in percentage of persons of age 80 years and above could be due to lower access to healthcare facilities, and a generally low standard of living of the bulk of the population aged 60 years and above. It could also be due to wrong age returns of a largely illiterate population at this stage of the life cycle. In numerical terms, however, the numbers have shown a rise. Between 1961 and

Table 1.14: Age distribution of persons aged 60 years and above, India, 1961 to 2050

Year	Age (in years)			
	60–69	*70–79*	*80+*	*Total*
1961	65.11	24.83	10.06	100.00
1971	65.37	24.84	9.79	100.00
1981	64.1	26.35	9.55	100.00
1991	62.79	25.88	11.32	100.00
2001	61.76	27.75	10.49	100.00
2010	59.44	31.04	9.52	100.00
2020	60.26	29.52	10.20	100.00
2030	57.46	31.73	10.80	100.00
2040	53.16	33.58	13.26	100.00
2050	52.17	32.56	15.26	100.00

Source: (i) For figures from 1961 to 2001, Census of India. Figures for 1981 do not include Assam, and for 1991 do not include Jammu & Kashmir. (ii) For figures from 2010 to 2050, *World Population Prospects, The 2002 Revision.*

2001, the number of persons aged 60–69 years has increased by 194 per cent, the number of persons aged 70–79 years increased by 247 per cent, and the number of persons aged 80 years and above by 223 per cent. In the next 50 years (2001 to 2050), the number of persons aged 60–69 years is projected to increase by 240 per cent, the number of persons aged 70–79 years by 372 per cent, and the number of persons aged 80 years and above by 486 per cent. In numerical terms, this would mean caring for 47 million persons aged 80 years and above in 2050, and 100 million persons aged 70–79 years.

In the ninety years period between 1961 and 2050, the demographic transition likely to take place will be that the percentage of persons aged 60–69 years will move down from about two-thirds in 1961 to about half in 2050, the percentage in age group 70–79 years will move up from one-fourth in 1961 to about one-third in 2050, and the percentage in age group 80 years and above will move up from about 10 per cent in 1961 to about 15 per cent in 2050. Figure 1.12 gives the data in graphic form.

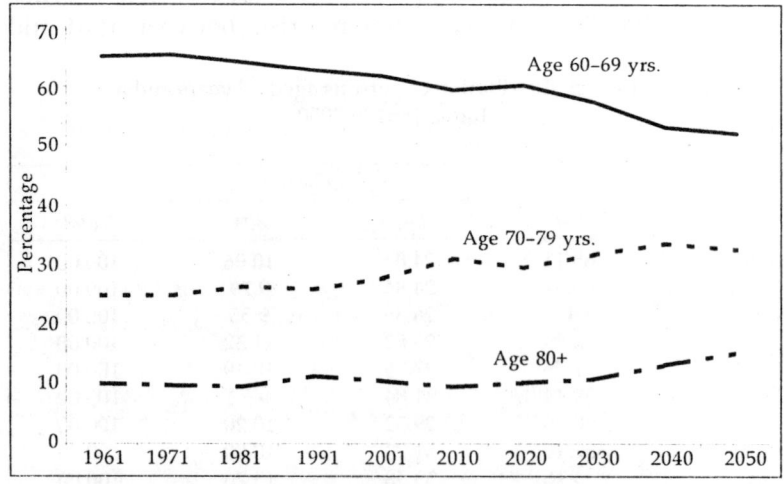

Figure 1.12: Percentage distribution of persons aged 60 –69 years, 70–79 years, and 80 years and above, India, 1961 to 2050

Dependency Ratio

The ratio of children (age 0–14 years) and old persons (age 60 years and above) to persons in the working age group (age 15–59 years) gives the dependency ratio. Table 1.15 gives the childhood dependency ratio, old age dependency ratio, and the total dependency ratio. These are, however, crude ratios since, as stated earlier, an increasing percentage of children continue to be dependents beyond age 14 years as they study in school/college, and many persons of age group 60 years and above continue to earn a livelihood. A fairly large percentage of women of age group 15–59 years are dependent even though they are in the working age group. Also, persons of age group 15–59 years are not a homogeneous category. The total dependency ratio (number of persons aged 0–14 years plus persons aged 60 years and above per 1000 persons aged 15–59 years) shows a fluctuating trend, an increase, followed by a decrease, and then again an increase. The data shows that the dependency ratio of children is declining, the dependency ratio of old persons is increasing.

Table 1.15: Dependency ratio, India, 1951 to 2050

Depen-dency ratio	1951	1961	1971	1981	1991	2001	2010	2020	2030	2040	2050
(0–14)/15–59	684.94	769.70	808.17	733.59	671.75	621.00	343.33	414.47	364.89	320.28	303.58
60+/15–59	98.01	105.62	114.73	120.32	121.97	131.23	139.82	171.34	217.61	264.52	328.79
60+/0–14	0.14	0.14	0.14	0.16	0.18	0.21	0.41	0.41	0.60	0.83	1.08
(0–14)+(60+)/15–59	0.78	0.88	0.92	0.85	0.79	0.75	0.48	0.59	0.58	0.58	0.63

Note: Ratio indicates number per 1000 of the denominator. Interpolated figures for Assam and Jammu Kashmir have been used for 1981 and 1991 respectively.

Source: For figures from 1951 to 2001, Census of India. For figures from 2010 to 2050, *World Population Prospects, The 2002 Revision,*.

Sex Ratio

The sex ratio in the age group 60 years and above given in Table 1.16 shows that between 1901 and 1951, the sex ratio was favourable to females, though in the general population (all ages), the reverse was the case. In 1961, the sex ratio in age group 60 years and above was evenly matched, but in the next three census years females aged 60 years and above were at a disadvantage. In 2001, again, the sex ratio (age 60 years and above) was favourable to females. Projections indicate that the trend will continue. Even then it is lower than in the more developed countries where it is projected to be 1282 females per 1000 males in 2050, or even in less developed countries where it is projected to be 1172. Figures on sex ratio in the age groups 60–69 years, 70–79 years, and 80 years and above indicate that the sex ratio favourable to females improves as the chronological age increases.

Table 1.16: Sex ratio in the older age groups, India, 1901 to 2050

Year	Sex ratio (total population)	Sex ratio 60+	Age (in years)		
			60–69	70–79	80+
1901	972	1192	N.A.	N.A	N.A
1911	964	1130	N.A	N.A	N.A
1921	955	1080	N.A	N.A	N.A
1931	950	1046	N.A	N.A	N.A
1941	945	1029	N.A	N.A	N.A
1951	946	1028	N.A	N.A	N.A
1961	941	1000	967	1038	1129
1971	930	938	921	941	1053
1981	934	960	952	962	1010
1991	927	930	935	924	917
2001	933	1029	1052	970	1051
2010	944	1108	1052	1170	1287
2020	953	1084	1007	1164	1367
2030	964	1085	1017	1123	1383
2040	976	1101	1027	1136	1346
2050	986	1115	1034	1146	1363

Source: 1. Figures from 1901 to 1951 from SB Mukhopadhyaya, *The Age Distribution of Indian Population.*
2. Figures from 1961 to 2001, from the Census of India.
3. Figures from 2010 to 2050, from United Nations, *World Population Prospects, The 2002 Revision.*

Rural and Urban Distribution

India is a predominantly rural country with 72 per cent of the total population living in rural areas in 2001. Data in Table 1.17 shows a disproportionately larger percentage of persons aged 60 years and above live in rural areas as compared to urban areas. This is possibly due to the age selective character of migration. Older persons tend to stay behind to look after assets in the village, or to perform other household functions as they would have fewer chances of employment outside the village. Problem of housing in urban areas is also a factor.

Table 1.17: Percentage distribution of rural and urban population aged 60 years and above, India 1961 to 2001

Year	Population 60+			Total population		
	Rural	Urban	Total	Rural	Urban	Total
1961	84.87	15.13	100.00	82.03	17.97	100.00
1971	83.40	16.60	100.00	80.09	19.91	100.00
1981	80.41	19.59	100.00	76.66	23.34	100.00
1991	78.12	21.88	100.00	74.29	25.71	100.00
2001	74.98	25.02	100.00	72.18	27.82	100.00

Source: (i) Figures of persons 60+, 1961 to 1991, from *Census of India, Ageing Population of India* ;(ii) Figures of total population, from *Census of India*, 1991, *Final Population Totals, Paper 2 of 1992*,.(iii) Figures of 2001, from *Census of India*.

Marital Status

Family formation through the institution of marriage is expected to provide in-built security for the care of older persons and other vulnerable groups. Data from Table 1.18 which gives the age, sex and marital status of males and females aged 60 years and above from 1961 to 2001, shows that marriage is near universal in the Indian population, more so for females. The percentage of unmarried females aged 60 years and above has shown a small rise. It was still, however, less 1.5 per cent. In the case of males, it was about 3 per cent. In numbers it meant about one million males and about 0.6 million females were likely to be vulnerable in terms of family care.

Table 1.18: Percentage distribution of persons aged 60 years and above by sex and marital status in rural and urban areas, India, 1961 to 2001

Rural/Urban	Year	Males						Females						Difference
		Never married	Married	Wi-dowed	Divorced or sepa-rated	Not speci-fied	Total	Never married	Married	Wi-dowed	Divorced or sepa-rated	Not speci-fied	Total	(widowed F-M)
Rural	1961	2.90	68.58	27.89	0.59	0.05	100.00	0.33	23.99	75.15	0.46	0.06	100.00	47.26
	1971	2.44	74.06	22.95	0.49	0.05	100.00	0.32	30.53	68.73	0.39	0.03	100.00	45.78
	1981	1.90	77.49	20.15	0.41	0.06	100.00	0.28	35.50	63.80	0.41	0.02	100.00	43.65
	1991	3.39	80.07	16.16	0.33	0.05	100.00	1.28	44.63	44.63	0.40	0.01	100.00	37.52
	2001	2.40	81.64	15.62	0.35	–	100.00	1.25	48.18	50.08	0.49	–	100.00	34.46
Urban	1961	2.64	71.71	25.12	0.45	0.07	100.00	0.84	22.20	76.52	0.38	0.05	100.00	51.50
	1971	2.36	77.76	19.41	0.28	0.19	100.00	0.61	27.61	71.38	0.30	0.10	100.00	51.97
	1981	2.19	81.14	16.27	0.29	0.10	100.00	0.72	32.42	66.46	0.37	0.03	100.00	50.19
	1991	3.69	83.00	12.98	0.26	0.08	100.00	1.79	42.52	55.29	0.39	0.01	100.00	42.31
	2001	3.00	83.66	13.06	0.29	–	100.00	2.25	44.84	52.40	0.51	–	100.00	39.34
Total	1961	2.86	69.06	27.47	0.57	0.05	100.00	0.41	23.72	75.36	0.45	0.06	100.00	47.89
	1971	2.43	74.67	22.37	0.46	0.08	100.00	0.37	30.04	69.17	0.37	0.04	100.00	46.80
	1981	1.95	78.19	19.40	0.39	0.07	100.00	0.36	34.89	64.33	0.40	0.02	100.00	44.93
	1991	3.45	80.70	15.47	0.32	0.05	100.00	1.39	44.16	54.04	0.40	0.01	100.00	38.57
	2001	2.55	82.14	14.98	0.33	–	100.00	1.50	47.34	50.66	0.49	–	100.00	35.68

Source: Census of India

The percentage of married males aged 60 years and above has increased in both rural and urban areas. It is also substantially higher than the percentage of widowed males. The percentage of married females has also increased. The percentage of widowed females aged 60 years and above has come down. This is a reflection of the increase in life expectancy of males, and a reduction in age difference of the couple. The percentage of widowed females in 2001 is, however, still a little higher than that of married females. The difference in percentage of married females and widowed females is getting reduced (Figure 1.13). Bhatt, using census data from 1961 to 1981, estimated that in India the difference in the age of the couple has come down from 8.4 years in 1961 to 7.0 years in 1981 . He also analyzed the mortality risks of men and women after 45 years of age and concluded that husbands of women have a higher mortality risk which is about 2.5 times that of their wives. Once widowed, both men and women, have a mortality risk. Among women, the risk is greater (Bhatt, 1998).

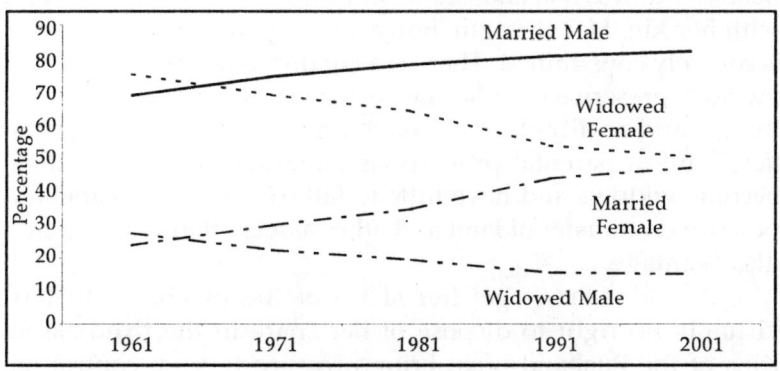

Figure 1.13: Percentage of married and widowed males and females aged 60 years and above, India, 1961 to 2001

The percentage of widowed females is far higher than that of widowed males in all the census years. There is a negative social attitude towards widow remarriage. Women generally do not remarry as compared to men, except when she is young and childless, belongs to certain castes where this is permitted, or lives in regions where levirate practice is followed among certain castes. A further factor is the inferior quality of grooms that become available at an older age as it is customary for women to marry men older than themselves. A remarried woman's social status is also not the same as that of a married woman.

Disaggregation of the population aged 60 years and above (60–69 years, 70–79 years, and 80 years and above) by marital status given in Table 1.19 shows that there is a far greater incidence of widowhood in the higher age groups among both males and females. For the first time in 1991, married females exceeded widowed females in the age group 60–69 years. However, in the higher age groups widowed women still outnumber married women. Also, the incidence of widowhood among women rises sharply as the age increases.

Widowed status makes the person vulnerable; however, the situation is far worse in the case of women. She has to face the problems of deprivation of fixed assets owned by her husband unless she chooses to stay on in the same household with her kin. Her strength, however, in getting her due status is severely constrained. There is a big difference between what the laws prescribe on inheritance, the customary practice, and the ground reality. Women have limited rights in accessing her share in parental property as daughters, even after they become widows and have little to fall back upon. Customary practice on transfer of land and other assets often works to her disadvantage.

A widow may get her share of the produce but has virtually no right to dispose of her share in the fixed asset. Kins of the husband often bring pressure to keep control on management and use of land, and other property resources. If she has no sons, her problems get aggravated and she may be forced to forfeit her dues in the use of property. Her participation in economic activity is severely restrained by socio-cultural taboos. Illiteracy, age, social stigma attached to widowhood, social isolation, ignorance of the ways of the world and on how to assert her rights in most matters, and absence

Table 1.19: Percentage distribution by age, sex and marital status of persons aged 60-69 years, 70-79 years and 80 years and above, India, 1961 to 2001

Age (in years)	Year	Males						Females					
		Never married	Married	Widowed	Divorced or Separated	Not Specified	Total	Never married	Married	Widowed	Divorced or Separated	Not Specified	Total
60-69	1961	2.88	73.45	23.06	0.57	0.05	100.00	0.41	28.73	70.29	0.51	0.06	100.00
	1971	2.41	78.85	18.20	0.46	0.08	100.00	0.38	36.05	63.10	0.43	0.04	100.00
	1981	1.96	82.52	15.13	0.39	0.00	100.00	0.36	42.35	56.84	0.46	-	100.00
	1991	2.30	85.42	11.95	0.30	0.03	100.00	0.72	52.54	46.30	0.43	-	100.00
	2001	1.96	86.80	10.91	0.33	-	100.00	1.13	56.21	42.12	0.54	-	100.00
70-79	1961*	2.81	60.46	36.11	0.56	0.06	100.00	0.40	14.80	84.39	0.35	0.06	100.00
	1971*	2.46	66.58	30.43	0.45	0.08	100.00	0.35	19.01	80.32	0.27	0.04	100.00
	1981*	1.94	70.52	27.15	0.39	0.00	100.00	0.38	21.73	77.59	0.30	-	100.00
	1991	2.44	77.59	19.65	0.30	0.03	100.00	0.86	32.69	66.09	0.36	0.01	100.00
	2001	2.76	78.30	18.61	0.33	-	100.00	1.13	56.21	42.12	0.54	-	100.00
80+	1991	12.19	61.71	25.39	0.46	0.26	100.00	6.40	23.42	69.78	0.33	0.08	100.00
	2001	5.42	65.29	28.94	0.36	-	100.00	3.51	25.09	71.01	0.39	-	100.00

* Includes 80 years and above.

Note: Figures for 1981, exclude Assam: Figures for 1991 exclude Jammu & Kashmir.

Source: Census of India, 1961, 1971, 1981, 1991, 2001.

of institutional structures which can help her to get her claim add to her vulnerability and exploitation. Widowed women thus get reduced much faster to a state of poverty.

The census figures have reported that less than 1 per cent persons aged 60 years and above are divorced/separated. This category is grossly under-reported. Many women have to face virtual desertion, particularly among the lower income groups. They represent a severely disadvantaged category.

The marital status of persons aged 60 years and above in the states shows an interesting variation, reflecting the socio-cultural variations in age at marriage and the mortality differentials. In the bigger states, in 2001, about 78 to 87 per cent of the males aged 60 years and above were married. In the case of females aged 60 years and above, however, the percentage of married ranged between 37 in West Bengal and Kerala, to 60 in Punjab and Haryana. In both these states, the practice of levirate marriage in several land owning castes accounts for a larger incidence of married status.

There is a larger evidence of widowhood in the southern states, Orissa, West Bengal and Assam. In all these states, the percentage of females aged 60 years and above was more than 55, with West Bengal having the highest percentage (60 per cent). The lowest percentage of widowed females aged 60 years and above was in Punjab (38 per cent) and Haryana (39 per cent). This phenomenon could be because of the large difference in age at marriage of couples in these states, the absence of levirate marriages and probably fewer instances of remarriage of widows. Using the census data of 1961, 1971 and 1981, Bhatt estimated the average age difference between husband and wife to be between 9 and 10 years in Karnataka and West Bengal, and between 8 and 9 years in Andhra Pradesh and Tamil Nadu. He also found a reduction in average age difference between husband and wife in all the states between 1961 and 1981 (Bhatt, 1998). Figure 1.14 gives the percentage of widowed females aged 60 years and above in the bigger states according to the 2001 census.

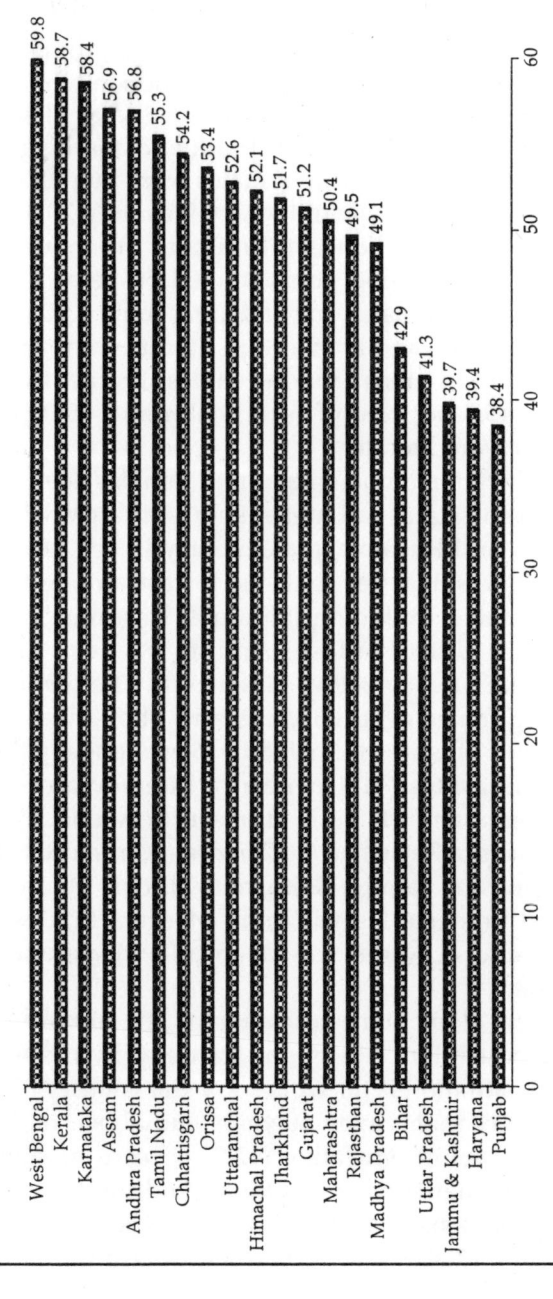

Figure 1.14: Percentage of widowed females aged 60 years and above in states, 2001

Literacy

India has very low level of literacy in the higher age groups, a reflection of the very poor state of their participation in schools in their younger days. Table 1.20, which gives the literacy level of persons aged 60 years and above in India and the bigger states, shows that while 52.8 per cent of males were literate, in the case of females the percentage of literacy was only 20.3.

There is a big difference between rural and urban areas in the level of education among persons aged 60 years and above for both males and females. In rural areas, only 13.0 per cent females aged 60 years and above were literate compared to 41.8 per cent in urban areas. Among males, literacy was somewhat better— 45.5 per cent of rural males and 75.0 per cent of urban males were literate.

The level of education among males and females aged 60 years and above in the states (all areas) shows a fairly wide variation. In Jammu and Kashmir, male literacy in age group 60 years and above was 32.5 per cent, the lowest among the bigger states. Five states, excluding Jammu & Kashmir, viz., Rajasthan, Haryana, Uttar Pradesh, Andhra Pradesh and Punjab, too, had male literacy below 44 per cent. The highest literacy rate among males aged 60 years and above was in Kerala (81.5 per cent). This was followed by West Bengal (68.8 per cent) and Maharashtra (61.4 per cent). Literacy among females aged 60 years and above is at a very low ebb. The lowest literacy rate was in Rajasthan (10.2 per cent). In six states, excluding Rajasthan, viz., Jammu & Kashmir, Bihar, Madhya Pradesh, Himachal Pradesh, Haryana and Madhya Pradesh, it was less than 15 per cent. Kerala was far ahead with a literacy rate of 58.1 per cent.

If one considers elementary education as the minimum desirable level of education, functional for daily living and other activities, the situation is far worse. For the country as a whole, 20.0 per cent of males aged 60 years and above had a middle and higher level of education (12.2 per cent in rural areas and 43.5 per cent in urban areas). Orissa, Andhra Pradesh, Madhya Pradesh and Rajasthan had less than 15.0 per cent males aged 60 years and above with this level of education. In

Table 1.20: Percentage distribution of persons aged 60 years and above by sex and level of education, India and states, 2001

India/States	Males						Females					
	Illiterate	Literate without educational level	Below primary	Primary	Middle	Matric/ Secondary and above	Illiterate	Literate without educational level	Below primary	Primary	Middle	Matric/ Secondary and above
India	47.17	3.57	14.78	14.53	5.88	14.08	79.75	1.93	6.99	6.29	1.96	3.08
Andhra Pradesh	56.79	3.47	9.52	15.58	2.63	12.01	83.90	1.84	4.27	7.04	1.03	1.92
Assam	41.45	2.78	22.44	13.78	7.12	12.42	78.93	1.41	10.21	5.40	1.83	2.22
Bihar	55.02	4.00	6.69	14.38	5.75	14.15	88.21	1.71	2.51	4.93	1.20	1.43
Gujarat	43.29	1.27	21.08	16.07	3.33	14.96	75.53	0.83	11.57	7.55	1.09	3.43
Haryana	57.84	1.94	6.94	10.43	7.30	15.55	87.03	1.43	2.36	4.75	1.72	2.71
Himachal Pradesh	52.35	2.51	10.55	12.28	7.93	14.39	87.32	1.63	3.16	4.55	1.38	1.96
Jammu and Kashmir	67.51	4.78	2.86	7.70	6.22	10.92	88.85	3.93	1.01	2.54	1.64	2.04
Karnataka	46.12	2.10	15.19	16.60	3.93	16.05	79.95	1.18	6.84	6.98	1.55	3.51
Kerala	18.56	2.63	31.95	22.53	7.78	16.56	41.95	2.27	27.98	16.69	4.43	6.68
Madhya Pradesh	51.49	3.58	19.45	11.43	4.84	9.20	86.45	1.82	5.19	3.39	1.33	1.81
Maharashtra	38.56	2.54	23.34	16.05	3.46	16.05	77.28	1.36	9.56	6.30	1.21	4.29
Orissa	39.72	3.59	27.18	18.70	2.80	8.01	84.34	1.22	7.73	5.32	0.54	0.85
Punjab	57.29	2.28	4.87	10.85	7.22	17.50	81.15	2.36	2.49	7.56	2.56	3.88
Rajasthan	59.30	4.95	11.67	10.69	4.23	9.17	89.77	1.94	3.18	2.87	1.04	1.20
Tamil Nadu	39.41	9.69	9.48	20.14	7.54	13.74	74.13	5.25	4.34	8.80	3.68	3.80
Uttar Pradesh	57.46	3.68	7.69	12.11	7.29	11.77	87.42	2.11	2.30	4.35	1.77	2.04
West Bengal	31.25	2.01	21.37	12.86	11.43	21.08	70.33	1.39	13.03	6.52	4.23	4.49

Source: Census of India, 2001.

the case of females aged 60 years and above, the situation is far worse. Only 5.0 per cent females of this age group in India had middle and higher level of education (1.6 per cent in rural areas and 15.2 per cent in urban areas). In four of the bigger states, it did not exceed 3 per cent. Figure 1.15 gives the data in graphic form. Education level of males of middle and higher level of education has been shown in the graph in ascending order. It will take about four to five decades for the lower age cohorts to reach the age 60 years and above, for a visible improvement in education, and the negotiating capacity and empowerment that it can provide.

Distribution in population aged 60 years and above in states

The number of persons aged 60 years and above in states in 2001, and the percentage of persons aged 60 years and above show considerable variation, and is a reflection of the varying size of population in the state. Among the bigger states, Himachal Pradesh had the lowest number of persons aged 60 years and above (0.55 million), while Uttar Pradesh had the largest number (11.65 million), followed by Maharashtra (8.46 million) and Andhra Pradesh (5.79 million). Figure 1.16 gives the population of persons aged 60 years and above in the bigger states in graphic form.

The percentage of population aged 60 and above, too, varies in different states. Table 1.21 gives the percentages in 2001. Assam had the lowest percentage (5.9 per cent) and Kerala the highest (10.5 per cent).

Several states, which are economically backward, have a large number of persons aged 60 years and above who need income security, health and other services. For instance, Uttar Pradesh, Bihar, Madhya Pradesh, Orissa and Rajasthan have nearly 37 per cent of the total population in India aged 60 years and above. Poor fiscal health of these states makes it difficult for them to cope with the needs of older persons. The organized sector of private employment in these states is very small, with very few workers having superannuation benefits.

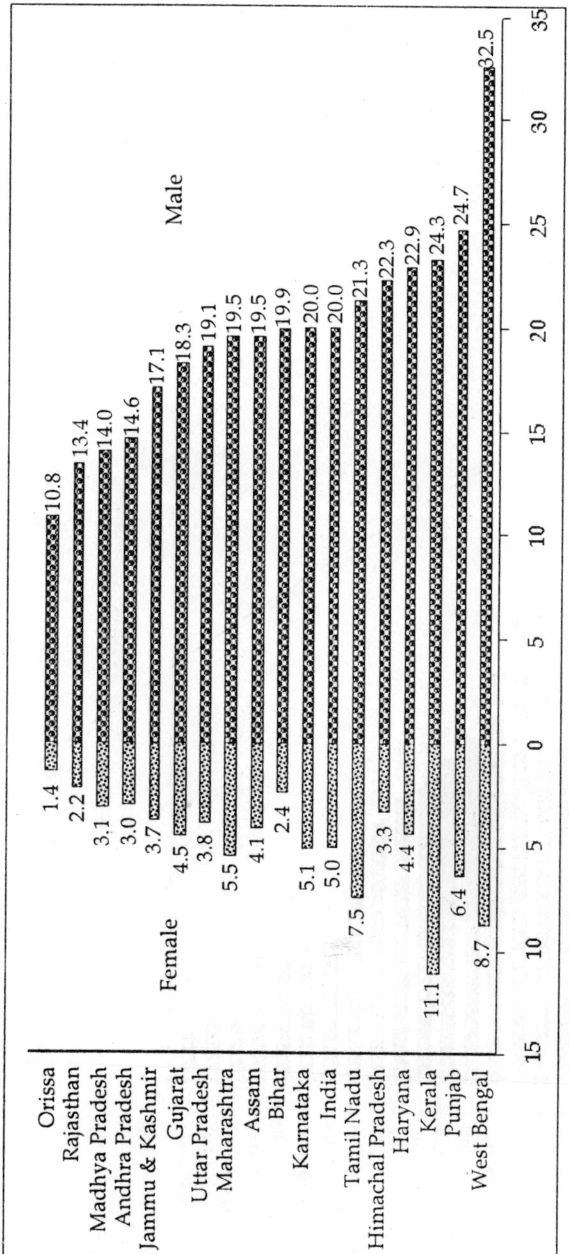

Figure 1.15: Percentage of persons aged 60 years and above in states with level of education middle and above by sex, 2001

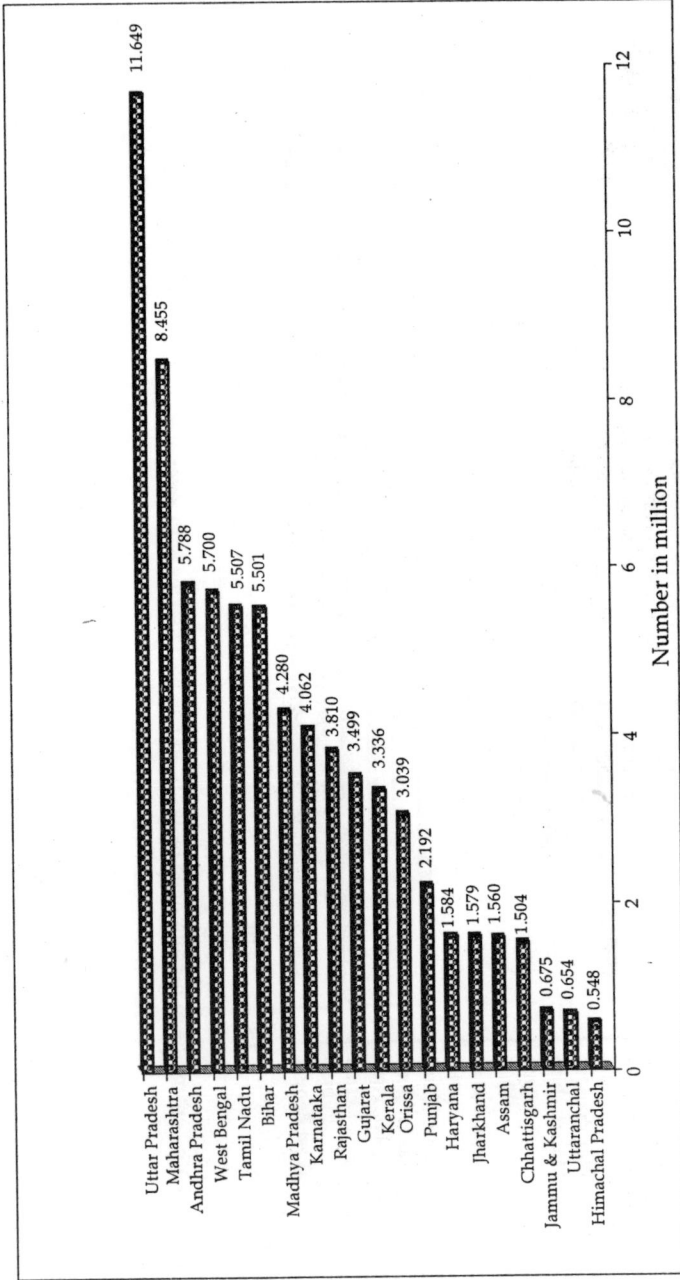

Figure 1.16: Number of persons aged 60 years and aove in states, 2001

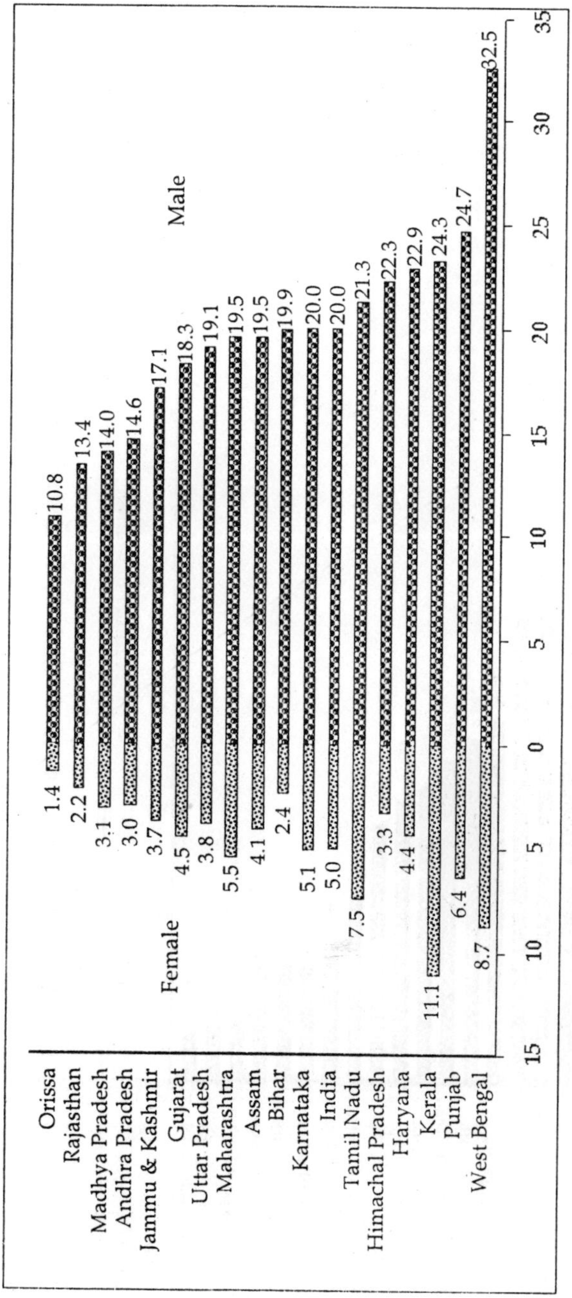

Figure 1.15: Percentage of persons aged 60 years and above in states with level of education middle and above by sex, 2001

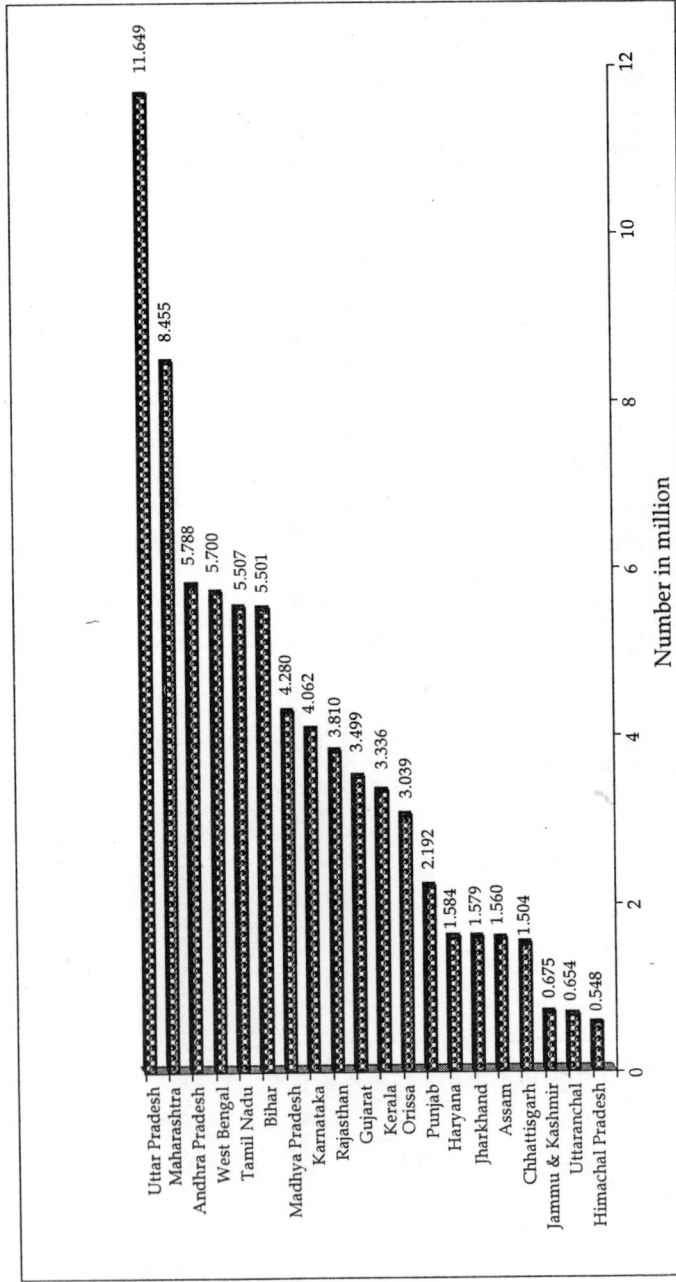

Figure 1.16: Number of persons aged 60 years and aove in states, 2001

Table 1.21: Percentage of persons age 60 years and above in states, 2001

<7.0	7.0 to 8.0	8.0+
Assam (5.9)	Uttar Pradesh (7.0)	Orissa (8.3)
Jharkhand (5.9)	Madhya Pradesh (7.1)	Maharashtra (8.8)
Bihar (6.6)	West Bengal (7.1)	Tamil Nadu (8.8)
Jammu & Kashmir (6.7)	Chhattisgarh (7.2)	Himachal Pradesh (9.0)
Rajasthan (6.7)	Haryana (7.5)	Punjab (9.0)
Gujarat (6.9)	INDIA (7.4)	Kerala (10.5)
	Andhra Pradesh (7.6)	
	Uttaranchal (7.7)	
	Karnataka (7.7)	

Note: Bigger states have been included here.
Source: Census of India, 2001.

Persons aged 60 years and above comprised 12.7 per cent of the electorate in 2001 (population aged 18 years and above), up from 8.7 per cent in 1941. This percentage will go on increasing with the rise in demographic ageing. Figure 1. 17 gives the trend.

The percentage of population aged 60 years and above in the electorate varies in different states, depending on the extent of ageing of population. Amomg the bigger states, the lowest percentage in 2001 was in Assam (10.33 per cent), followed by Jharkhand. The highest percentage was in Kerala (15.30 per cent). Figure 1.18 gives the variation between different states.

Persons aged 60 years and above, if they are well organized, can play a very effective role in interacting with political parties and negotiating with them on the facilities and benefits that could be accorded to them. The segment represents the most secular minority, cutting across all ideological philosophies. In the developed countries, associations of older citizens have organized themselves to promote their interests and engage in welfare activities. They have formed pressure groups, and negotiate through advocacy, media, research and dissemination for enhanced social security benefits and social services from the state, employers, non-governmental organizations and other bodies. This is unfortunately not the case in India where only a few senior citizens' associations exist in urban areas of retired professionals and superannuated government employees, without any mass base.

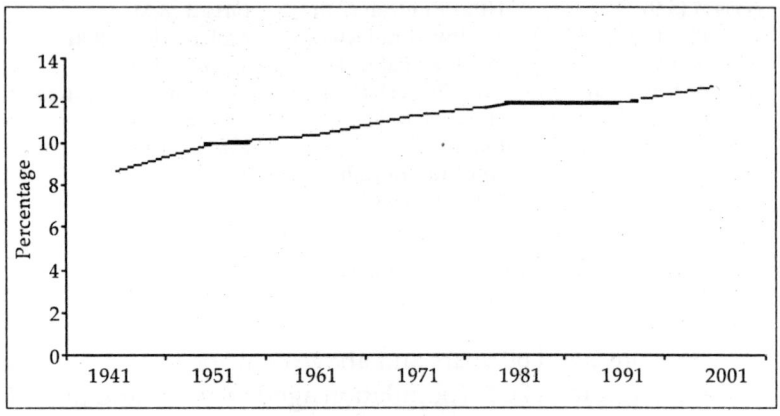

Figure 1.17: Percentage of persons aged 60 years and above in the electorate, India, 1941 to 2001

Summing Up

The world is undergoing a major demographic change which is affecting society and economy. The process of ageing is universal though the rate of transition varies from one country to another. In 1950, 8.2 per cent of the world's population was 60 years and above. In 2000, it increased to 10.0 per cent. In 2050, the population aged 60 years and above is projected to increase to 21.4 per cent. In 1950, 46.4 per cent of the world's population aged 60 years and above was in the mcre developed regions, and 53.6 per cent in the less developed regions. In 2000, the percentages were 38.2 and 61.8 respectively. In 2050, the projected percentages are 20.6 in the more developed regions and 79.4 in the less developed regions. The median age of population has shown an increase. In the more developed regions, it has increased from 28.6 years in 1950 to 37.3 years in 2000 and is projected to increase to 45.2 years in 2050. In the less developed regions, it has increased from 21.3

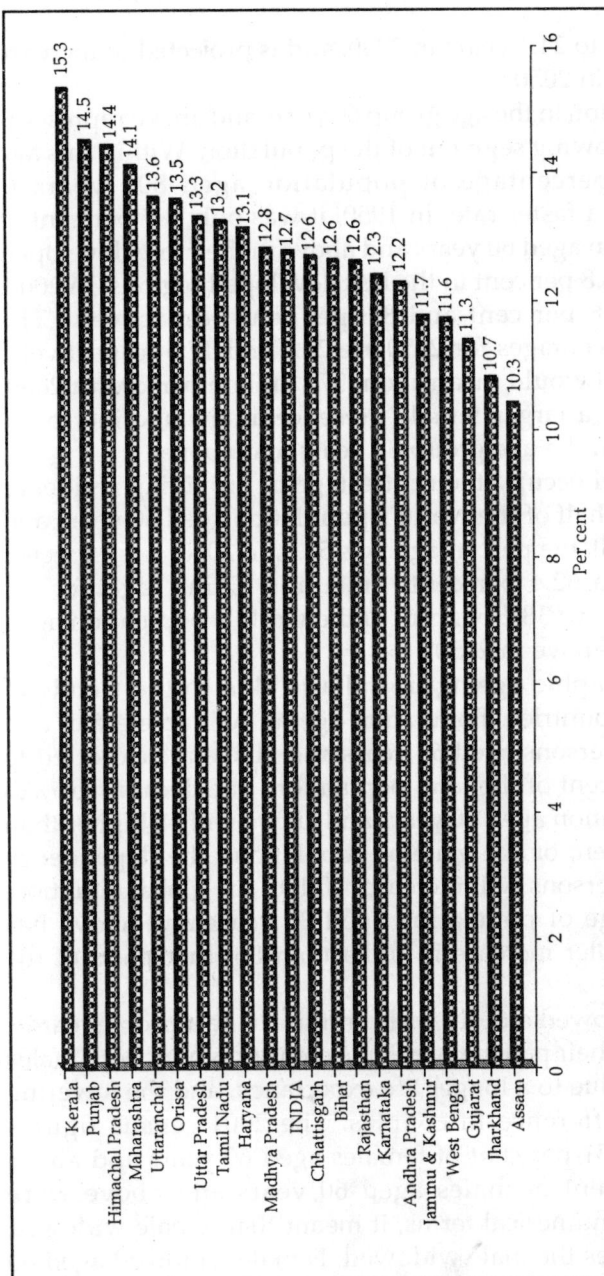

Figure 1.18: Percentage of persons aged 60 years and above in the electorate in states, 2001

years in 1950 to 24.1 years in 2000, and is projected to increase to 35.7 years in 2050.

Population in the age group 60 years and above represents the fastest growing segment of the population. Within this age group, the percentage of population aged 80+ years is increasing at a faster rate. In 1950, it was only 8.9 per cent of the population aged 60 years and above in the more developed regions and 4.8 per cent in the less developed regions. In 2000, it rose to 15.8 per cent and 8.6 per cent, respectively. The projected percentages for 2050 are 28.6 and 17.5 respectively. In numbers, it would mean about 377 million persons in 2050.

There is a larger female presence as the age increases, particularly in the age group 80 years and above.

Asia will occupy the centrestage in providing residence to more than half of the world's population aged 60 years and above. In 2000, the percentage was 53.1. In 2050, it is expected to increase to 62.4 per cent. India and China together are projected to have 38.1 per cent of the world's population aged 60 years and above in 2050.

Demographic ageing in India is akin to the trends in developing countries. Population ageing will accelerate, and in 2050, the persons aged 60 years and above are expected to reach 20 per cent of the total population. The decadal growth rate of population aged 60 years and above will be higher than that of children, or the general population. The dependency ratio of old persons will increase. Unlike the global situation, the percentage of population aged 80 years and above has shown a smaller increase in India than in other parts of the world.

The widowed elderly will continue to be a problem area. It is true that their percentages have come down for both males and females due to a longer life expectancy, and the lowering of the age difference in couples. The 2001 census figures indicate that 51 per cent of females aged 60 years and above and 15 per cent of males aged 60 years and above were widowed. In numerical terms, it meant that female widowed were 3.48 times the male widowed. Female widowed aged 60 years and above represent the most disadvantaged group.

Persons aged 60 years and above have a very high illiteracy rate, much higher than other segments of the population. In 2001, 47 per cent of males and 80 per cent of females aged 60 years and above were illiterate. In seven of the 17 bigger states in 2001, female literacy in age group 60 years and above was less than 15 per cent. The level of education of persons 60 years and above was poor. Only 20 per cent of males and 5 per cent of females aged 60 years and above had a middle and higher level of education.

There is considerable variation in the number of persons aged 60 years and above in different states because of difference in their size of population. Among the bigger states, Himachal Pradesh had only 0.55 million persons aged 60 years and above in 2001. Uttar Pradesh, on the other hand, had 11.65 million persons in the same age group. Assam had the lowest percentage of persons aged 60 years and above (5.9 per cent), while Kerala had the highest in this age group (10.5 per cent). Several states, which are economically backward and have poor fiscal health, have to cope with providing services to this segment of the population.

The median age of population in India in 2000 was 23.4 years. It is projected to increase to 30.3 years in 2025 and to 37.9 years in 2050. Older persons (aged 60 years and above) comprised 12.7 per cent of the electorate (18 years and above) in 2001, up from 8.7 per cent in 1941. It is projected to increase further with the ageing of population. The percentage of population aged 60 years and above in the electorate varies in different states, depending on the extent of ageing of population. In 2001, Kerala had the highest percentage of older persons in the electorate (15.3 per cent). Assam had the lowest percentage (10.3 per cent). Older persons need to organize themselves, form a pressure group to pursue their interests, and negotiate with political parties, the government, employers, non-governmental organizations and other bodies for better social security benefits and social services. This is unfortunately not the case in India where only a few senior citizens' associations exist in urban areas of retired professionals and superannuated government employees, without any mass base.

2

Financial Security in Old Age

Responsibility of sons to look after their parents in old age is enjoined by tradition and custom. Preference for male children in eastern societies, including India, has been an in-built social security measure, cutting across religious, caste and socio-economic boundaries. The prevailing social norm and public policy laid down that in old age the family had the responsibility to look after the older person's needs. Taking assistance from persons other than family members met with great social disapproval even if it was due to circumstances beyond its control. It meant a loss of face for the individual, the family and the kin. It was only in case of destitution that religious orders, charitable trusts and the state were expected to step in.

The National Sample Survey Organization, in its 42nd Round, 1986–87, and 52nd Round, 1995–96 studied the situation of aged population in India. It investigated the current degree of dependence among persons aged 60 years and above by sex in rural and urban areas. The data given in Table 2.1 shows that almost nine-tenths of females and almost half the males are fully or partly dependent on others, in both rural and urban areas. The survey also shows that most persons aged 60 years and above, who are economically dependent, are supported by their children and grand children. About 14 per cent are supported by their spouse and about 7 per cent by others (NSSO, 1998). However, nearly half the males and nearly 12 per cent of the females aged 60 years and above were not economically dependent on others, may be because they still work, or have earnings from land holdings or other sources of sustenance.

Table 2.1: Distribution per 1000 of aged persons by state of economic
independence, India, 1986–87 and 1995–96

NSSO survey	Residence	Sex	State of economic independence			
			Not depen-dent on others	Partially depen-dent on others	Fully depen-dent on others	Total (includ-ing no response)
NSSO 52nd	Rural	Male	485	180	313	1000
Round		Female	121	146	706	1000
1995–96		Person	301	163	511	1000
	Urban	Male	515	169	297	1000
		Female	115	110	757	1000
		Person	311	· 139	532	1000
NSSO 42nd	Rural	Male	511	162	327	1000
Round		Female	88	137	775	1000
1986–87		Person	340	152	508	1000
	Urban	Male	457	169	374	1000
		Female	48	91	861	1000
		Person	289	137	574	1000

Source: NSSO, *The Aged in India: A Socio-Economic Profile*, 52nd Round, July
1995–June 1996.

Building Old Age Security in Working Life

It is now being recognized, even in developing societies like
India, that informal networks based on family, kinship and
community ties are no longer sufficient for meeting financial
needs in old age. Sole dependence on children may not be
enough due to changes in family size, composition and
structure. Also, there are more instances of nuclear households.
In rural areas, households even when they become nuclear,
continue to interact and assist. Neighbours, often from the same
caste, help because of their close proximity and long
association. In urban areas, however, physical dispersal and
distance act as a deterrent factor.

Family obligations of children towards their parents are
undergoing a change. There is deviation from the norm. The
extent, however, may vary in different households. Financial
responsibilities of children, too, have increased. Fewer children
can imply a larger share of dependency on their shoulders,

specially in the case of a single earning member. A wide range of expenses have to be met by children. Sons have to shoulder the responsibility of educating their children which may extend to 20 to 25 years, and require large expenses as good education and training come at a price. Even for education in government/local authority schools where tuition is free and text books and some other incentives are provided to students, parents still have to bear some expenses. In urban areas, they are further required to meet the increased costs of rent, transportation and other expenses. The immediate consumption needs of households are fueled by bank loans which have to be repaid on an instalment basis. Sons and their wives become more concerned with the immediate gratification of their needs, including that of their children. The current family environment puts a stress on the amount that can be spared for sending regular remittances to parents to provide food and shelter on a sustained basis, and meet their medical and other expenses, some of which may entail a heavy financial outgo, specially in view of the increase in life expectancy after 60, and the escalating costs of medical treatment. Earning children will also have to find ways of meeting not only their current needs but also to save for incurring expenses pertaining to marriage of daughters, healthcare and other social obligations. They also need to save for meeting their needs in old age, and invest in housing for a place to stay after retirement from economic activity. When parents stay on in the same household as the son, discriminatory care can arise. Decision making also passes to the hands of the son. Parents tend to feel marginalized and lonely, as they are not integrated into the functioning of the household.

Financial requirements for old age security of individuals for about a decade and a half to two decades after they reach age 60 years have, therefore, to be designed differently. People in their working life span have to think early enough to invest in long-term saving instruments and/or build capital assets to generate income in old age when they are no longer working. This is particularly true for most persons who have no retirement benefits (provident fund, pension, gratuity) from their employment. The working period, when a person is economically active (a span of about 40 to 45 years for males, and a somewhat shorter period for females), is thus the best period to initiate steps to plan for meeting financial needs in old age for self and spouse as a safeguard against a decline in standard of living. Individuals have to assess their short and long term expenditure requirements in old age, the nature and extent of which will vary as they grow older. Trends in inflation will also have to be taken into account in estimating the costs.

It is important first to see the extent of economic participation of persons in India in their working age to ascertain to what extent they would be able to meet their current needs and, hopefully, to make savings and investments which can sustain them in old age.

We look first at the work participation rate at age 15–59 years given by the 2001 census which is normatively the working age. The data given in Table 2.2 shows that in 2001 in the age group 15–59 years, 72 per cent of rural males and 70 per cent of urban males were main workers (employed for six or more months in a year). Among females, the percentages were 27 in rural areas and only 14 in urban areas. The percentage of marginal workers was less than 12 for males in rural areas and 5 in urban areas. It was higher in the case of females, 22 per cent in the case of rural females aged 15–59 years, and above 4 per cent in the case of urban females aged 15–59 years.

Figure 2.1 gives the pattern of work participation rate (main + marginal) in graphic form for males and females in rural and urban areas in different age groups. The 2001 census data shows that in the case of both males and females, work participation (main + marginal) rises in the younger ages. Females, however, have a far lower work participation rate in all age groups. The difference between male and female work participation rates in the age group 15–59 years in rural areas was 34 per cent and in urban areas 57 per cent. Putting it differently, in rural areas, work participation rate in the age group 15–59 years among males was about 1.7 times that of females while in urban areas, it was almost 4.3 times that of females.

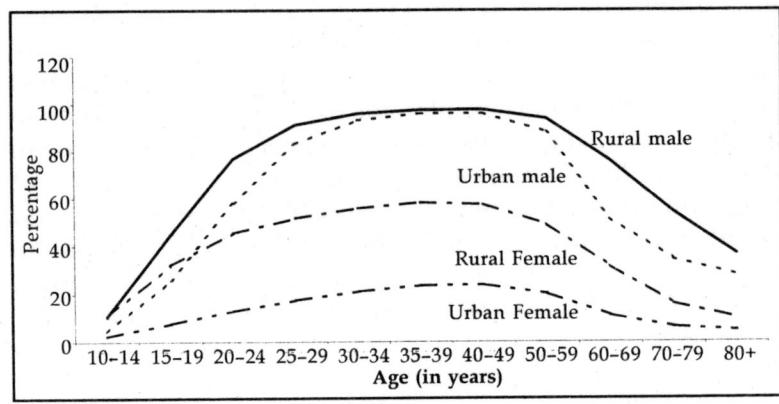

Figure 2.1: Work participation rate (main + marginal workers) in
rural and urban areas by age and sex, India, 2001

Data in Table 2.2 also shows that in the case of rural males,
the difference between the percentage of main workers aged

Table 2.2: Work participation rate in age group 15–59 years, and in age
group 60 years and above by sex in rural and urban areas, India, 2001.

Resident	Sex	Age group	Work participation rate				Total
			Main workers	Marginal workers	Main + Marginal workers	Non-workers	
Rural	Male	15–59	71.76	11.59	83.35	16.65	100.00
		60+	56.83	8.77	65.60	34.40	100.00
	Female	15–59	27.23	22.24	49.47	50.53	100.00
		60+	13.73	11.21	24.94	75.06	100.00
	Total	15–59	50.05	16.78	66.83	33.17	100.00
		60+	35.01	10.01	45.02	54.98	100.00
Urban	Male	15–59	70.05	4.84	74.89	25.11	100.00
		60+	40.70	3.43	44.13	55.88	100.00
	Female	15–59	14.08	3.53	17.61	82.39	100.00
		60+	6.81	2.15	8.96	91.04	100.00
	Total	15–59	43.80	4.22	48.02	51.98	100.00
		60+	23.43	2.78	26.21	73.79	100.00
Total	Male	15–59	71.23	9.48	80.71	19.29	100.00
		60+	52.81	7.44	60.25	39.75	100.00
	Female	15–59	23.33	16.69	40.02	59.98	100.00
		60+	11.99	8.93	20.92	79.07	100.00
	Total	15–59	48.15	12.96	61.11	38.90	100.00
		60+	32.11	8.20	40.31	59.69	100.00

Source: Based on *Census of India, 2001.*

15–59 years and main workers aged 60 years and above is 15. Non-working dependents are higher among urban males as compared to rural males. In the case of rural females, the difference between the percentage of main workers aged 15–59 years and main workers aged 60+ is 13.5. In the case of urban females, the difference is 7.3 per cent. Non-working females are far higher in urban areas as compared to rural areas.

The data indicates far more males than females would notionally be in a position to save for the future in view of the difference in work participation rates. There is a much higher dependency status among females as reflected in Table 2.1.

In the age group 60 years and above, different census years have shown a very high work participation rate for males in both rural and urban areas. Work participation rate in 2001 in age group 60 years and above for rural males was 79 per cent of the work participation rate in the age group 15–59 years. In the case of rural females, there was a much greater decline of work participation rate, from 50 per cent in the age group 15–59 years to 25 per cent in the age group 60 years and above. Rural female work participation rate in age group 60 years and above was 50 per cent of the rural female work participation rate in the age group 15–59 years.

In urban areas, work participation rate among males aged 60 years and above was 44 per cent (41 per cent as main workers and 3 per cent as marginal workers), which was 59 per cent of the work participation rate in the age group 15–59 years. Among females, work participation rate in the age group 60 years and above was 9 per cent which was 51 per cent of work participation rate in the age group 15–59 years. Figure 2.2 gives the comparative work participation rates in age groups 15–59 years, and 60 years and above in graphic form.

Rural males aged 60 years and above are about 2.6 times as economically active as rural females. In urban areas, males are about five times as economically active as females in the same age group.

Figure 2.2 gives in graphic form the data on work participation rate in age group 15–59 years, and 60 years and above in rural and urban areas for the country as a whole in 2001.

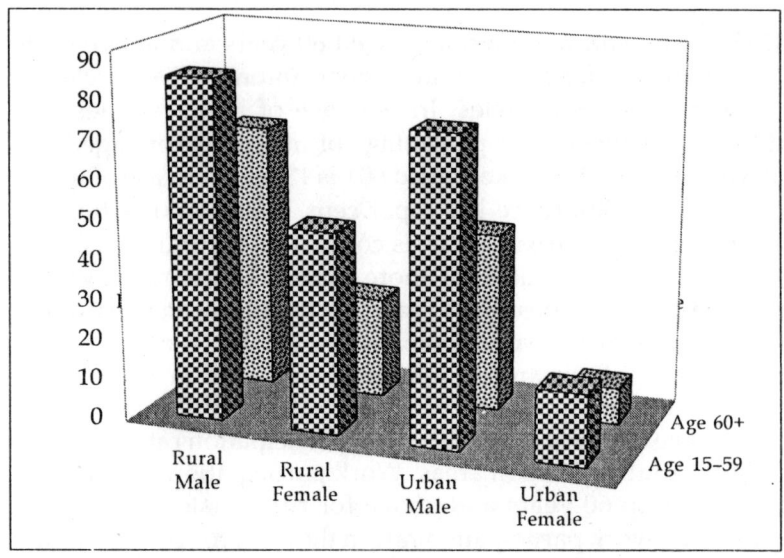

Figure 2.2: Work participation rate in age group 15–59 years, and 60 years and above, by sex in rural and urban areas, India, 2001

Work participation rate in age group 15–59 years (main + marginal) in the 20 bigger states in 2001, given in Table 2.3, shows that there is considerable inter-state variation among females. Four states have less than 30 per cent work participation rates among females. Kerala has the lowest female work participation rate (22.5 per cent), while Chhattisgarh has the highest (64.0 per cent), a difference of nearly 42 per cent. In the case of males, however, there is far less difference in work participation rates of states. Kerala has the lowest work participation rate (73.4 per cent) and Gujarat the highest (84.2 per cent), a difference of nearly 11 per cent. Twelve out of 20 states have a male work participation rate which is more than 80 per cent.

In a large number of states, there is a low female work participation rate due to customary practices, absence of employment opportunities nearer home, low levels of education and skills necessary for employment in a modernizing economy, and the demands of time for performing household duties. The remuneration paid to women is lower than that of males despite the existence of the

Table 2.3: Work participation rate (main + marginal) in age group 15–59 years in states, 2001

Sex	Work participation rate			
	20–39	*40–59*	*60–79*	*80 & above*
Males			Kerala (73.35) Uttaranchal (74.10) Jammu & Kashmir (75.58) Assam (77.82) Uttar Pradesh (78.13) Jharkhand (78.83) Orissa (79.70) Himachal Pradesh (79.93)	Maharashtra (80.41) Bihar (80.62) INDIA (80.71) Haryana (80.89) Punjab (81.10) Tamil Nadu (81.14) West Bengal (81.54)) Madhya Pradesh (83.35) Andhra Pradesh (83.46) Rajasthan (83.73) Karnataka (83.73) Chhattisgarh (83.73) Gujarat (84.18)
Females	Kerala (22.45) Uttar Pradesh (27.43) West Bengal (28.13) Punjab (28.66) Bihar (32.12) Assam (33.25) Jammu & Kashmir (34.33) Orissa (37.70)	INDIA (40.02) Gujarat (42.56) Uttaranchal (42.96) Jharkhand (43.54) Haryana (43.60) Tamil Nadu (44.26) Maharashtra (46.93) Karnataka (47.80) Andhra Pradesh (51.89) Madhya Pradesh (54.33) Rajasthan (54.99)	Himachal Pradesh (63.44) Chhattisgarh (63.97)	

Source: Census of India, 2001.

Table 2.4: Work participation rate in age group 60 years and above (main + marginal) in states, by sex, all areas, 2001

Sex	Work participation rate 60+				
	Less than 15	15 – 29	30–44	45 –59	60 & above
Male			Kerala (40.49)	Haryana (48.77) Gujarat (51.20) West Bengal (53.73) Maharash- tra (55.12) Punjab (56.00) Rajasthan (56.12) Karnataka (58.02) Uttaranchal (58.66) Andhra Pradesh (58.98)	INDIA (60.25) Tamil Nadu (60.31) Jharkhand (60.87) Orissa (61.83) Himachal Pradesh (63.14) Madhya Pradesh (63.95) Jammu & Kashmir (64.03) Chhattisgarh (65.25) Assam (66.27) Bihar (70.86) Uttar Pradesh (71.12)
Female	Kerala (8.81) West Bengal (11.25) Punjab (14.06)	Assam (16.28) Gujarat (17.19) Orissa (17.92) Haryana (18.23) Bihar (18.58) Jammu & Kashmir (18.71) Uttar Pradesh (18.81) INDIA (20.93) Karnataka (22.00) Jharkhand (22.13) Rajasthan (23.06) Andhra Pradesh (24.00) Tamil Nadu (26.06) Maharashtra (27.69) Uttaranchal (27.93) Madhya Pradesh (28.37)	Chhattis- garh (33.33) Himachal Pradesh (38.18)		

Source: Census of India, 2001.

equal remuneration legislation. They are also primarily engaged in lower paid occuaptions. Fewer women would thus have the capacity to save from their earnings for a long duration. Generating newer opportunities for women's work (conventional and non-conventional) would help them to supplement the family's income and to save for the future.

Work participation rates in age group 60 years and above (main plus marginal) in the 20 bigger states in 2001, given in Table 2.4, shows that it is fairly high for males. In Kerala, it is the lowest (40 per cent), while in Uttar Pradesh and Bihar it is 71 per cent. Work participation rate among males aged 60 years and above was higher among economically backward states, probably because they have to work even in old age to survive. Among females, three states have a work participation rate less than 15 per cent. Kerala has the lowest rate at 9 per cent. In seven states, it is between 15 and 20 per cent. There is a big difference in work participation rates between males and females aged 60 years and above. In all the states, the difference is more than 30 per cent.

Work participation rate (main + marginal workers) in age groups 60–69 years, 70–79 years, and 80 years and above given in Table 2.5 shows a high work participation rate for males, even after 70 years of age. In the case of rural males, 76 per cent in the age group 60–69 years and 54 per cent in the age group 70–79 years were workers. In the case of urban males, the percentage are 51 and 34 respectively. The difference between rural and urban areas is probably because of different patterns of work that are available. In the case of females, the

Table 2.5: Work participation rate (main + marginal workers) in age group 60–69 years, 70–79 years, and 80 years and above in rural and urban areas by sex, India, 2001

Residence	60–69 years			70–79 years			80 years & above		
	Male	*Female*	*Total*	*Male*	*Female*	*Total*	*Male*	*Female*	*Total*
Rural	76.04	31.35	53.05	54.12	15.77	35.38	36.76	9.97	23.25
Urban	51.13	10.98	30.76	34.37	6.17	20.18	27.83	4.68	15.39
Total	69.73	26.30	47.46	49.30	13.32	31.58	34.83	8.57	21.28

Source: Census of India, 2001.

percentage of workers in the age group 60–69 years and 70–79
years is far less in both rural and urban areas. The presence of
a large percentage of male workers of age 60 years and above,
or even at age 70 years and above, could be by choice or could
be reflective of the need to earn a living as they have little to
fall back upon. Their sons may have migrated to urban areas
to seek employment. A large number are self-employed with
no pre-determined age of retirement. Hence, they participate
in an economic activity, as long as they can, to cater to their
financial needs. Chronological age, work participation and age
of withdrawal from work vary for the workers in the
unorganized sector who constitute more than 90 per cent of
the workforce.

High work participation rates in older age groups would,
in general, indicate the virtual absence of social security benefits
in old age. Persons have to continue to work to subsist. This is
in sharp contrast to the situation in the developed countries
where persons have the benefit of pensions and other welfare
benefits and can choose to retire after the mandatory age. Some
countries facing skilled manpower shortage problems, do
permit their employees to continue for some more years after
the age of superannuation under a flexible retirement system.
But even in these countries, the work participation rate is far
lower than is the case in India.

A new trend is now emerging among superannuated
workers in urban areas who have general as well as technical
education and work experience in diverse services. A number
of them have high professional qualifications and skills. Some
private sector companies and autonomous bodies choose to
hire superannuated experienced persons on contract as
consultants or as administrative personnel to get a good quality
of output at a lower cost to themselves. Many superannuated
workers are physically and mentally fit, and wish to work after
retirement because of family responsibilities, such as daughters
to marry, sons to settle, or a house to be built or extended.
Some seek employment for meeting their financial
requirements to run the household. Some also work as they
consider it more useful and productive way to occupy time
and to fill the vacuum which is created after retirement. They
find re-employment as a means to interact with workers

professionally and socially. They continue to have a status socially which an employed person has. Within the household, too, there is virtually no decline of role as would be the case if a person becomes totally retired. Presence of twenty-four hours stay within the home can also create problems and may lead to interference in household matters which are primarily in the domain of the housewife.

Persons over 60 are a huge untapped resource which needs to be developed through skill development and entrepreneurship training programmes, and given facilities for credit and other inputs required. In many countries of the world it has been seen that older workers can be equally, if not more productive and sincere for certain types of jobs. Age related stereotypes and discriminations against employment of older workers must end. Agewell and some other NGOs have set up employment exchanges to register persons seeking employment.

The category of work, to some extent, gives an indication of the likely earnings. The percentage distribution of main workers aged 15–59 years, and main workers aged 60 years and above by category of work is given in Table 2.6. The 2001 census data are not yet available. The 1991 census data show that a large percentage of workers in rural areas, both males and females, are engaged in agriculture and allied activities. Rural female workers show a high percentage as agricultural labourers. Even among cultivators, a large percentage is likely to belong to small and marginal farmers. It is unlikely that most of the poor rural workers, who are busy meeting their daily needs, have the capacity to save for a long period of time to meet their financial needs in old age. Empirical studies in rural areas in Maharashtra and Karnataka and in several other states have indicated that personal savings by the poor for social security in old age have been a very difficult proposition due to insufficient earnings during their working years which was entirely spent to meet their immediate needs for daily living; at times debts had to be incurred to meet exigencies. Dandekar, in her survey of 601 elderly persons in rural Maharashtra drawn from four regions, found that most of the rural poor had no cash savings at all. This was also true of the inmates in old age homes (Dandekar, 1996). A study in

Table 2.6: Percentage distribution of main workers, 15–59 years and 60 years and above, by industrial category and sex in rural and urban areas, India, 1991

Industrial category	Rural						Urban					
	Males		Females		Total		Males		Females		Total	
	15–59	60+	15–59	60+	15–59	60+	15–59	60+	15–59	60+	15–59	60+
I. Cultivator	50.3	66.9	39.0	44.0	47.4	63.4	4.4	13.3	4.9	9.7	4.5	12.9
II. Agricultural labourer	25.9	20.5	48.2	46.7	31.6	24.6	5.1	8.3	15.0	22.4	6.4	9.8
III. Livestock, forestry, fishing and allied activities	2.2	1.6	2.1	1.3	2.2	1.5	1.7	2.0	1.6	1.6	1.7	2.0
IV. Mining and quarrying	0.6	0.2	0.3	0.1	0.5	0.2	1.2	0.5	0.7	0.3	1.2	0.5
V. Manufac- a) Household industry	1.9	2.0	2.9	2.5	2.2	2.1	2.4	4.0	7.2	8.7	3.0	4.5
turing, process- b) Other than household industry ing, servicing and repairs:	4.2	2.0	2.3	1.2	3.7	1.8	23.4	16.4	14.0	10.2	22.2	15.8
VI. Construction	1.4	0.6	0.3	0.1	1.1	0.5	5.4	4.2	3.3	2.2	5.1	4.0
VII. Trade and Commerce	4.2	3.0	1.1	1.9	3.4	2.8	23.5	29.6	9.9	16.7	21.8	28.2
VIII. Transport, storage and communication	1.8	0.4	0.1	0.0	1.4	0.3	9.6	4.7	2.0	0.8	8.6	4.3
IX. Other services	7.4	2.9	3.7	2.1	6.4	2.8	23.2	16.9	41.3	27.4	25.6	18.1
Total	100.0	100.0	100.0	100.0	100.0	100.0	100.0	100.0	100.0	100.0	100.0	100.0

Source: Based on Census of India, 1991.

rural Karnataka, too, indicated the poor fianncial status of persons belonging to the low income groups (Gurumurthy, 1998). Workers with slightly better earnings could save if proper institutional structures suited to their needs and pattern of earnings are set in place. Even in urban areas, the bulk are in trade and commerce, manufacturing and other services, and do not belong to the organised sector with retirement benefits. Their earnings may be higher than rural workers, but so also are their expenses. It is unlikely that most of such workers will have the capacity to save for old age to sustain them for 15 to 20 years.

The employment status of workers, given in Table 2.7, shows that for the country as a whole, in 1999–2000, 53 per cent were in self-employment, 14 per cent in regular salaried employment and 33 per cent in casual employment. In rural areas, the percentage of self-employment and regular salaried employment have come down, while that of casual workers has increased, which would mean a higher percentage of workers with low and insecure earnings. In urban areas, while the percentage of self-employment has shown hardly any change, regular salaried employment has shown a modest fall, and casual employment has shown a rise. Aggregate figures for rural and urban areas indicate that for the country as a whole, casual employment has increased from 23.2 per cent in 1972–73 to 33.2 per cent in 1999–2000. Also, self-employment has decreased from 61.4 per cent in 1972–73 to 52.9 per cent in 1999–2000. Figure 2.3 gives the trends. For such workers and others of small means, financial security in old age is important. Regular salaried employment is mainly an urban phenomenon, and has about the same percentage as the self-employed during the period 1977–78 to 1999–2000. Some salaried employees have employment related retirement benefits. Among the urban self-employed, there are some categories (lawyers, doctors, architects, consultants, businessmen) who have the education and the earnings to save for old age. There will thus be a wide spectrum of workers in self-employment in need of saving measures through a proper institutional framework to meet their financial needs in old age.

Table 2.7: Percentage distribution of workers by status of
employment, India, 1972–73 to 1999–2000

Residence	Year	Category			
		Self employment	*Regular salaried employment*	*Casual employment*	*Total*
Rural	1972–73	Not available			
	1977–78	62.6	7.7	29.7	100.0
	1983	61.0	7.5	31.5	100.0
	1987–88	59.4	7.7	32.9	100.0
	1993–94	58.0	6.4	35.6	100.0
	1999–2000	56.0	6.7	37.3	100.0
Urban	1972–73	Not available			
	1977–78	42.4	41.8	15.8	100.0
	1983	41.8	40.0	18.2	100.0
	1987–88	42.8	40.3	16.9	100.0
	1993–94	42.3	39.4	18.3	100.0
	1999–2000	42.1	40.1	17.8	100.0
Total	1972–73	61.4	15.4	23.2	100.0
	1977–78	58.9	13.9	27.2	100.0
	1983	57.4	13.9	28.7	100.0
	1987–88	56.0	14.4	29.6	100.0
	1993–94	54.8	13.2	32.0	100.0
	1999–2000	52.9	13.9	33.2	100.0

Note: Figures refer to classification of 'usual status' employment (NSSO).
Source: Report of Task Force on Employment Opportunities, Planning
            Commission. Compiled by the Task Force from NSSO surveys.

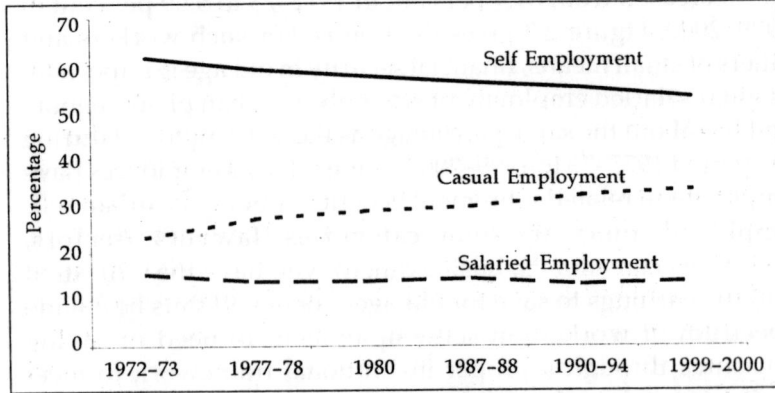

Figure 2.3: Percentage distribution of workers by status of employment,
1972-73 to 1999-2000

The type of employment is often categorized into the organized and the unorganized sectors. The former provides higher emoluments, better employment conditions and retirement benefits. In India, out of the total employment of 397 million workers in 1999–2000 (NSSO data, usual status), only 281 million (7.1 per cent) were in the organised sector (Table 2.8).

Employment in the private organized sector has grown from 75.5 lakhs in 1983 to 87 lakhs in 1999–2000, an increase of only 11.5 lakhs. In the public organized sector, employment has grown in the 1980s but has remained almost constant in the 1990s. In the 1980s and 1990s, private organized sector constituted about 30 per cent of the total organized sector of

Table 2.8: Total employment and employment in the organized sector, India, 1983 to 1999–2000

				(in lakhs)
	1983	*1988*	*1994*	*1999–2000*
Total employment	3027.5	3242.9	3744.5	3970.0
Employment in organized sector:				
(a) Private	75.5	73.9	79.3	87.0
(b) Public	164.6	183.2	194.4	194.1
Total	240.1	257.1	273.7	281.1
Percentage of employment in organized sector	7.93	7.93	7.31	7.08
Percentage of private organized sector in total organized sector	31.45	28.74	28.97	30.94

Source: Report of Task Force on Employment Opportunities, Planning Commission, 2001.

employment. In view of the policies followed by government to curtail public sector employment, any growth in the number and percentage of employment in the organized sector will depend on its growth in the private sector. This has, however, to contend with the growing tendency of the organized sector to outsource their needs and utilize the unorganized sector to avoid the problems of complying with labour legislation and to save costs. In the near future, retirement benefits in the organized sector, even on assuming an optimistic scenario, will, at the most, be available to less than 10 per cent of the workforce. The rest will have to depend totally on their own savings/investments, and to depend on their children.

Another indicator of the income saving capacity of individuals is the percentage of people below the poverty line. Table 2.9 gives the number and percentage of poor persons from 1973–74 to 1999–2000, and the projections for 2006–07. The poverty ratio has come down from 55 per cent in 1973–74 to 26 per cent in 1999–2000. It is expected to decline further. In numbers, it still means a staggering figure, 260 million in 1999–2000, which is projected to decline to 220 million in 2006–07. Rural areas have a higher percentage of persons below the poverty line. The trends are given in Figure 2.4. The computation of poverty by the Planning Commission has not indicated the weight given to expenses other than food (calorie consumption), variable over a period of time. Moreover, definition of poor should be based on extent of deprivation of basic needs by different segments and regions. If the percentage of persons, who are in low income groups but are not now categorized as poor, is included, about half of the earners, even in 1999–2000, will be ill-equipped to save or make investments for future security in old age.

Table 2.9: Percentage of population below the poverty line, India, 1973-74 to 2007

Year	Number (in million)			Percentage		
	Rural	*Urban*	*Total*	*Rural*	*Urban*	*Total*
1973-74	261.290	60.046	321.336	56.44	49.01	54.88
1977-78	264.247	64.648	328.895	53.07	45.24	51.32
1983	251.957	70.940	322.897	45.65	40.79	44.48
1987-88	231.879	75.169	307.049	39.09	38.20	38.86
1993-94	244.031	76.337	320.368	37.27	32.36	35.97
1999-2000	193.243	67.007	260.250	27.09	23.62	26.10
2006-07	170.526	49.567	220.094	21.07	15.06	19.34

Source: Planning Commission.
Figures on projections for 2006–07, from Tenth Plan.

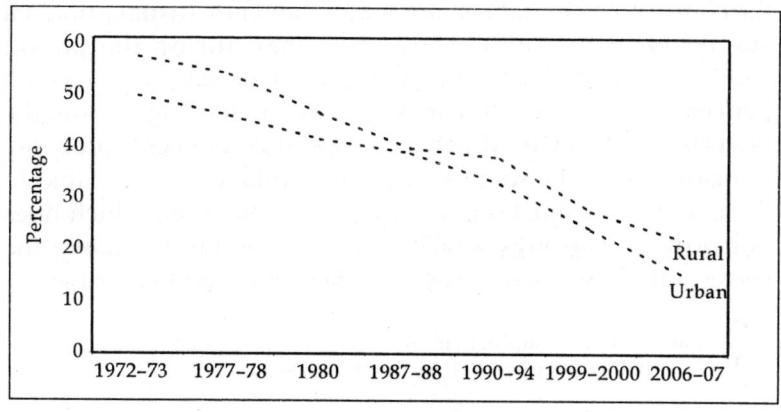

Figure 2.4: Percentage of population below poverty line in rural and urban areas, 1973–74 to 2006–07

State-wise distribution of percentage of persons below the poverty line shows that among the bigger states, 10 states had more than half the population below the poverty line in 1973–74. In 1999–2000, the percentage has come down in all the states. However, Orissa and Bihar still had more than 42 per cent of their population below the poverty line. Punjab, Haryana and Himachal Pradesh had the lowest percentages. Projections for 2006–07 indicate that Bihar and Orissa will continue to have more than two-fifths of their population below the poverty line. Bihar (undivided), Madhya Pradesh (undivided) and Uttar Pradesh (undivided) together had 48 per cent of the country's poor in 1999–2000. There is a growing incidence of casual employment in these states. There are hardly any social security benefits as the organized sector of employment is small. If West Bengal and Maharashtra are added, the percentage below the poverty line in these five states would be about two-thirds of the country's population. Poverty of families would continue to act as a deterrence for long-term savings needs. Blocks/districts in states which are poorer than the rest need special employment generating programmes to increase their incomes to meet present and future needs.

An interesting dimension of the poverty scenario is that it is apparently not related to the extent of unemployment in the country. NSSO data on unemployment rate (usual principal status) given in Table 2.10 shows that during the period 1987–88 to 1999–2000, the unemployment rate was about 3 per cent or lower in rural areas. Yet, the percentage below the poverty line has varied between 39 and 26 per cent, probably indicating the low quality of rural employment available in the country for most segments of the population, which does not provide earnings which can keep the family above the poverty line. In urban areas, too, the same trend is visible.

Table 2.10: Unemployment rate and percentage of population below the poverty line, India, 1987–88 to 1999–2000

Year	Unemployment rate (usual principal status)			Percentage of persons below poverty line		
	Rural	Urban	Total	Rural	Urban	Total
1987–88	3.07	6.56	3.77	39.09	38.20	38.88
1993–94	1.80	5.21	2.56	37.27	32.36	35.97
1999–2000	1.96	5.23	2.81	27.09	23.62	26.10

Source: NSSO; Planning Commission.

Public Assistance to the Old

(1) *Old Age Pensions*

A number of persons, who struggle during their earning days, have to face destitution in old age. They are without means of support and unable to find a place in old age homes. They have to depend for survival on fiscal transfers by the state as a welfare measure. The old tradition of setting up endowments and charitable institutions to set up and maintain old age ashrams are no longer adequate. The sources of funding of such institutions are also drying up.

With independence, public policy began to be guided by welfare and development. The 1950s and 1960s witnessed the launch of public assistance schemes by state governments for persons facing a virtual state of destitution. They were conceived as a long-term relief measure and were different from interim gratuitous relief given from pre-independence days to old persons as a part of famine relief, or any other calamity relief code. The basic philosophy underlying the concept of old age pension as a public assistance programme was that persons in their working life were expected to save or build income generating assets for their needs in old age, and/or depend on the family or close kin to take care of them in their twilight days as part of the moral responsibility of children. When a small percentage of persons due to their poverty, lack of foresight, or special circumstances were unable to provide for their needs in old age, had no family member to support them, and faced a virtual state of destitution, it became a fit case for the State to step in. The programme when it started, and even now, was not intended by the State to substitute the family for taking care of all older persons. The scheme was, in a sense, a surviving trace of the Elizabethan poor law with the difference that it was not the local authority but the state government which stepped in to provide relief. Also, unlike the Elizabethan poor law, it did not carry a label. The Indian scheme was given a different title (old age pension) and, in a sense, granted as a sort of entitlement of such persons to get relief for a long period. The criterion of near destitution was, nonetheless, an over-riding consideration in the operation of old age pension schemes.

Uttar Pradesh was the first state to launch the old age pension scheme in 1957, mainly due to the initiative of the Chief Minister who had been aware of problems of older persons, who had neither a source of sustenance nor a family member who could provide support. Problems of ill-health were an added reason. When the scheme was being formulated it had to counter a number of arguments from the state's bureaucracy and the planners. Among these were:

- non-availability of funds for long-term welfare measures;
- allocations to such schemes were 'non-developmental and populist' and would not promote thrift among persons in their working life period; family responsibility would be eroded and a sense of dependency promoted;

- persons in need of relief could find refuge in old age homes (these were, however, too small in number, located in urban areas, and costed many times more);
- absence of information on the number of such persons could end up with a large budgetary requirement which the state may find it difficult to sustain.

Fortunately, the political will was able to overcome such opposition and a pension scheme, even though a modest one, was sanctioned by the state. Though the amount of pension was small, it provided great assistance to poor old persons and their families who were on the verge of destitution.

Following the example set by Uttar Pradesh, Chief Ministers of other states were convinced of the need to provide relief to old persons without any means of support. Kerala was the second state to launch the scheme in 1960, followed by Andhra Pradesh in 1961, and Tamil Nadu and West Bengal in 1962. Other states followed gradually. The year of launching of old age pension scheme in different states is given below:

1950–59   Uttar Pradesh
1960–69   Andhra Pradesh, Chandigarh, Haryana, Himachal Pradesh, Karnataka, Kerala, Punjab, Rajasthan, Tamil Nadu, West Bengal.
1970–79   Bihar, Dadra and Nagar Haveli, Delhi, Goa, Daman and Diu, Gujarat, Jammu and Kashmir, Lakshwadeep, Madhya Pradesh, Mizoram, Nagaland, Orissa, Tripura.
1980–89   Andaman and Nicobar Islands, Arunachal Pradesh, Assam, Maharashtra, Manipur, Meghalaya, Pondicherry, Sikkim.

The scheme of old age pension was not backed by any statutory right granted to old persons. It was given through administrative orders and was, therefore, discretionary in character. A residual approach was followed in allocating resources. Funds that could be spared determined broadly the quantum of pension that could be given to a beneficiary and the number of pensions that could be sanctioned.

The scheme was welcomed by political parties that were in power in different states. Opposition parties lent support to the scheme. Most of the north-eastern states took a longer time to adopt the scheme, may be because the problem of destitution here was less apparent than in other states.

State governments have laid down the criteria for determining eligibility for old age pension. Initially, these were characterized by the principle of 'exclusion' to keep down the number of claimants. Over the years, there have been some changes and a more humanitarian approach was adopted, though administrative and financial factors played an important role. The criteria currently followed are as follows:

Age: When the scheme was first launched in Uttar Pradesh, the minimum age of eligibility was 70 years, mainly to reduce financial liability as there were few persons living beyond that age. Kerala, Andhra Pradesh and West Bengal, too, adopted the same criterion. Currently, most states have prescribed a minimum age of either 60 or 65 years. Some adopt a higher age for males (65 years) as compared to females (60 years), the consideration being that women enter into widowhood earlier than males, and have no income to support them. In the case of divorced women, or persons suffering from physical or mental handicap, a lower age limit has been prescribed. In the administration of the scheme, complaints of persons being left out have been voiced because old persons, who are mostly illiterate and are resident in rural areas, do not have a certificate on the date of their birth. They are required to get it from the doctor in Primary Health Centre/ Community Health Centre. A medical examination for an age certificate is not easy. There is also a degree of arbitrariness in deciding on age, specially when elected representatives (state/ local authority) have a say in the selection of beneficiaries. Extraneous factors are known to play a role. Malpractices can, and do occur, in deciding eligibility on the bases of age.

Domicile: Beneficiaries are required to be domiciled within the state, usually for three or more years. The intention is to spend the state's finances for the benefit of its residents, and exclude short duration migrants from taking advantage.

Destitution: State governments usually define a destitute as a person who is not capable of doing remunerative work, has no source of income, no assets (land/house/jewellery), no family member/adult relatives to support him/her in old age, and not dependent on others. In a large number of states, if a person is very poor and earns an annual income far below the basic minimum necessary for survival, or if the children are too poor to support the person, they still qualify on the basis of the means test as it would be too harsh, both to the person and to the poor family with whom the person resides, to leave the person out. Most pensioners living in a very poor family feel that the pension makes the old person less of a burden on the family, and gives the person a sense of dignity and better acceptance by the family. Assistance to old persons is thus based on special circumstances. The revenue official/social welfare officer/panchayats certify the income status. They also check that there is no earning member staying in the household.

The definition of family responsibility, in the early years when the scheme was launched, was based on the premise that members of the family covered the joint family and not just the household. Even the brother and his children were included. For instance, the scheme of old age pension, when it was launched in 1957 in Uttar Pradesh, defined the persons who constituted family members. A person was eligible for the pension if he "has no relatives of 20 years and over of the following categories: (i) son, son's son, son's wife; (ii) real brother, real brother's son; (iii) married daughter, daughter's son (provided the custom of the locality, community, sector, class, permits a person to get support from them; (iv) husband, wife, husband's real brother; (v) married sister, sister's son; (vi) father's real brother's son" (Hasan, 1963). With changes taking place in the structure and composition of families, and in the actual discharge of family responsibilities, it was recognized by the State that the inclusion of such a wide range of relatives would adversely affect the interests of older persons to qualify for a pension, and would serve to exclude rather than include those in need. The concept of the nuclear family in deciding family responsibility has now been adopted. The

Financial Security in Old Age

criterion followed is that a person will be eligible to receive assistance if immediate family members who can provide support are not present. These include son, son's children, husband/wife.

A person who has children who are earning but refuse to send remittances or provide support to an old person, becomes ineligible on the ground that it is the moral responsibility of the children to support the parent. It would be too much of a legal hassle for the poor, illiterate, old person to ask the Court under Section 125 (a) of the Criminal Procedure Code to intervene. Thus many persons, who have sons but who provide no support, are not considered eligible. A case study of a Kerala widow has been cited to illustrate the issue. She had crossed the age of 60 years, qualified on the basis of a means test, but was disallowed grant of pension because she had earning sons who did not send a remittance to support her, nor did they agree to live with her (Gulati and Gulati, 1997). Such instances have also been referred to in the case studies reported for Maharashtra (Dandekar, 1996).

The Working Group on Social Security of the Economic Administration Reform Commission has commented on the criterion of destitution as followed by state governments:

> "In particular, the destitution criterion is unreasonably restrictive since it filters out many deserving cases of old-aged poor who, although not entirely destitute, depend on children or other relatives who are themselves below the poverty line. In fact, a total destitute with no earning power or assets would have starved to death before securing an old age pension. Enquiries to establish destitution can also be time consuming and subject to arbitrary judgments and corruption (GOI EARC, 1984).

Institutional Care: Persons who receive institutional care, free of cost, are not given old age pension as they do not satisfy the criterion of destitution. Some states have a provision that if a payment has to be made for staying in an old age home, the person can apply for a pension in which case the grant is made to the institution.

Other requirements: In some states, grant of old-age pension is consistent upon a good conduct. The person should not have been convicted of a serious crime or of moral turpitude. Beggars are also excluded in some states.

Fixing of Quantum of Pension

To fix the quantum of pension or its revision from time to time, the criteria to be followed in determining the extent of needs of older persons to be covered by the pension, have been debated upon. A norm could be that the pension would cover food, shelter, fuel, clothing, health and other needs. States, in trying to strive a balance between a limited budgetary provision and the numbers to be given pension, have got round the normative requirement by observing that the scheme can only provide assistance to an old person who lives in a household that cannot totally take care of the person's needs. The amount of monthly pension in a state currently varies between Rs. 75 to Rs. 250, with most states giving a pension between Rs. 100 and Rs. 200, depending on political sensitivity and the state's resources. Goa provides a pension of Rs. 500 per month. If subsidized foodgrain from the public distribution system is made available, the pension in most states would cover about four weeks' of food ration for a person plus a very small sum to meet other needs.

States have altered, with the passage of time, the pension rate and the number of pensioners. They have also liberalized the eligibility criteria. The poor old become important when elections are held. Candidates are keen to show their concern. The ruling party promises to increase the rate of pension, and to expand the number of beneficiaries. Other parties, too, make similar announcements. They distribute application forms to get a good impression of their concern for the old. The promises, however, are soon forgotten. Normally, the number of pensioners in a state should go up because people are living longer, and a larger number is crossing age 60. In actual practice, this does not happen. When finances are limited, additions depend on vacancies created by current pensioners. A person who is granted a pension in a year does not automatically get it in the subsequent years, though many states allow it based on some verification, not often foolproof. In several states, the number of persons given pension has shown an erratic trend, depending on the financial outlay that can be provided, and the administrative ability to implement the scheme.

Tamil Nadu pensioners are entitled to meals in the Nutritious Meal Programme Centres. Free supply of half a kilogram of rice per week per head is also given. Persons not taking meals at these centres are entitled to one kilogram of rice per week per head. In some states, old age pensioners, are entitled to free medical treatment.

Budgetary Provisions

Budgetary provisions for old age pension schemes were made till the Seventh Five Year Plan (1985–86 to 1989–90) by the states from their non-plan head which, because of its inelastic character, put a severe strain on the state's ability to expand the scheme or to increase the rate of pension. The Planning Commission refused to accept the proposal as a plan scheme on the plea that it was non-developmental in nature, would give no returns on investments made, and any allocation made for it would be at the cost of other plan programmes. States were finding it extremely difficultt to finance what it considered an essential welfare measure, and approached the Finance Commission which dealt with non-plan budgetary allocations between the Centre and the states. The Seventh Finance Commission (1979–80 to 1983–84) took a liberal view. It recommended the ceiling of old age pension to be raised to Rs. 60 per month as compared to Rs. 25 to Rs. 45 which the states were paying earlier. It allowed devolution to the states for grant of old age pensions to 0.1 per cent of the total population. In monetary terms, it meant Rs. 264 crores to 22 states for the period 1979–80 to 1983–84. As a result of the award of the Finance Commission, six states and three union territories, which did not have old age pensions, launched the scheme. The Commission, however, worked the financial estimate on the basis of 0.1 per cent of the total population

(1971 census) or only 1.7 per cent of the total population aged 60 years and above as the intended coverage. In actual practice, however, the number in need of such a scheme was far greater. The Commission's award did indicate, however, that the scheme was important enough to make a provision for devolution of resources to states in the non-plan budget. The Eighth Finance Commission, too, allowed the devolution of resources to the states on account of the scheme, adopting a per capita rate of Rs. 4.60 for purposes of forecasting.

The states continued to urge the Planning Commission for inclusion of old age pension schemes in the state plan. From mid–1980s onwards, Chief Ministers of states pleaded with the Planning Commission to include old age pension as a plan scheme, as the non-plan budgets of states were unable to meet the cost. This was conceded on the plea that net increases in the scheme will be met from the plan funds, while maintenance levels will be met by the states. In actual practice, over the years, as financial stress on the states increases, most of the disbursement is made from plan schemes.

Till the middle of the Ninth Plan (1992–97), old age pension schemes were treated as the sole domain of state governments. It was in mid–1995 that the Government of India decided for the first time to contribute to old age pension scheme, even though there was no mention of it in the Ninth Five Year Plan (1992–97). It thus accepted the principle that social security for all segments of the population was, as stated in the Constitution, a concurrent subject. It acted on what the Working Group on Social Security set up by the Economic Administrative Reforms Commission had submitted in June 1984, viz., that the Centre should share responsibility with the states for a basic uniform pattern. The Central scheme was announced by the Prime Minister in his address to the nation on 30 July 1995. It was launched on 15 August 1995 as a major component of National Social Assistance Programme (NSAP). It was classified as a centrally sponsored programme. NSAP covered, apart from the National Old Age Pension Scheme (NOAP), two other programmes of social assistance, viz., the National Family Benefit Scheme (NFBS) and the National Maternity Benefit Scheme (NMBS).

Under NOAP, the central government provides assistance for a beneficiary at the rate of Rs. 75 per month. The beneficiary, male or female, should be over 65 years of age and must be facing near destitution, having little or no regular means of subsistence of his own or from family members. The scheme highlights the role of local authorities in implementing the scheme. Panchayats/municipalities are required to play an active role in the identification of beneficiaries, and help in administering the scheme. State and district level committees have been set up to streamline implementation. States are expected to ensure wide publicity, make available application forms and process the applications. Grants are released by the Centre to the districts. Pension benefits are payable to the bank account of beneficiaries in post offices/banks or by postal money order. The scheme permits payment of pension in public meetings, preferably of *gram sabhas* in villages and of neighbourhood/mohalla committees.

NOAP is not meant to take over the state's own responsibility in implementing state sector old age pension schemes. It seeks to share with the states the payment of a minimum old age pension throughout the country. States can and do provide assistance over and above the Rs. 75 provided by the central government to persons aged 65 years and above. States are also expected to continue to give pensions to persons below 65 years, if the state scheme under operation has fixed the criterion of minimum age of 60 years. For instance, in Uttar Pradesh, the quantum of old age pension has been fixed at Rs. 125 per month which is more than the grant of Rs. 75 per beneficiary given by the central government. The minimum age prescribed is 60 years. Pension to beneficiaries from age 60 to 64 years is met from the budget of the state government. For beneficiaries from age 65 years, the state government adds Rs. 50 to the central grant of Rs. 75, for a uniform pension rate. NOAP also permits grant of medical care and other benefits to the old and the poor.

Central assistance under NOAP is based on financial entitlement of a state. The scheme has worked out ceilings for every state and the qualifying financial assistance from the central government. The advance/reimbursement to the state is dependent on the actual expenditure incurred by it. To calculate the ceiling for a state, the following procedure is followed: Total population (1998) in the state; percentage of persons in the state below the poverty line (1993–94); percentage of population who are 65 years and above. From the number thus arrived, 50 per cent of the population has been assumed to be destitute. For the country as a whole, the numerical ceiling in 1995 when the scheme was formulated was 53.4 lakhs, and the qualifying financial entitlement for the states Rs. 480.20 crores. This was subsequently raised to 68.8 lakh beneficiaries, and the qualifying financial entitlement Rs. 619.29 crores.

Information on implementation of the scheme is reported directly from the district to the Centre. In view of the large number of districts in the country, there are drawbacks in the consistency of information. There is little checking done at the district level on the information sent on socio-economic categories covered by the scheme.

Allocation on NOAP by the central government and the expenditure reported by states is given in Table 2.11. These show variability from one year to another. During the period

Table 2.11: Allocation, expenditure and beneficiaries under NOAP, India, 1995–96 to 2001–02

Year	Allocation (Rs. in lakhs)	Expenditure reported (Rs. in lakhs)	Numerical ceiling of beneficiaries (in lakhs)	Number of beneficiaries reported (in lakhs)	Percentage to the ceiling
1995–96	29,707	10,733	53.36	26.59	49.73
1996–97	50,737	32,004	53.36	47.60	89.22
1997–98	46,397	36,300	53.36	73.24	106.44
1998–99	45,685	46,716	68.81	50.80	73.84
1999–2000	47,624	45,710	68.81	52.81	76.75
2000–01	51,261	47,698	68.81	51.54	74.90
2001–02	45,499	46,469	68.81	54.30	78.91
2002–03	Not available	42,862	68.81	41.80	60.75

Source: Department of Rural Development.

1998–99 to 2001–02, about three-fourths of the number of potential beneficiaries as per ceiling prescribed was covered. In 2002–03, it declined to 61 per cent. Shortfalls indicate inability of the states to identify and sanction the allotted quota of beneficiaries.

States have been asked to give preference to Scheduled Caste and Scheduled Tribe beneficiaries, and disadvantaged sections in the selection of beneficiaries. The percentage of Scheduled Caste beneficiaries between 1997–98 and 1998–99 has varied between 21.0 and 27.4, and of Scheduled Tribe beneficiaries between 4.4 per cent and 10.6 per cent. Some states have reported a higher percentage of old age pensions given to Scheduled Castes and Scheduled Tribes than their proportion in the state.

In the case of women beneficiaries, the percentage for the country as a whole has varied between 27.5 per cent and 35.6 per cent in the years between 1997–98 and 2001–02. This indicates that women appear to be at a disadvantage in getting selected, even though women live longer, become widowed earlier, have no assets, and would satisfy the criterion of destitution in large numbers than men. Some states, however, have given preference to women in the selection of beneficiaries and report a larger number of women beneficiaries than men (SDS, 1999; HelpAge India, 2003). There are large unexplained inter-district variations in percentage of old persons sanctioned pensions.

The scheme has been transferred to the states from 2002–03. Funds are released by the Ministry of Finance as additional central assistance to the state plan. States have been given the flexibility to operate the scheme. The decision to transfer the scheme, even when there are operational problems, indicates the low priority given to the subject. The central government has virtually divested itself of the responsibility of monitoring the implementation of the scheme, which even earlier was inneffectively done.

Old age pension schemes continue to face implementation problems. Persons are aware of the scheme mainly through word of mouth. Because of their illiteracy, they are ignorant of

the eligibility criteria and the procedures to be followed. There
are instances of wrong selection of beneficiaries, fake sanctions
and irregular payments, factors which characterize virtually
every relief and welfare programme. Touts, in connivance with
the officials, extort commissions, either for selection of
beneficiaries or for payment, even when it is by cheque (HT,
1999; HelpAge India, 2003). At some places, petty politicians
extract a share for listing the person as a beneficiary. The
Comptroller and Auditor General of India, in its report on the
Government of Delhi, 2001, revealed that huge sums of money
remained undisbursed and unclaimed in post-offices. Over
10,000 cheques amounting to Rs. 1.35 crores remained
undistributed. The Department issued sanctions without
exercising any checks, as prescribed in the scheme, on the basis
of members' recommendations, with the result that a large
number ineligible persons were given pensions. The audit
report showed 37 per cent sanctions to ineligible persons or
persons of questionable eligibility. Even dead persons were
paid pensions (Statesman, 2001). When a pensioner dies, the
authorities are not informed. Yet the pension is fraudulently
drawn with the connivance of officials. A state government,
while celebrating one year in office, declared that one lakh
bogus claimants of old age pension by the previous government
have been detected. Evaluation and media reports, too, have
indicated cases of corruption in the implementation of the
scheme.

For no apparent reason, names of eligible persons get
struck off. The very old find it very difficult to rectify and
include their name once again in the list. Women have a lower
share in the list of beneficiaries in most states because of greater
problems of identification and age verification. Similarly,
persons who are very old and infirm, or are physically
handicapped, get left out because they are unable to present
their case for age and other factors which require verification.
Visits have to be made a number of times to get the prescribed
form which is often not available. They have to be repeated to
check on the status of their application. This requires time, cost
of travel and other expenses which the old can ill-afford. The
process of sanction can take between six months to two years.
No acknowledgement is given when the form is submitted.

The apathy of officials and their absence at the time of visit, adds to the problems. Banks through whom payments are made at many places, are not keen to open their accounts because these give little return and are seen as more of a botheration. Opening of a bank account by a beneficiary with a photograph, introduction from an account holder, and requirements of minimum balance are seen as problem areas. States are discouraging the use of postal money orders because of the costs involved. At times, payments of pensions, are not done on a quarterly basis. They are given half-yearly or even on an annual basis (SDS, 1999).

The quantum of pension paid per person has, for a number of years, remained the same in most states despite an increase in the cost of living index. Even the central pension of Rs. 75 per month has not changed since 1995 when it started. It is unfortunate that while the government goes on adding dearness allowance for its employees, current and superannuated, depending on the rate of inflation, no such need has been felt for the deprived and destitute old even though the real value of Rs. 75 has significantly declined due to inflation.

Some norms for the scheme of old age pensions by states need to be formulated. These are given below. These are the minimum norms. States must examine to what extent they can upgrade them.

1. The minimum age limit for old age pension in the states should be 60 years for males. There is also an annual increase of eligible persons because of the demographic surge. In the case of women, the age for eligibility should be 58 years as they withdraw from the workforce much earlier and have no assets. Since the main support of a woman is from the husband who is older, the difference of age is justified. The fixation of age limit can be reduced by about 15 years if the person is physically handicapped or is a widow/divorcee/deserted woman.

2. A pensioner once selected should be eligible to receive it till his/her death, unless there is a change of

circumstances due to which the criteria of eligibility is transgressed.

3. The definition as to who is a destitute has to be reworked. Apart from persons without any source of income to maintain himself/herself, a person with a meagre income should also be eligible. States have different sets of criteria on the maximum income beyond which a person will not qualify. It is necessary to develop a uniform set of criteria for all states to follow. The National Commission on Rural Labour (1991) and the second National Commission on Labour (2002) recommended that old persons, even when they have very low levels of income which cannot sustain them, should be entitled to old age pension. Increase in cost of living should lead to revision of amount of pension paid. The fixation of amount of pension should be linked to consumer price index, and periodically revised.

4. The minimum quantum of pension fixed at current prices should be Rs. 300 per month, to be equally shared between the central and state government as social security is a concurrent subject.

5. Husband and wife, if individually eligible, should each be paid the full amount of pension.

6. Domicile requirement by the state for old age pension needs to be revised, if not removed, so that only temporary migrants are left out, specially since the central government is also contributing to the scheme.

7. The selection of beneficiaries should be characterized by full transparency. The criteria of eligibility should be widely disseminated, including word of mouth by panchayat members and officials. Verification procedures have to be clearly prescribed. Time consuming and arbitrary judgments on age and income have to be remedied. Procedure for redressal of grievances have to be indicated and written replies on rejections have to be furnished.

8. To prevent leakages, payment of pension has to be through Post Office, Savings Bank Account, or Postal

Money Order so that full payment is received by the beneficiary.

9. There should be a simple procedure for verification that the person is still alive. This should be made known to the beneficiaries.

10. Monitoring of the scheme needs to be streamlined. Data reported on the implementation of the scheme suffers from several shortcomings which need to be remedied. Up and down movements in number of pensions paid in a state, the inter district variations and the socio-economic categories of beneficiaries covered need to be closely watched.

Some states, on their own initiative, are implementing pension schemes for older workers of specific categories, in addition to the old age pension schemes meant for the 'destitute' old. They were launched in the 1980s. They, too, are non-contributory in nature and are of the nature of a public assistance programme. Some of these schemes are listed below:

1. Andhra Pradesh Landless Agricultural Workers Pension Scheme, started in 1984.
2. Gujarat Old Age Pension for Agricultural Labour, started in 1981.
3. Kerala Agricultural Workers Pension Scheme, started in 1982.
4. Kerala Old Age Pension Scheme for Craftsmen.
5. Tamil Nadu Old Age Pension for Destitute Agricultural Labourers, started in 1981.
6. West Bengal Farmers Old Age Pension Rules, started in 1980 for landless agricultural workers.
7. Indira Gandhi Aged Landless Labourers' Assistance Scheme for landless old labourers.

Sanction of pension under these schemes is at the discretion of the State Government and may be refused or discontinued. The Andhra Pradesh Landless Agricultural Workers Pension Rules, 1984 stipulate that for refusal or discontinuity no reason has to be given nor is it subject to any question in a court of law. The Kerala Agricultural Workers' Scheme, however, has given the right to appeal in case of rejection of his application.

These schemes prescribe an age limit of 60 years (males/ females). Ceiling of individual and family income below which a person will be entitled to qualify as a beneficiary have been prescribed. Domicile requirements are necessary for eligibility.

A few local authorities grant old age pensions to the destitute old, often on the recommendation of elected representatives. Here, too problems of identification and selection of beneficiaries, and making of fake payments arise.

(2) *Pensions for Other Categories of Senior Citizens*

For freedom fighters, the Government of India is operating a Swatantrata Sainik Samman Pension Scheme (SSSP). It started in 1669 as the Ex-Andaman Political Prisoners Pension Scheme to honour freedom fighters. A regular scheme for grant of pension was introduced in 1972, which was liberalized and renamed as SSSP in 1980. The chief criterion laid down for entitlement under the scheme is that the person should have been a freedom fighter. No income criterion has been prescribed. Up to 2001–02, the number of sanctions for freedom fighters and their eligible dependents (widow/widower, unmarried/unemployed daughter, mother/father) numbered 164,516.

The quantum of pension paid has increased since the inception of the scheme. It started with only Rs. 200 per month. It was raised periodically and increased to Rs. 1500 per month in October 1994. On the occasion of the 50th anniversary of independence, the quantum of paid pension received a big jump. Currently, Ex-Andaman Political Prisoners are paid a pension of Rs. 4000 per month, freedom fighters who suffered outside British India are paid Rs. 3500 per month, and other freedom fighters (including Indian National Army) are paid Rs. 3000 per month. Widows/widowers of above categories of freedom fighters are paid Rs. 3000 per month. Dependents are paid at a lower rate. From August 2003, dearness relief has been made payable at 39 per cent of the monthly pension. The pension is given to the beneficiary as a 'Samman' or honour. In 2003–04, the expenditure incurred on payment of pension was Rs. 258.77 crores, and on free railway passes, Rs. 29.36 crores. Pensioners receive, in addition, free medical facilities (OPD and indoor) in hospitals/dispensaries under the central government health scheme, government hospitals, and empanelled private hospitals/nursing homes. It covers consultancy, medicines, surgery and other expenses as per CGHS rules. Pensioners are also entitled to housing facility in the government general pool, accommodation in the Freedom Fighters' Home (for persons who have no one to look after them), and some other ancillary benefits (MHA, 2004).

State governments have their own freedom fighters' pension scheme. The Government of NCT Delhi, for instance, gives a monthly pension. In 2002, the amount was Rs. 2251. No dearness relief is, however, given. A person can draw pension from both the central government and the state.

(3) Food Rations to Older Persons

Annapurna Scheme was launched by the central government in April 2000 to meet food security needs of poor persons over 65 years who, though eligible for old age pensions, had not yet been covered by NOAPS or State Pension Schemes. The criterion of destitution, as in the old age pension schemes of states, is followed in this scheme too. Persons selected for the scheme are given 10 kg. of foodgrains every month, free of cost. Beneficiaries are selected by the Gram Sabha/Gram Panchayat which gives them entitlement cards to draw the ration.

Performance of the scheme has not been satisfactory. Some states are not implementing the scheme. In 2000–01, against an allocation of 1.65 lakh tonnes of foodgrains, the total quantity of foograins lifted from the public distribution system amounted to only 19,084 tonnes (11.6 per cent of the allotment). Against a targeted coverage of 13.47 lakh beneficiaries, only 4.83 lakh beneficiaries (35.9 per cent) were reported to have been covered. Also, against an allocation of Rs. 99.05 crores in 2000–01, actual expenditure was only Rs. 17.44 crores (17.6 per cent). In 2001–02, 1.62 lakh tonnes of foodgrains were allotted. The offtake was only 93,000 tonnes. Against a targeted coverage of 13.4 lakh persons, the actual average was 203,000 (15 per cent). The state administration was unable to identify beneficiaries, an indication of their lackadaisical manner of functioning. The scheme has been transferred to the states from 2002–03. Funds are being released by the Ministry of Finance as additional central assistance to the State Plan.

A complementary scheme, the Antodaya Anna Yojana (AAY) was announced by the central government in December 2000 to benefit the poorest among persons below the poverty line (BPL). It aims at providing foodgrains at a subsidized cost from the public distribution system to about 1 crore families. Each Antodaya family was initially given 25 kg. of foodgrains at almost half the rates charged for BPL families. In April 2002, the amount was raised to 35 kg. per family for a year. In 2001–02, against an allocation of 19.60 lakh tonnes of foodgrains, offtake by the states was 16.78 lakh tonnes (86 per cent). In 2002–03, against an allocation of 41.27 lakh tonnes of foodgrain, offtake by the states was 35.38 lakh tonnes (86 per cent). During 2003–04, against an allocation of 45.56 lakh tonnes, the offtake was 38.24 lakh tonnes (84 per cent) (DFPD, 2004). Old persons living in such families are also expected to benefit. In June 2003, the target number of BPL families was expanded to cover, in addition, 50 lakh families 'below poverty line' which comes to about one-fourth of the households below the poverty line. Priority is given to: (a) households headed by widows, terminally ill persons, disabled persons or persons aged 60 years and above with no assured means of subsistence; (b) persons (widows, terminally ill persons, disabled persons, persons aged 60 years and above, single women, single men) with no family or social support or assured means of subsistence; (c) primitive tribal households; (d) landless agricultural labour, marginal farmers, rural artisans/ craftsmen, slum dwellers and poor persons engaged on a casual basis in the informal sector (DFPD, 2004, 2005).

The public distribution system suffers from poor implementation, particularly where matters of relief are concerned. Foodgrains are available at infrequent intervals and in lower quantity. There are repeated complaints of beneficiaries not getting their due share. Corrupt politicians and officials slice off the subsidized foodgrains to benefit themselves. There is diversion of foodgrains meant for the poor as the cost is far below the market price. The Tata Economic Consultancy Services, in its survey in 1997 carried out in 22 states and union territories, assessed the extent of diversion of foodgrains to be 36 per cent for wheat, 31 per cent for rice, 23 per cent for sugar and 55 per cent for edible oil. There are, in addition, complaints of wrong selection of beneficiaries (DFPD, 2003).

Financial Security in Old Age for Workers in the Unorganized Sector

Financial security in old age for workers currently in low income categories in the unorganized sector have remained virtually unattended. Their fragile state has been highlighted by the National Commission on Rural Labour, National Commision on Labour, National Commission on Self-Employed Women and Women in the Informal Sector, and various other bodies set up by government to inquire into their conditions. Informal sector workers are primarily engaged in rural areas as small and marginal farmers, landless workers, fishermen, craftsmen and small traders. In urban areas, they are engaged as casual labour, street vendors, small traders, mechanics, vehicle drivers, domestic workers, home based workers in self-employment, contract workers and the like. Their earnings are used to meet their immediate consumption needs.

Workers in the unorganized sector have not only low earnings, whether employed on wages or as self-employed. The income is also uncertain and irregular. It varies depending on the market situation. There are also problems arising from the migratory character of labour in several sectors of employment. In wage employment, the minimum wages fixed by law are often not paid to them. In self employment, workers have to face the vagaries of market conditions; their lack of organization leads to exploitation by middlemen and moneylenders. Home based workers form yet another exploited category. Vulnerability of such workers arises when there are exigencies to be faced like ill-health, disability, periods of unemployment and natural calamities, or when personal needs (such as marriage, funeral) have to be met. Unfortunately, such exigencies get repeated. Often the workers are forced to borrow money from informal money markets at exorbitant rates of interest which lands them in indebtedness.

Working families in the unorganized sector, particularly women, save in informal ways. Chit funds among urban informal sector workers for getting loans to be paid in instalments are popular, even though they are exposed to risks. Self-help groups are currently being formed to obtain credit to be paid in instalments, and also generate savings. Co-operative societies also help but are rather few in number. The earnings are mostly spent on meeting immediate consumption needs. They find it difficult to invest in long-term saving schemes or in insurance. Workers in the informal sector place a much greater value on liquidity of their savings than on saving schemes which have a long gestation period.

Formal means of saving for meeting financial needs in old age have, by and large, not made a dent on income groups in the unorganized sector. There are no institutional structures which take cognizance of the patterns of earning in their working life. Insurance companies and mutual funds, particularly those in the private sector, do not expect stable clients from this segment. The reasons usually advanced are:

- Absence of a sustained regular income from which savings can be made to enable the clients to pay regularly for a long period;
- Organizational inputs necessary for mobilizing clients from this segment would be large and expensive;

- Ability of clients to conform to the regulations is uncertain;
- Attitudinal problems could arise whereby immediate needs are perceived as far more important than future needs; the liquidity factor is considered more important than the stability factor.
- Uncertainties of clients about risks of payment in long saving ventures, and the real value of such payments due to inflation.
- Absence of supplementary saving mechanisms which can be drawn upon to meet immediate cash needs in order to protect the long-term savings plan;
- Migratory character of workers which may create problems of tracking;
- Illiteracy/semi-literacy/lower levels of education of the workers which may affect sustainability of the account for its full tenure.

It is thus evident that problems of income security of workers in old age flow from the nature of work in the unorganized sector and the attitude of workers towards long-term savings. Earners need a regular income with proper wages to meet their current expenses, to tide over any exigencies in their working life and to make a saving for old age. In other words, right to work with adequate remuneration is the key to social security in the working life of persons in the unorganized sector, and also in old age. This will imply the formulation and implementation of employment policies which enhance considerably the quantity of employment, improve its quality through better training, inducting technology, marketing, credit and entrepreneurial skill development, and creation of job opportunities through appropriate investment policies in the public and private sector. The manpower asset base of the poor needs considerable strengthening. The level of their income has to be significantly raised through employment which can guarantee sustainable income, enable them to acquire assets, provide access to basic social services and save for old age. They must also remember that the ability to earn, in the case of manual workers, whether wage earners or self employed, declines with age. Savings must, therefore, start early in life.

The threat of destitution in old age can become a reality if there are no sons/grandsons to fall back upon, or when the economic security of the family itself is fragile. Workers have to imbibe the attitude that just as one must earn to live well in their earning days, they have to save and invest to live in reasonable comfort in the post-earning phase.

The government has been considering ways to extend social security to workers in the unorganized sector whose condition may worsen in old age. In July 2001, the Ministry of Labour, Government of India, launched the Krishi Shramik Samajik Suraksha Yojana through LIC in 50 selected districts. The scheme was intended to cover 20,000 agricultural labourers aged 18–50 years from each district over a period of three years. The worker was required to contribute Rs. 365 in a year (Re. 1 in a day), while the Government of India would contribute Rs. 730 per beneficiary per year (Rs. 2 in a day) from the Social Security Fund. The scheme has a provision for cash benefits in the case of death or disability before age 60. After this age, the scheme has provision for pension ranging from Rs. 100 to Rs. 1900 per month, depending on the age of entry to the scheme. A lump sum payment is also provided to the family on the death of the beneficiary (MOL, 2004).

The Government of India has also launched the Unorganized Sector Workers' Social Security Scheme in January 2004 on a pilot basis in 50 districts. It is voluntary in character. The scheme envisages three benefits to unorganized sector workers who become its members, viz. old age pensions, personal accidental insurance, and medical insurance. Under the old age pension scheme, a pension will be paid from the age of 60 years or in case of permanent/total disablement. It is based on pension points which accrue to the worker during the contributory period. Pension will be payable to a member on attaining the age of 60 years, till his death. To receive the full monthly pension of Rs. 500, the number of pension points to be accumulated must reach 480. If the pension points accumulated are less, a proportionate quantum of pension will be paid. Family pension is paid to the widow in case of the death of the worker. Another benefit is the Personal Accident Insurance cover of Rs. one lakh. A third benefit is entitlement to Universal Health Insurance Scheme for the member and his family. The scheme reimburses hospitalization expenses up to Rs. 30,000 in a year and, in case the worker is hospitalized due to accident/illness, a compensation of Rs. 50 per day is given up to a maximum of 15 days, after an initial period of three days. The scheme also covers death of workers due to accident (up to Rs. 25,000).

The scheme covers unorganized sector workers, including the self employed, having an income below Rs. 6500 per month. A contribution of Rs. 50 per month is to be made by workers joining the scheme in the age group 18–35 years, and Rs. 100 per month for workers joining the scheme in the age group 36–50 years. The contribution from the employers, whenever identifiable in both the age groups, is Rs. 100 per month. Self employed workers in the age group 36–50 years are required to contribute the employer's share in addition to their own share. Contribution by the government is at the rate of 1.16 per cent of the monthly wage of the workers which, in 2004, amounted to Rs. 250 per annum. Implementation of the scheme has been vested in the Employees' Provident Fund Organization (EPFO) which provides single window service to workers for all the components of the scheme. EPFO will provide a unique national social security number, and issue identity cards so that workers can deposit their contribution and receive benefits in any part of the country. Response to the scheme has not been encouraging, particularly in the matter of enrolment of unorganized sector workers in rural and semi-urban areas. Infrastructure facilities are still not in place for implementing the scheme. The low rate of contribution by the member is likely to make the scheme unsustainable in the long run, unless the state enhances its contribution to meet the deficit. Since the scheme is voluntary in character, contribution from the employer cannot be enforced.

Some states have set up Funds for providing social security to workers in specified occupations. Kerala set up a number of such Funds in the 1980s. In 1985, it constituted the

Kerala Fishermens' Welfare Fund Act. Later, the state covered other areas such as Kerala Cashew Workers Relief and Welfare Fund Act, 1989; Kerala Handloom Workers Welfare Fund Act, 1989; Kerala Coir Workers Welfare Fund Act, 1989; Kerala Construction Workers Welfare Fund Act, 1989; and Kerala Khadi Workers Welfare Fund Act, 1989. These schemes also provide a small amount of pension (below Rs. 100 per month) after age 60. The source of financing the schemes varies. It includes contributions from workers, employers, government, and a cess collected from sales in the case of some Funds (Rajan, Mishra, and Sarma, 1999).

At the central level, the Ministry of Social Justice and Empowerment, the nodal Ministry for older persons, set up an Expert Committee in 1999 for devising a pension system for informal sector workers in India. The report titled Project OASIS (Old Age Social and Income Security), which was submitted in 2000, draws the outline for pensions for all segments, including those in the unorganized sector.

Project OASIS has proposed a pension scheme to be financed through thrift and self help by accumulating savings in the working life of the person through a modest contribution. The Report observes the features of informal sector workers: "Unorganized sector workers may change jobs, opt for spells of self-employment, move from one location to another, and also face temporary unemployment during their working life". It visualized that a pension system for this class should thus be flexible and useful to such workers, and not just confine itself to workers in the organized sector who have a regular monthly salary and have limited job mobility within the sector. The role the government can play is to create the necessary institutional infrastructure.

The Report has argued:

"........Regular savings at the rate between Rs. 3 to Rs. 5 per day through the entire working life easily suffice in escaping the poverty line in old age, provided the pension assets are invested wisely. This is an extremely heartening feature of pension system design in India, since we can visualize an extremely large number of people in India today who can save between Rs. 3 to Rs. 5 per day, and thus prepare themselves for old age income security. These numbers also remind us that low contribution rates are not the essence of the problem."

The features of the system proposed by OASIS are as follows. The subscriber will have a unique Individual Retirement Account (IRA) throughout his life, and will be given a pass book where he can see the balance which will reflect his contribution and the accumulation. The individual would save into this account in his working life, subject to a minimum of Rs. 100 per contribution and Rs. 500 in total subscription in a year. Individuals can decide when and how much they would subscribe, without the pressure of having a fixed monthly contribution. The account will stay, even when the individual changes jobs across geographical locations, or have spells of unemployment. The subscriber will be empowered in having a say of how the pension assets will be invested. Upon retirement, the pension assets can be used to buy annuity from annuity providers (insurance companies) who will convert the lump sum assets at retirement for a monthly pension (regular or variable).

A regulatory framework has been suggested in the scheme to provide safety from problems of risk management and prevention of fraud. An additional safety mechanism suggested is that if, for any reason, the final pension assets are smaller than the sum total of the contribution paid, an insurance cover would reimburse the difference.

The system works on Points of Presence (POP) located in post offices, banks and other such agencies. An individual can visit any POP to access his account and conduct transactions. This will become feasible through a sound information technology to be put in place.

Six professional Pension Fund Managers (PFM) have been suggested to manage the retirement funds. Each Pension Fund will offer three styles – Safe Income, Balanced Fund, and Growth, containing 18 schemes in all for the individual to choose from. The subscriber can alter the risk profile in an optimal fashion from high risk high return investments at a young age, to a low risk low return portfolio when approaching retirement.

The scheme is proposed as voluntary. At age 60 (assuming a contribution from age 25), the IRA account holder will be able to derive benefits from his retirement account. From the accumulation, the first Rs. 2 lakhs would be used for buying an annuity, and the remaining for other purposes.

The scheme also speaks of integrating a micro-credit facility into the pension system whereby individuals can have access to loans against their pension savings.

For premature withdrawal before the age of 60, the scheme suggests that this should be permitted on specific grounds, once an individual accumulates Rs. 2 lakhs in the account, the maximum being 33 per cent of the balance above Rs. 2 lakhs, subject to a withdrawal tax of 10 per cent. In other words, a disincentive has been provided for premature withdrawal.

OASIS Project Report suggests that advocacy and strong publicity through informal and formal means are important for the success of the scheme. It would be desirable to tie up with self-help groups, cooperative societies, non-governmental organizations, trade unions, federations of self-employed workers and other bodies to mobilize support for the programme.

.   The scheme depends solely on the contribution of members. It rests on the optimistic assumption that every informal sector worker will be able to make a contribution for the entire period of his working life. It sidelines the fact that many workers earn too little, and that too in an intermittent manner which varies from week to week and from season to season. Empirical studies in rural areas have shown that among the rural poor, earnings are just sufficient to meet their immediate needs (Dandekar, 1996; Gurumurthy, 1998). It also gives little weight to the outlook of workers who look for cash and benefits in the short run, rather than deferring it for a longer period. The state makes no contribution to the scheme, even though the State has the basic responsibility of providing social security to all, and not just to its own superannuated employees.

There are several other issues which need consideration. Accumulation of a worker in the pension fund will depend on the age at which a worker joins the scheme. Norms will need to be worked out on the transaction cost in administering the scheme as that will have a bearing on the net amount which will be available to the worker when he crosses the age of 60 years. The members have been given the choice to choose the type of Fund and the scheme for investing. Since most workers are illiterate/semi-literate or have a low educational standard, they are ignorant of the stock market. Their capacity to choose is, therefore, a leap in the dark. The exercise of their choice is thus more notional than real, and can be regarded as illusory in character. The scheme is very optimistic of returns from investments in equity. The Report has indicated that in the long run, the average rate of return on the equity index in India is 18.5 per cent "which has the potential to revolutionize the accumulation over a worker's life time". Returns, however, depend on the choice of companies in which professional managers invest, assuming that this is always rationally done. In developing countries like India, there are high risks, bordering on speculation. Finance companies with professional managers have given no returns for some mutual fund schemes; even the net asset value has been found to be lower than the price at which it was offered. Prices of equity stocks depend not only on the performance of the company but also on economic policies, political stability, global political and economic climate, trade fluctuations, sectoral performances, efficiency and transparency of the regulator. Stock market scams infect the prices of stocks giving them an unpredictable volatile character. There will always be a nagging anxiety of a person not receiving even the real value of the contribution he has made, not to speak of additional returns.

Provident Fund/Pensions to Workers of Industrial Establishments in the Organized Sector

Prior to independence, some private companies extended provident fund to its employees. In 1952, the central government brought forward a legislation for the establishment of provident fund for employees specified in the Act. The main object was to provide a retirement benefit to the worker and security to his dependants in case of early death. The Act made it compulsory for the worker in establishments covered by the Act to join the Fund, the assumption being that the worker would imbibe the spirit of savings from his earning years for use in his twilight years, by getting a lump sum after retirement. In 1971, after about 18 years of operation of the scheme, the employees family pension scheme became a part of the Act through the creation of a Family Pension Fund by diverting a portion of the contribution of workers and employers, supplemented by a contribution from the central government. In 1976, the Act was further amended to make provision for the Employees' Deposit Linked Insurance Scheme, to provide insurance cover to the members, without payment of any additional premium. The Act was amended again in 1995 to include the Employees' Pension Scheme, which replaced the family pension scheme of 1971. The Act as it now stands makes provision for payment of provident fund on superannuation, and for pension after retirement. The family is protected in case of death. The government also benefits as it is able to borrow a large volume of money for utilization in development projects. The financial sector/capital markets can benefit from an additional funding source as the Fund can also invest up to 10 per cent in capital markets (private sector bonds/securities). An annual pre-determined rate of interest is credited to the account of the worker based on his balance. The Provident Fund contribution, additionally, has the advantage of providing to the worker incentives for saving by giving rebate in income tax (under section 88). The annual interest in the Provident Fund account, and the lump sum on withdrawal, are free of income tax. EPF also has provision for a pension for the worker. It is thus a saving scheme with several plus points.

When the Employees' Provident Fund and Miscellaneous Provisions Act was launched, it covered only 6 specified industries. In 2003–04, it covered 180 specified industries/ classes of establishments. The categories covered are given in Table 2.12.

Table 2.12: Industries/Classes of establishments covered by EPF, 2003–04

Category	No.	%
Primary Sector		
Agriculture, forestry and fishing	10	5.55
Mining and quarrying	36	20.00
Manufacturing including repairs	91	50.56
Electricity, gas and water	1	0.56
Construction	1	0.56
Hotels	6	3.33
Service Sector		
Transport, storage and communication	8	4.44
Financing, insurance, real estate and business services	9	5.00
Community, social and personnel services	18	10.00
Total	180	100.00

Source: Employees' Provident Fund Organization.

Most members covered by the EPF are from 5 industries: (i) Electrical, Mechanical or General Engineering; (ii) Textiles; (iii) Trading and Commercial Establishments; (iv) Bidi; and (v) Heavy and Fine Chemicals. Together, they constitute 28 per cent of the total membership. An establishment, which is not otherwise covered by the Act, can be brought within its purview with the mutual consent of the employer and the majority of its employees. In March 2004, the number of establishments voluntarily covered was 30,059, which was about 8 per cent of the total number of establishments covered by the Act. The number of members in EPF in 2003–04 was 401 lakhs, and the number of establishments 370,386. Table 2.13 gives the growth in number of establishments covered, and number of members. Out of 370,386 establishments, 2491 were in the exempted category. These are establishments which have their own provident fund schemes which give better or equivalent returns. EPFO monitors their operation.

Table 2.13: No. of establishments covered by EPF and number of members, 1995 to 2004

Year	No. of establishments covered	No. of EPF members (in lakhs)
1995	251,013	187.24
1996	266,645	194.85
1997	277,555	202.88
1998	299,204	212.19
1999	318,430	231.19
2000	326,541	245.37
2001	340,013	263.01
2002	357,747	274.18
2003	344,508	394.98
2004	370,386	400.92

Note: Figures refer to 31 March of the year and cover both exempted and non-exempted establishments.
Source: Employees Provident Fund Organization.

An employee, on joining an establishment covered by the Act, has compulsorily to contribute to the Provident Fund. The employer, too, makes a contribution. Statement below gives the contributions and the benefits. The Fund operates on the twin principles of defined contribution and defined benefits.

The Employees' Provident Fund Organization also administers the Employees' Deposit Linked Insurance Fund which came into force in August 1976. It provides lump sum benefit upon death, based on a formulae. No contribution is payable by the employee for availing the insurance cover. Employers are required to pay contributions to the Insurance Fund at the rate of 0.5 per cent of pay (basic wages, dearness allowance including cash value of food concession, and retaining allowance, if any). During 2003–04, a sum of Rs. 175.36 crores was deposited as contribution from employers. In the same year, 19,874 claims were settled and an amount of Rs. 50.78 crores authorized for payment. At the end of 2003–04, there was a total investment corpus of Rs. 3904 crores under the scheme.

	Employees' Provident Fund Scheme, 1952	*Employees' Pension Scheme, 1995*
Benefits	Accumulation plus interest upon retirement, resignation, death. Partial withdrawals allowed for specific expenses such as house construction, higher education, marriage, illness.	Monthly benefits for superannuation/ retirement, disability, survivor widow (er), children. Amount of pension based on average salary in the preceding 12 months of the employee, and total years of employment. Minimum pension on disablement Past service benefit to participants of Family Benefit Pension Scheme,1971
Contribution (% in wages)		
Employer	3.67% (for 175 industries) 1.67% (for 5 industries)	8.33%
Employee	12% (for 175 industries) 10% (for 5 industries)	Nil
Government	Nil	1.16%
Administrative charges:		
Unexempted (% in wages)	1.10 %	16% of the total expenditure of the EPFO to be charged to the EPS Fund.
Inspection Charges:		
Exempted	0.18 %	Not applicable

Source: Employees' Provident Fund Organization.

Provident Fund contributions have shown an increase. In 2003–04, the contribution rose to Rs. 12,356 crores, up from Rs. 4,030 crores in 1991–92. Table 2.14 gives the contributions received each year.

Table 2.14: Provident Fund contributions received, 1991–92 to 2003–04

Year	Total contribution (Rs. in crores)
1991–92	4030.23
1992–93	4666.42
1993–94	4954.85
1994–95	5076.89
1995–96	5765.87
1996–97	5971.06
1997–98	6818.19
1998–99	7795.54
1999–2000	9682.22
2000–01	10728.44
2001–02	11188.26
2002–03	11388.14
2003–04	12355.97

Source: Employees' Provident Fund Organization.

Contributions received by the Employees' Provident Fund Organization are invested as per the pattern prescribed by the central government. The exempted establishments are required to follow the same pattern of investments. Most of the investment is made in securities, bonds, deposits guaranteed by the government. The Board of Trustees has been permitted to invest up to 10 per cent in private sector bonds/ securities which have an investment grade rating from at least two credit rating agencies. This is considered by some financial experts as restrictive of the returns which could otherwise come from the Fund. The members get a return from their deposits in the Fund through a rate of interest credited annually to the account. The rate is recommended annually by the Board of Trustees for endorsement by the central government. It rose from 3 per cent annually in 1952–53 to 12 per cent in 1990–91 where it remained till 1999–2000. The interest declined to 11 per cent in 2000–01. It has been fixed at 9.50 per cent in 2001–02, 2002–03 and 2003–04. Trade unions and left parties supporting the government are keen that the existing rate of interest should continue while the government would like it to drop in view of the policy to soften interest rates. High interest rates on EPF do not seem to be sustainable, given the current investment policies of the Fund. It has been estimated that an interest rate of 8 per cent on EPF account will have a surplus (income-liabilities) of Rs. 39.35 crores. Any increase in interest rate will lead to a deficit. At 8.50 per cent, the estimated deficit would be Rs. 365.89 crores, at 9.00 per cent it would be Rs. 771.13 crores and at 9.50 per cent, it would be Rs. 1176.37 crores (Dhoot, 2005). Higher than sustainable interest rates would thus imply a heavy subsidy. It is possible that exempted establishments, instead of managing their own funds, may opt for joining the EPFO, as they may not be able to give the high interest rates.

EPFO has a sanctioned staff strength of about 23,276 employees on 31 March 2004. It has 21 Regional Offices, 87 Sub-Regional/Sub Accounts Offices, 12 Service Centres and 163 District Offices. Administrative expenditure on the Provident Fund Scheme is met out of: (i) charges received from employers of unexempted establishments. Currently, this amounts to 1.10 per cent of the basic wages and dearness allowance on which Provident Fund contribution is payable; (ii) inspection charges from employers of exempted establishments. Currently, this is 0.18 per cent of basic wages and dearness allowance on which Provident Fund contribution is payable. During 2001–02, Rs. 498.86 crores were collected as cost of administration from both the categories.

Arrear demands from employers continue to be a problem with the Employees' Provident Fund Organization. On 31 March 2004, there was an outstanding arrear demand of Rs. 1862.80 crores. On 31 March 2003, it was Rs. 1511.79 crores. A large part of the amount is in the unrealizable category due to disputes in courts, factories which have gone into liquidation, factories declared sick by Board of Industrial and Financial Reconstruction, and recovery barred by Acts of central/state governments. The private sector in the unexempted category accounted for about seven-tenths of the arrears in 2003–04. Efforts are being made to collect the arrears as far as possible. In 2003–04, the arrears collected amounted to Rs. 1832.70 crores.

The effectiveness of provident fund as a compulsory long-term savings instrument through which a member can get a lump sum (contribution plus interest) at the time of super-annuation gets diluted when members make partial withdrawals from the account, which *ipso facto* becomes a payment before the date of maturity. Workers seem to value liquidity and discount future requirements. The number of claims for partial withdrawal has been rising. In 1994–95, it was 4 lakhs. In 2003–04, it rose to 4.67 lakhs. In 1999–2000, the amount authorized for payment for partial withdrawal cases was Rs. 781.95 crores. In 2003–04, the amount rose to Rs. 1876.13 crores. The average amount of partial withdrawal from provident fund in 2003–04 was Rs. 40,203 per claim settled. In the previous year, it was Rs. 29,746. The grounds for withdrawal were house building, marriage, education, illness of members, temporary closure of establishment, and other factors.

Defaults in annual statement of accounts to members of Employees' Provident Fund is a matter of concern. In 2001–02, annual statements were pending for 93.81 lakh members. In 2003–04, it rose to 119.31 lakhs.

The National Commission on Labour, 2002 reported that provision for premature withdrawal of provident fund by a member should be restricted. The withdrawal is mainly due to resignation. Even though EFPO allows for transfer of accounts when a person takes up another job, members prefer to withdraw the amount instead of getting them transferred. In 2003–04, 20.40 lakh claims of provident fund were settled and Rs. 5772.99 crores authorized for payment. The average claim per case settled in 2003–04 was Rs. 28,293. Most of the claims, almost 90 per cent, were due to resignation. The other reasons were superannuation, death, retrenchment and other factors.

Several suggestions have been made to enable EPF to serve fully the purposes for which it was framed, viz., a long-term saving instrument for old age, to be available after superannuation. These are:

• Lowering the minimum number of workers in

industrial establishments and cooperative societies so that they, too, are covered.

- Stringent action against employers who default on payment to EPF establishments.
- Better investment of EPF funds to bring a higher rate of return which will, in turn, provide better interest rates for EPF members. Some commentators are of the view that returns from investments made by EPFO can be improved by investing some portion in the equity stock market which, in the long run, has been found to provide better returns than government securities in developed countries.
- Partial withdrawal from EPF account to be considerably reduced through stringent regulations indicating the percentage amount that can be withdrawn under different heads, the minimum period after which withdrawal can be made, and the minimum balance necessary, so that at the time of its maturity full benefit can be obtained.
- A predetermined rate of bonus should be given to those members who do not withdraw from the account.
- Some workers, like those in construction industry, which have a large extent of migration from one employer to another, have not been happy about deductions being made for provident fund because of problems of crediting it to their accounts. Many accounts remain frozen and become inoperative. Such problems have to be resolved. The National Commission on Labour, 2002 observed that the provision to cover persons on casual or on contract basis were operating largely to the disadvantage of the workers. The employers deduct contributions from their wages but do not remit them to the EPFO. Thus the deduction operates as an unauthorized deduction.
- Inclusion of self-employed workers in EPF would help a large number of persons in getting the benefits of provident fund. A separate set of provisions can be made for them in the Act.
- The age of superannuation at 58 years is too low,

keeping in view the increase in life expectancy. The post-retirement period has been extended due to longer life expectancy, even though the earning years have remained the same. Extending the age will imply lowering the period of liability. The member will also have the advantage of getting access to a higher provident fund in his account.

- The salary period used to calculate the period of pension payment could be raised if, on examination, it is found to have been abused by some employers who tend to substantially raise the salary at the time of retirement to benefit the workers.

The suggestions given above need to be considered after a detailed empirical study of contributions and withdrawals by EPF members covering different industries and states. This will help the Consultant/Review Committee to consider objectively the solutions, keeping fully in mind the primacy of workers' interests.

The state of West Bengal has launched a state assisted scheme of provident fund for unorganized workers, including the self-employed. Details of operation of the scheme are yet to be known.

Employees' Pension Scheme under Employees' Public Provident Fund and Miscellaneous Provisions Act, 1952

The Employees' Provident Fund and Miscellaneous Provisions Act, 1952 provides for a pension scheme to workers on superannuation or permanent total disablement. The scheme is compulsory for : (i) all persons who were members of the Provident Fund (including those employed in exempted establishments) and were contributing to the erstwhile Family Pension Scheme, 1971 which has now ceased to operate; and (ii) persons who became members of the Provident Fund from 16 November 1995, i.e. the date of introduction of the pension scheme.

Entitlement to pension under the scheme accrues from a minimum of 10 years of contributory service, and is payable on attaining the age of 58 years. If the member ceases employment before 58 years, pension may be availed before hand, but not before 50 years. Early pension is subject to a discounting factor of 3 per cent for every year of shortfall from 58 years. The quantum of monthly pension varies depending upon the pensionable salary and pensionable service. The pension scheme also provides for commutation up to one-third of the pension amount. On the death of the pensioner, the pension is provided to widow/widower for life or till remarriage. Children (two at a time) are also entitled to pension. Dependent father/mother is entitled to pension in cases where the member dies leaving behind his family and no nominee. The scheme ensures guarantee of pension to a member even in case of default on the part of the employer. It provides for annual valuation and additional relief to pensioners.

No additional amount (beyond provident fund contribution) is payable by the employee or the employer for coverage under the scheme. The Fund gets its resources by partial diversion of the employer's contribution to the provident fund (8.33 per cent of the wages). The central government contributes to the Pension Fund at the rate of 1.16 per cent of the wages.

The number of members of the Employees' Pension Fund has been rising. In 1998–99, it was 204.81 lakhs. In 2003–04, it increased to 280.90 lakhs. The cumulative number of pensioners (including Employees' Family Pension Scheme, 1971) has also been rising. In 1995–96, it was 219,445. In 2003–04, it increased to 1758,841, showing that within a period of eight years, the cumulative number has increased to about eight times. The number of pensioners is about 6.3 per cent of the number of members of the pension fund.

Table 2.15 gives the number of EPF pension beneficiaries by category. The number of superannuated pension beneficiaries is about one-fifth of the total number of pension beneficiaries. An interesting point to note is that the number of early pension beneficiaries is larger than the number of superannuated pension beneficiaries. It has increased from 17.7

Table 2.15: Number of pension beneficiaries, 1999–2000 to 2001–02

Category	1999–2000		2000–01		2001–02	
	Number	%	Number	%	Number	%
1. Member's Pension						
(i) Early pension (50–57 years)	166,046	17.70	238,335	25.43	328,438	28.10
(ii) Superannuation pension	157,235	21.31	194,747	20.78	247,153	21.15
(iii) Disablement pension	605	0.08	832	0.09	1021	0.09
Subtotal	323,886	43.89	433,914	46.30	576,612	49.33
2. Widow/widower pension						
(i) Death in service	267,708	36.27	296,468	31.64	331,858	28.39
(ii) Death away from service	7,778	1.05	13,208	1.41	16,418	1.40
Subtotal	275,486	37.33	309,676	33.05	348,276	29.80
3. Nominee pension	833	0.11	2600	0.28	4413	0.38
4. Orphan pension	1966	0.27	2975	0.30	4260	0.36
5. Children pension	135,827	18.40	187,961	20.06	235,218	20.13
Grand Total	737,998	100.00	937,126	100.00	1168,779	100.00

Note: The figures include widow pensioners and children pensioners.
Source: Annual Reports.

per cent in 1999–2000 to 28.1 in 2001–02. The percentage of widow pension due to death in service is quite high

The entire accumulation in the erstwhile Family Pension Fund constitutes the corpus of the Pension Fund. On 16 November 1995 the corpus was Rs. 8,252 crores. This increased to Rs. 39,050 crores in 2001–02 (securities + public account). The scheme provides for investment of the Pension Fund. The Family Pension corpus and the central government's contribution is invested in the Public Account of the Government of India. Other accretions to the Pension Fund are invested as per the pattern prescribed for the Employees Provident Fund Scheme, 1952. Investment of Pension Fund during 2001–02 was Rs. 5833 crores.

The Employees' Provident Fund Organization administers the pension scheme. EPFO is streamlining its operations for a quick settlement of pension claims. The percentage of claims settled to work load has increased from

68 per cent in 1998–99 to 78 per cent in 2003–04. EPFO is developing a Unique Identification Number for every subscriber regardless of geographical location to help him in matters connected with his account. A computerized public grievances cell has been introduced. Lok Adalats have been organized for redressal of grievances.

Valuation of the scheme by panel of actuaries has shown that the scheme in its present form is unsustainable. The sixth valuation, which submitted its report on 31 March 2002, showed a big valuation deficit. A number of suggestions have been made, such as an increase in the age of retirement from 58 years to 60 years, increase in rate of contribution of employers, increase in reduction rate for pension for early withdrawal from 3 per cent to 5 per cent, and better returns from investments. It has also been suggested that any changes in future should be done after an actuarial assessment (EPFO, 2004).

Provident Funds also exist for coal mine workers, seamen, Assam tea plantation workers, and some other categories which, too, provide somewhat similar benefits.

Public Provident Fund for Self-Employed and Others

There are several long-term saving instruments for the general public. Prominent among them is the Public Provident Fund (PPF), introduced in 1968–69 to enable self-employed persons mainly in business, professions, consultancy and other service providers at middle and higher income levels to meet their financial needs in old age. PPF account can be opened in designated branches of the State Bank of India and the post offices. Government employees having a GPF/CPF account can also open a PPF account and get a facility for continuation of the account beyond the age of superannuation. Deposits in the PPF account can vary between Rs. 500 and Rs. 70,000 (erstwhile, Rs. 60,000) in a year, and has to be paid from taxable income. The scheme thus allows enough flexibility to those who do not want to commit themselves to a fixed amount every year. The minimum tenure of the account is 15 years. It can be continued thereafter for every five years, with or without a further contribution. However, it continues to draw the same benefit. At the end of the 15 year period (or more, as the case may be) even when no further deposits have been made, the scheme provides for a lump sum withdrawal or for an annual withdrawal for as long as the balance lasts.

PPF is generous in tax benefits as a long-term saving instrument. It provides incentives for investment, accumulation (tax free income, in regard to income and wealth tax) and withdrawal (no tax, as amount withdrawn from PPF is not treated as income). PPF has liquidity as loans/ withdrawals are permitted. It carries no risks because it gives assured returns by way of interest. This makes PPF different from equity/mutual funds. PPF has defined benefits since interest on it is decided upon by the government and is generally linked to GPF account of government employees.

Though Public Provident Fund is meant for meeting financial needs in old age, it is often used as a device for tax planning, particularly by those in the middle and higher income groups. Tax consultants are always busy advising on withdrawals from PPF for meeting household or business expenses, and making deposits into it from taxable income to get tax benefit. To that extent, the real benefit of income security in old age suffers a decline, and the object of the scheme is partly diluted. Savings for needs in old age are discounted against current needs.

The policy of the government is now to reduce interest rates. PPF interest rates, which were 12 per cent per annum in the 1990s, have been gradually reduced. In his budget speech dated 28 February 2003, the Finance Minister has proposed a further reduction of interest in view of the stated policy to reduce interest rates to make cheaper credit available to industry. The interest rate in 2003–04 was 8 per cent on the savings, which is lower by 4 per cent from what it fetched earlier. This has, undoubtedly, not been received well by PPF savers as it will make a dent on accumulations in the PPF account, and particularly affect retiring/retired persons who have no pension or other superannuation benefits.

PPF is a good long-term saving instrument for the general

public as it has total security, flexibility, liquidity and maximization of returns. However, it has not been publicized well enough as an investment for old age security, and is used often as a medium period saving instrument, useful for tax saving. PPF can be promoted to cover larger segments of the population beyond metropolitan areas in rural, semi-urban areas and towns by having well trained agents with a higher level of educational qualifications and marketing skills. The accounting system should be so designed as to facilitate deposits in any selected post office or branch of the State Bank of India, and to get the pass book periodically updated giving current balance, as has been suggested in the report of the OASIS Committee for a pension scheme for workers in the unorganized sector. PPF could do well with some modifications. Some disincentives for withdrawals may be introduced by deducting a penalty from the amount withdrawn. A bonus may be provided to persons who do not make any withdrawal or loan for at least 15 years. A slightly higher bonus can be paid for persons who make no withdrawal for 20 years. On maturity, the account holders may be encouraged to have annual withdrawals (annuities) for as long as the balance lasts, rather than to take the amount as a lump sum, as there is always the possibility of the money being used without ensuring that it will last for the full period of survival. The maximum annual contribution to PPF should be raised. OASIS suggested that a Public Pension Scheme should be initiated under PPF in which 10 per cent of the annual contribution to PPF should be mandatorily earmarked, with a minimum contribution of Rs. 500 per year.

Retirement Benefits

Employees in the organized sector (central and state governments, public sector undertakings and industrial establishments) get benefits on superannuation in the form of: (i) leave encashment, (ii) gratuity, (iii) general provident fund, and (iv) pensions.

These benefits are often legislatively and administratively

defined, and provide a cushion for meeting financial needs after superannuation/death/disability.

Leave encashment

Central/State government employees are permitted to encash earned leave to their credit at the time of their superannuation for a maximum period of 300 days. The amount is not treated as a taxable income and is exempt from income tax. Employees in quasi-government undertakings and a number of private sector establishments are also permitted facilities of leave encashment. The amount, too, is exempt from income tax, subject to certain conditions laid down in the income tax rules.

Gratuity

Gratuity is an additional retirement benefit paid in lump sum to persons who have completed the minimum service requirement. The Payment of Gratuity Act, 1972 applies to factories, mines, oil fields, plantations, ports, railway employees, shops and commercial establishments having 10 or more workers. Some other establishments are also included by notification. A continuous service of at least five years is required for entitlement to gratuity which is paid at the rate of 15 days' wages for every completed year of service or part thereof, subject to a ceiling of Rs. 3.50 lakhs.

Benefit of gratuity to central government employees was granted on the recommendations of the Third Central Pay Commission. It was extended to employees of state governments and quasi-government undertakings. Dearness allowance is now included in the last pay drawn for calculating the amount of gratuity, based on acceptance of the recommendation of the Central Fifth Pay Commission.

Several companies, even before the passing of legislation, had introduced gratuity for their employees. It was an added incentive for the staff as it enhanced the employment rating of the company, and helped in retaining manpower. Payment of gratuity by the employer is treated as an expenditure and is not treated as taxable income for the company. Gratuity covered by the Payment of Gratuity Act, 1972 is exempt from income tax in the hands of the retired person to the extent of 15 days' salary (7 days in the case of employees of seasonal establishments) for each completed year of service, subject to a ceiling of Rs. 3.50 lakhs. Gratuity paid to an employee in excess of this amount is taxable in the hands of the assessee.

Contributory Provident Fund

Contributory Provident Fund is a long-term saving instrument payable in lump sum at the time of superannuation. It is intended to provide financial security in old age. It applies to government/quasi-government employees who do not have pensions. Such employees have compulsorily to subscribe to the Fund. The employee is required to contribute a minimum of 10 per cent of his emoluments to the Fund. The maximum amount can be his total emoluments. Contribution from the employer equals 10 per cent of the emoluments of the employee. For purposes of advances/withdrawals from CPF, only the employees' contribution and interest thereon is considered, and not the total CPF accumulation which includes that of the employer.

Accumulation in CPF has a defined benefit. It provides a fixed rate of interest every year (determined by government). The interest is free of taxation. Initially the rate of interest was 12 per cent; it began to fall in view of the policy of the government to soften interest rates. In 2004–05, the rate of interest was 8 per cent. Partial withdrawals are permitted from the CPF account for specified purposes. Such a provision, if liberally utilized by the account holder, reduces the amount available on superannuation, and can thus become a contributory factor to financial insecurity in old age. Annual contribution to CPF provides an incentive to the employee as tax relief is provided. CPF balance received by the employee at the time of superannuation is free of taxation. CPF, thus, has the same advantages as PPF—it provides incentives for investment, accumulation and withdrawal.

Several companies have formulated their own scheme of contributory provident for the employees not covered by the Employees' Provident Fund and Miscellaneous Provisions Act, 1952. The rate of interest paid in the member's account is predetermined.

General Provident Fund

General Provident Fund (GPF), too, is a long-term saving instrument payable in lump sum on superannuation/death/ disability. GPF is compulsory for all pensionable employees of central and state governments, and quasi-government undertakings. An employee, who has joined the Contributory Provident Fund, cannot join the GPF. The employee intimates the amount of the monthly subscription from his salary, the minimum quantum of which is 6 per cent of the total monthly emoluments. The maximum monthly amount that can be contributed is his total emoluments. Accumulation in the Fund has a defined benefit. The annual interest in the GPF account is free of income tax. The amount of interest is notified by the government from time to time. Between 1986–87 to 1999–2000, the rate of interest was 12 per cent. It was reduced to 11 per cent in 2000–01 and 9.5 per cent in 2001–02. It has been reduced further. The GPF balance received by the employee at the time of superannuation is free of taxation. Annual contribution to GPF provides an incentive for investment in the account as a deduction has been provided in the income tax rules, subject to a ceiling.

The utility of a long-term accumulated saving instrument can be lost by employees who make withdrawals to meet immediate cash needs. The purposes, and the terms and conditions of withdrawal from GPF, have been specified – illness, higher education, marriage, building of a house (including addition, alteration, reconstruction), purchase of a motor vehicle, and other purposes indicated in the rules. The amount withdrawn is at times used for purposes different from the stated purpose. It is also used for purposes of tax planning. Withdrawals from GPF often results in a lower sum at the time of superannuation than would be the case if GPF was left intact.

In order to get over the problem of withdrawal, a suggestion has been made for giving an incentive to those who do not withdraw from their GPF till the date of superannuation by paying an additional interest or bonus at the time of termination. Suggestions have also been made that employees may be permitted to retain their accumulations in the Fund for a period of two years after superannuation, and get paid the usual GPF interest on the amount so retained.

The issue of pass books to GPF subscribers was recommended by the Fifth Central Pay Commission so that the issue of missing contributions can be sorted out well in advance. The Third and Fourth Central Pay Commissions had made similar recommendations to enable contributors to know the latest status of their provident fund accounts. These are yet to be fully implemented.

Employees in banks, insurance companies and several other public sector undertakings have now opted for non-contributory provident fund, which is based entirely on contribution by the employee (as in the case of central and state government employees) so that they, too, can have pensions.

Pension from Government

Pension given by central and state governments, public sector undertakings and some other bodies is a secure and valid provider of income security on superannuation/death. The Supreme Court, in its landmark judgement in the case of D.S. Nakara and others vs Union of India (1983), gave the principles for pension payments. It stated that a pension scheme, consistent with available resources, must provide that the pensioner would be able to live 'free from want, with decency, independence and self-respect' and 'at a standard equivalent at the pre-retirement level'. It held that pension is "neither a bounty nor a matter of grace depending upon the sweet will of the employer. It is not an ex-gratia payment, but a payment for past services rendered. It is a social welfare measure, rendering socio-economic justice to those who, in the hey day of their life, ceaselessly toiled for the employer on an assurance that in their old age, they would not be left in the lurch". Based on the court's judgement, the Fifth Central Pay Commission observed that the pension of superannuated persons should be treated as 'their statutory, inalienable, legally enforced right'. It also said that the pension rates should, accordingly, be fixed, revised, modified and changed in ways not entirely dissimilar to the salaries granted to serving employees.

Pension is paid from the budget in the case of central and state government employees, and the general revenue in the case of other undertakings. No pension contribution is made by the employee during the period of his service. From 1 January 2004, a separate system of financing pensions has been introduced. for new entrants in central government service. The current employees, however, will continue to be governed by the existing rules of pension payments.

The qualifying service for payment of pension is 20 years. Full pension is paid on a service of 33 years or more. Public sector undertakings, too, are now providing pension, and changing from contributory provident fund to non-contributory provident fund which has only the employees' contribution, plus accumulated interest. Longer life expectancy, and the view that pension payments when indexed to cost of living is a better deal than receiving instant cash, have brought about this transition. An added factor now is the falling rate of interest.

Pensions provide a sustained value to superannuated employees because it provides a monthly payment which cannot be nibbled at, except at the time of the decision to commute a portion of the pension at the time of superannuation. It is, therefore, a far more stable return and is intended to last for the whole life of the person (and the person's spouse after his death). It is, also, not subject to the risks of wrong investment policies as can be the case if a lump sum is received, and invested in equity markets or in business enterprises, exposing the person to risk and market uncertainties. The indexing of payment of pension with dearness relief (as in the case of serving employees) has made it far more attractive compared to Contributory Provident Fund.

Pensions to central government employees have shown some major changes over the years. In the past:

- No dearness relief was paid to compensate for the rise in cost of living. This eroded the pensioner's purchasing power and led to a decline in standard of living. Later, a relief was granted, which was at half the rate given to serving employees.
- There was gross disparity between pensions drawn by persons of the same rank but retiring at different points of time. In the past, a person retiring later could draw pension higher than a person retiring earlier on a similar or a senior scale.
- Commuted value of pensions was upto one-third of the pension amount.
- Commuted value of pension was not restored to the pensioner.
- There was no family pension.
- Pension was earlier calculated on the average pay drawn in the last 36 months before retirement, and fixed at three-eighths of the average emoluments (i.e. 37.5 per cent).

Pension has now been made more attractive, more so after the Fifth Central Pay Commission submitted its report. Effective from 1 January 1996, pension is calculated on the basis of 50 per cent of the average salary drawn during the last ten months of service. Full pension is paid if the employee has worked for more than 33 years. Dearness relief is granted at the same rate as for serving employees. Payment of pension is now adjusted on the basis of current pay scales of employees irrespective of the date of their superannuation (one rank one pension regime). Amount paid as commuted pension is free of income tax. No medical examination is required if the option is exercised within one year of retirement. The percentage of pension which can be commuted has now increased to 40 per cent as compared to 33 per cent earlier. Commuted pension is now restored after 15 years from the date of superannuation. This has been made possible after the judgment of the Supreme Court in favour of restoration of commuted value of pension.

The initiative was taken by Common Cause, an NGO, which filed a writ petition that it is inequitous for the central government to continue to deduct the commuted part of the pension throughout the life of the pensioner. It cited the cases of a number of very old pensioners in their eightees and nineties from whom the government had taken two to three times or more of the amount they were given on commutation as a lump sum. After a series of arguments and counter arguments, the Supreme Cout decided in favour of the pensioners, which was made applicable to civil as well as defence pensioners, effective from 1 April 1985. The commuted value of the pension was restored; pensioneers were entitled to full pension after 15 years of the date of retirement (Common Cause, 1987). The High Level Expert Group on New Pension System considered restoration as unique to the pension system in India, not found in other countries. Family pension is now 30 per cent of the pensionary amount plus 100 per cent neutralization of dearness relief. For purposes of family pension, dependent parents, widowed/divorced daughters have been included, whereas these relations were not considered earlier for family pension. There is also an increase in the minimum rate of pension paid. The ceiling on pension has been raised to Rs. 15,000 per month (50 per cent of the highest pay). The current system is thus a defined benefit pension scheme, and is indexed not only to rates of inflation but also to the salary structure of current employees.

The number of central government pensioners has been increasing. Rise in central government employment in the late 1950s and 1960s is being reflected in the large number of persons who are superannuating now. Retirees are now living longer. The attrition rate has been lower than the additions. Pension reforms, such as a lower number of salary structures, increase in promotional avenues, and an increase in minimum pension, are leading to an escalation in expenditure.

The Fifth Central Pay Commission compiled the number of central government pensioners from 1990–91 to 1994–95. The data in Table 2.16 shows that in a five year period the number grew from 27.33 lakhs in 1990–91 to 32.33 lakhs in 1994–95, a growth of 18.3 per cent.

Table 2.16: Number of central government pensioners, 1990–91 to 1994–95

(no. in lakhs)

Category	1990–91	1991–92	1992–93	1993–94	1994–95
Defence (including armed forces)	15.74	15.85	16.00	16.13	16.66
Railways	6.86	7.26	8.19	8.63	9.00
Postal	1.51	1.58	1.65	1.72	2.00
Telecom	0.43	0.47	0.51	0.58	0.66
Other Civil Departments	2.79	3.06	3.37	3.64	3.92
Total	27.33	28.22	29.72	30.70	32.23

Source: Report of Fifth Central Pay Commission.

The High Level Expert Group on a New Pension System, appointed by the Government of India in June 2001, indicated that in 1999–2000 in the Ministry of Defence there were 168 pensioners to every 100 employees. In the Ministry of Railways, it was 68 persons per 100 employees, in Postal Service it was 54, in Telecom it was 34 and in the case of civil services it was 55 (DPPW, 2002). Estimates have been made of the projected total number of pensioners in central government. In 1999–2000, the number was 38.29 lakhs. It is projected to increase to 48.28 lakhs in 2009–10 at a compound annual growth rate of 2.3 per cent. Even without any further pay revision, the pension liability will increase due to increase in numbers and indexing of pension to inflation (Swain and Sen, 2004).

Enhancement of pension payments as a result of the recommendations of the Fifth Central Pay Commission, and increase in the number of pensioners, has led to a big increase in pension expenditure. Table 2.17 gives the trends between 1990–91 and 2001–02. The data shows that central government pension expenditure rose from Rs. 3,272 crores in 1990–91 to Rs. 22,410 crores in 2001–02, showing an increase by a factor of 6.85 in twelve years. The highest growth rate of pensions took place from 1997–98 to 1999–2000 as a result of acceptance of the recommendations of the Fifth Central Pay Commission by the government without carefully scrutinizing the future implications of pension liability. Figure 2.5 gives the trend. Of the 5 major sub-categories of pension paid by central government, nearly 50 per cent are accounted for by Defence.

Table 2.17: Trends in central government expenditure on pensions,
1990–91 to 2001–02

(Rs. in crores)

Year	Posts	Civil	Defence	Railways	Telecom	Total	% increase
1990–91	150	480	1670	886	85	3272	
1991–92	182	583	1840	1040	103	3748	14.54
1992–93	204	701	2313	1251	117	4585	22.35
1993–94	227	818	2531	1488	142	5206	13.54
1994–95	253	934	2704	1686	156	5733	10.13
1995–96	312	1103	3197	2117	199	6928	20.83
1996–97	384	1425	3683	2509	252	8253	19.12
1997–98	558	1948	4947	3509	413	11376	37.84
1998–99	677	2803	7270	4144	452	15346	34.90
1999–2000	682	3286	11024	4018	437	19446	26.72
2000–01	815	4021	10539	5167	575	21117	8.59
2001–02	835	4320	10770	5800	685	22410	6.12
Compound annual growth rate (%)	25	23	21	20	19	21	

Note: Due to rounding off, figures in Total column may not tally. The percentage annual increase in the last column has been calculated on the basis of total expenditure upto 2 decimal places.

Source: Working Group on Pensionary Liability, Department of Expenditure, Government of India, 2001 as quoted in report of High Level Expert Group on New Pension System.

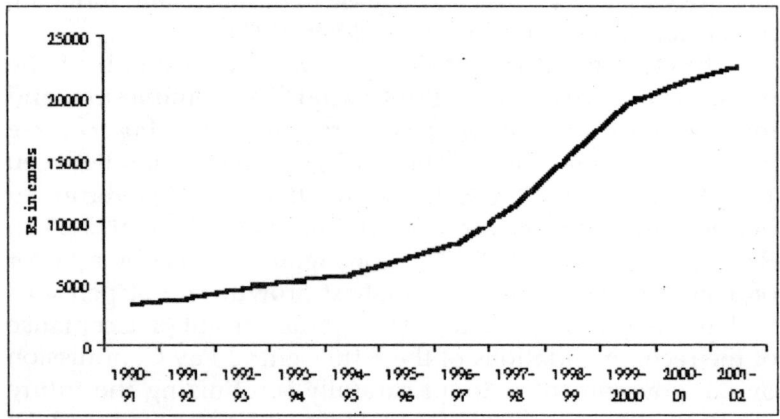

Figure 2.5: Trends in central government expenditure on pensions,
1990-91 to 2001-02

The pension liability of the Railways and Telecom is not met from the Consolidated Fund of India. Pension expenditure as a percentage of GDP grew from 0.6 in 1990–91 to 0.7 in 1997–98 and 1.0 in 1999–2000. Pension expenditure (defence and civil) as a percentage of net revenue receipts rose from 4 in 1995–96 to about 7 in 2000–01 (MOF, 2002). The Fifth Pay Commission had assumed that the financial liability on account of its recommendations would be Rs. 1170 crores per year. In actual practice, pension expenditure surged from Rs. 8253 crores in 1996–97 to Rs. 22,410 crores in 2001–02. This has happened despite some recommendations of the Pay Commission not being accepted such as, for instance, restoration of the commuted value of pension after 12 years instead of the current 15 years, and payment of an additional pension when the superannuated person has done more than the minimum of 33 years of service. Such huge expenditures became possible because the government was meeting the expenses from its revenues. There was no cap. Expenses were met depending on the requirement. Since the future beneficiaries were the current decision makers, the large increase in expenditure on pension was allowed to continue even though it meant diversion of funds that would have been available for development.

Pension liabilities of the central government would go up further. The Eleventh Finance Commission commented on a very rapid growth in government budget for payment of pensions at the Centre. Successive Pay Commissions could be expected to increase pension liability of the Central Government through more liberalized payments due to pressure from central government employees who have a decisive influence in deciding on their emoluments, when in service or after their retirement.

Absence of data on pensioners affects projections on future payment liabilities. It would be necessary to have a data series prepared on number of pensioners/family pensioners each year, longevity of pensioners by gender and category, and annual rate of attrition/addition for assessing the outcome of future policy decisions on pension payment. The expected revisions in pensions due to recommendations of new Pay Commissions which may be constituted in the future provide a big element of uncertainty. The information may also help the pensioner in deciding on commutation of pension at the time of superannuation, as instant cash, at least for some, has more value than payments over time.

Expenditure on pensions of the central and state governments as a percentage of the total tax revenue has shown a rising trend. As stated earlier, expenditure on central government pensions has increased from Rs. 3272 crores in 1990–91 to Rs. 22,410 crores in 2000–01, an increase of 575 per cent during this period. Pensions of state governments increased from Rs. 3,131 crores in 1990–91 to Rs. 25,452 crores in 2000–01, an increase of 713 per cent in a ten year period. The total tax revenue also increased during this period from Rs. 87,722 crores in 1990–91 to Rs. 319,787 crores in 2000–01, an increase of 333 per cent, indicating that it has been outpaced by the rise of pension expenditure. The percentage of total pension expenditure of central and state governments increased from 7.30 per cent in 1990–91 to 14.56 per cent in 2000–01 (Anand and Ahuja, 2004). Estimates have also been made of the extent of pension liability of the government in the coming decades. These vary widely, depending on the assumptions, handicapped as these were because of paucity of data. The future liability on account of pension payment as per the current method of financing it was considered as unsustainable.

Most state governments have adopted the pattern of the central government for grant of pensionary benefits. Changes in pension rules of the central government were also usually adopted by the state governments. Some adjustments have also been made. Punjab grants a special allowance equal to 5 per cent of its basic pension on attaining the age of 65 years and 10 per cent on attaining the age of 75 years, on account of the higher costs involved in maintaining life in old age. No dearness relief is, however, paid on the special allowance. Some state governments allow restoration of the commuted value of pensions after 12 years, some on completion of 14 years or on the pensioner attaining the age of 70 years, whichever is later. Punjab gives its pensioners, once in every block of two years, a month's basic pension as a grant to meet expenditure on travel in lieu of the Leave Travel Concession admissible to serving employees.

Pension payments in the states have recorded a fast increase. Pension expenditure of state governments in 1990–91 was Rs. 3131 crores. In 1995–96, it rose to Rs. 7813 crores, and in 2000–01 it rose to Rs. 25,452 crores. Thus in a ten years period, pension expenditure increased to about 8 times the figure in 1990-91 (Anand and Ahuja, 2004,). The Eleventh Finance Commission (for 2000–05) reported that during the period 1991–95, pensions in the states, on the average, rose by 19.59 per cent (Table 2.18). During the period 1995–99, expenditure on pension grew by 26.64 per cent. For some states, the average annual increase in pensions was below 18 per cent (Andhra Pradesh 16.54 per cent, Assam 17.13 per cent, to name

Table 2.18: Annual growth rate of pensions of states

States	Average 1991–95	Average 1995–99	1998–99
Andhra Pradesh	23.43	16.54	20.58
Assam	35.74	17.13	22.38
Bihar	24.58	21.94	31.88
Gujarat	15.92	35.15	62.29
Haryana	18.47	44.72	106.06
Himachal Pradesh	17.10	27.94	34.36
Jammu & Kashmir	30.25	42.87	90.05
Karnataka	15.95	20.01	20.10
Kerala	18.00	19.87	26.43
Madhya Pradesh	23.10	32.10	51.87
Maharashtra	14.74	18.60	3.68
Orissa	22.32	30.86	50.02
Punjab	14.73	35.73	65.63
Rajasthan	17.68	31.23	47.63
Tamil Nadu	18.60	27.86	31.45
Uttar Pradesh	23.84	38.84	68.58
West Bengal	21.64	26.18	27.86
All States	19.59	26.64	38.71

Note: Figures for the bigger states are given here.
Source: Report of the Eleventh Finance Commission.

some) while in other states it was more than 35 per cent (Haryana 45 per cent and Uttar Pradesh 39 per cent, to name some). Thus states, despite a wide variation in their fiscal health, have sanctioned an increase in the quantum of pensions of its superannuated employees, following the example of the central government. The Eleventh Finance Commission also commented that in the states, pension payments have been the fastest growing item of expenditure. Annual growth rates in future will depend, to a large extent, on the increase in superannuated employees due to rise in employment in the 1970s and 1980s, increase in rates of pension payments and the longer life expectancy.

Rising pension payments are causing serious concern to the government as it results in a reduction in the resources available for growth and development.

The Eleventh Finance Commission (for 2000–2005) reported:

"The immediate impact of the pay and pension revision of employees of central government ministries and departments including defence services (excluding Telecom, Post and Railways) was a rise in their salary bill by 33.6 per cent and pension bill by 35 per cent in 1997–98. Salaries and pensions as a percentage of the revenue receipts of the Centre in 1998–99 worked out to 20.8 as against 17.4 per cent prior to the revisions. In the case of the States, the impact has been even more severe, as the revisions were extended not only to employees of the government administration but also to those of aided institutions and local bodies. This has been further aggravated, as in some States, pay-scales are higher than the pay-scales of the Central government employees of certain categories. While reliable and comprehensive figures of payments under the head salaries and pensions for the States are not available, in several States, salary related expenditure absorb over two-thirds and in some (e.g., Maharashtra), nearly three-fourths, of their revenue receipts. Apart from aggravating the budget imbalances, the sharp rise in salaries has resulted in inadequate provision for spending on materials essential for running public services efficiently and maintaining assets in workable conditions. Salary intensity in social services went up in all States leaving too little for efficient delivery of services in vital areas like healthcare and education.

The impact of pay and pension revision on the budget was compounded by the slowdown in the growth of revenue receipts. In 1997–98, the net revenue receipts of the Centre increased by a mere 6 per cent while revenue expenditure grew by 13.5 per cent. In 1998–99, the respective growth rates were 11.7 per cent and 20.6 per cent. Revenue receipts of the states also registered a growth of only 2.8 per cent in 1998–99 while their revenue expenditure increased by 17 per cent".

The Reserve Bank of India, in its report on state finances 2002–03, has also drawn attention to the sharp rise in pension payments, particularly during the second half of 1990s. It observed:

"During the period 1995–96 to 2000–01, the annual average increase in pension expenditure was as high as 27.1. In 2000–01, pension payments pre-empted more than 10 per cent of the revenue receipts. With the increase in the number of retirees, the pension liabilities are expected to increase and could, therefore, emerge as an important expenditure item for the states. Some of the states have proposed to introduce a new contributory pension scheme for the newly recruited employees" (RBI, 2003).

Some public sector undertakings, banks and the insurance sector had introduced pension schemes in lieu of contributory provident fund. They, too, will have to take a view on how best to resolve the increasing load of pension payments.

Concerned about the rapid rate of increase of pension expenditure, the Government of India appointed working groups to find a solution to the problem. The Working Group on assessment of pension liability of the central government submitted its report in 2001. Subsequently, a high level expert group on new pension system (chaired by B.K. Bhattacharya) submitted its report in 2002 "to provide a roadmap for introducing a new system" for fresh employees. It projected the extent of pension liability if no reform was carried out for a time span of 80 years based on an exercise done by the National Institute of Public Finance and Policy. The projected expenditure if no reform was carried out, was estimated at Rs. 33,932 crores in 2110–11, Rs. 51,214 crores in 2020–21, Rs. 66,903 crores in 2030–31, and Rs. 52,203 crores in 2040–41. The Report was discussed in detail and a somewhat modified system was adopted by the central government.

A new system of payment of pension was approved by the central government on 23 August 2003, and notified on 22 December 2003. It introduced a radical reform in payment of pension for fresh entrants in central government service on or after 1 January 2004, excluding defence personnel.

The pension scheme was expected to have two tiers. Tier I was mandatory for all new central government employees who thus become its captive members. It provides for a defined contribution shared equally by the employee and the government, the former making a monthly contribution of 10 per cent of salary plus dearness allowance, which will be matched by the central government as its employer. Contribution made by the employees and the government, and the returns from investments in Tier I would be deposited in a non-withdrawable Tier I Account. The employee will be given an Individual Retirement Account (IRA) to which all contributions will be made. The account will be transferable even when the employee takes up a new job. Labour mobility will, therefore, not be a problem in retaining the IRA and making contribution to it. Employees can exit the system on the date of retirement. At the time of exit, it is mandatory for the employee to invest 40 per cent of pension wealth to purchase an annuity to provide pension throughout his life, and to his dependent parents/spouse. The remaining 60 per cent of pension wealth will be paid in a lump sum at the time of exit. The system will have several Fund Managers which will offer three options. Under Option A, investment will be made predominantly in fixed income instruments; there will also be some investments in equity. Under Option B, there will

be greater investment in equity. Under Option C, balanced investment in fixed income and equity is visualized (MOF, 2004).

Tier II was proposed as voluntary in character. Central government employees in Tier I could, in addition, also join Tier II in which the employee can open and deposit any amount, and withdraw in part or in full from this Account. Deposits in Tier II will not have any special tax treatment as the contribution is not treated as pension investment. The government makes no contribution to a Tier II Account. It is thus an account which provides additional investment options to the employee. Apart from central government employees, workers in the private sector, self-employed professionals and others will have the option to join Tier II on a voluntary basis. Attractiveness of Tier II will not depend just on tax rebates that may be allowed for such schemes by the government, but also on the returns that the Funds are expected to yield. It is also anticipated that account holders of Tier II will opt for a certain percentage of funds to buy an annuity when they retire.

The scheme promises to bring big savings in government expenditure which will accrue after about three decades when the fresh crop of employees reach the age of superannuation. It is also expected to expand and deepen the operation of capital markets by making available huge funds that can be invested. Labour mobility will also be facilitated. It will provide an option to private sector employees and the self-employed to access a pension system

A Pension Fund Regulatory and Development Authority (PFRDA) was set up by an Ordinance in December 2004 to promote, regulate and develop the pension market and set up norms/guidelines and disclosure norms for investment of funds by Fund Managers, and protect the interests of subscribers. Details will be known on the objectives, scope, functions and regulatory mechanisms once the law has been passed. A Central Record Keeping Agency will maintain the Account and give an individual retirement account number in which all contributions will flow. The Pension Fund Manager will provide updates to the account holder on how the accumulations are growing.

The new system proposed differs from the current

pension scheme which the government has decided to phase out. While the existing pension scheme for current employees is a defined pension scheme, the reformed pension scheme for fresh employees has transformed itself into a defined contribution scheme. It will no longer be non-contributory. Nor will it be entirely financed by taxes paid by the public. It will also not have the benefit of a defined payment of pension, indexed to inflation, and subject to revision depending on the revisions in salary structure of current employees. It is not known whether there will be a facility of commutation of pension and its restoration after 15 years, as per the current practice. The deposits in Tier I cannot be withdrawn (even one's own contribution) till the date of superannuation when 60 per cent can be withdrawn, and the remaining 40 per cent will be compulsorily used to buy an annuity. Before accumulating a sufficient amount in Tier I, if a member dies young, his family will face problems of income insecurity as there will be no fixed system of payment of pension. Such uncertainties could perhaps be rectified by some sort of group insurance which can pool the risks.

Contributions made to the pension fund are viewed to provide higher returns due to the appointment of highly rated professional fund managers who hopefully will steer through the market risks and the volatile nature of stock prices. The account holder will, however, be unsure about the real gains in returns after retirement, taking into account the annual rates of inflation. It will be desirable for the government to bear the contingent liability if the investments suffer a decline due to wrong investments or stock market scams. The PFRDA will have to set norms to protect the interests of the account holder in the long run. This will include ceilings on costs of administering the fund so that maximum benefit can accrue to the investor. The performance of Fund managers and of the regulator are expected to help in the development of the financial market, and generate awareness to save early enough in the working life of a person and not defer it.

The PFRDA ordinance lapsed. The Pension Fund Regulatory and Development Bill was not introduced in Parliament. It was referred to the Parliamentary Standing Committee which approved it in principle but suggested a large number of changes in its basic structure. There is strong opposition, particularly from the left parties. They are apprehensive of the ability of Pension Fund Managers to get expected returns from the stock market which is highly speculative and volatile. If the investments are made in wrong stocks, the subscribers will tend to loose. Several parties wanted some kind of guarantee from the government that the investments will be in safe hands. There is also opposition to participation by foreign institutional investor. The Government is considering the Report of the Parliamentary Standing Committee. The revised structure will be discussed with different political parties. After the Bill has been passed by Parliament and enacted into a law, its features and the role of PFRDA will be known (TOI, 2005).

Pensions from Insurance Companies and Mutual Funds

Persons of medium and higher income groups, who do not have an employer related pension scheme or who are self-employed, often look to a long-term saving instrument which will give them an annual payment when the person may no longer be earning, as the savings they have may not be enough to last the post-retirement phase which could be about 15 to 20 years or more. Annuity plans offered by insurance companies and mutual funds provide the option. They are entirely paid for by the policy holder. Even for persons whose employment provides a pension after retirement, schemes offered by insurance companies provide coverage of risk, long-term savings and tax incentives, and can be an added option for security in old age.

Pension plans by insurance companies offer 'money back' policies which, on maturity, gives the sum assured plus bonuses declared annually. Risks of life to the person insured, and disability, are usually covered. Premiums paid (annually, quarterly, monthly) depend on the sum assured, the age at which insurance is taken, mortality rates as per actuarial figures, and tenure of the policy. Some offer a single premium policy, mainly for those who have got a lump sum from bonus, sale of property, or other means, and do not wish to invest every year. Some schemes offer variable payment schedules to enable the policy holder to meet expenses at different stages of the life cycle. Some companies have policies to guarantee a minimum rate of return for the premiums paid after the policy has matured, plus additional amounts depending on the returns. Others provide a variable return depending on accruals from the investments made out of the pension fund. In some policies, there is provision for choice of investments by the insured person for a part of the premiums paid. Several investment packages are offered by the company in the pension scheme so as to make the investments partly participatory. Some policies provide that at the end of the tenure, the policy holder may also like to take a part of the amount as a lump sum, and for the remaining amount he can get an annuity for as many years as he chooses. He could also opt for getting the entire sum as pension payment throughout his life. The risk of a lump sum on maturity is that it can be subject to wrong investments which may denude its value. An annuity, on the other hand, will give him a guaranteed income. Some policies (such as LIC's Future Plus) offer a second income (pension) from a particular age, and provide options of life cover, accident and critical illness.

Tax incentives are given for pension schemes. Contributions made (premium) are eligible for rebate from gross income. However, when the assessee or his nominee surrenders the annuity before the maturity date of such an annuity, the surrender value is taxable in the hands of the assessee or his nominee, as the case may be.

Insurance companies are increasingly not providing guaranteed returns to the premiums paid. Additions (or subtractions) to the premium paid by the policy holder will now be dependent on accruals from investments made by the insurance company.

Pension schemes are now being offered not only by the public sector Life Insurance Corporation of India, but also by private insurance companies licensed to do so by the Insurance Regulatory and Development Authority. This has opened up a wide variety of options for the public to choose from. Since the premium rates vary between public and private insurance companies, it would be necessary to assess their relative merits in accordance with the pension needs. The private sector is more market savvy, using professional marketing personnel and fine tuned advertisement campaigns to woo customers. The insurance sector has expanded considerably with the entry of private players, and is expected to go up further due to competition and aggressive selling. Since most schemes offered are becoming open-ended in terms of returns, accrual to the policy holder on maturity will depend on the returns from investments made by the relevant insurance fund.

Mutual funds, too, have begun to offer retirement benefit plans. Tax concessions given vary with the prevailing tax laws. Investments in mutual funds are, however, subject to market risk and the net asset value (NAV) would depend on returns by the fund in the securities market.

Some insurance companies offer group superannuation schemes. Contributions made to it are deductible from gross income for calculation of tax liability of the policy holder. A few schemes also allow the scheme to be linked to life insurance. On superannuation, a choice of pension payments can be made either to take the entire sum , an annuity, or a combination of both.

Pension payments (annuities) by insurance companies are taxable in the hands of the policy holder, same as for pension schemes by central/state government/quasi-government bodies. However, they are not entitled to a standard deduction under section 16(1) of the Income Tax Act as would be the case when a person receives pension after superannuation from his employer. This is so because there exists no relationship of employer and employee. Pension from insurance companies/ mutual funds are treated as 'income from other sources' and are liable to income tax for the entire amount. The pension paid to policy holders is also not entitled to dearness relief and would be subject to inflationary pressures which could deflate the real value of the money.

Insurance schemes are basically an urban phenomenon, and are primarily taken by the educated policy holder to cover risk of life/disability, and provide some savings for old age. It would be necessary to promote them among workers in the active working years in towns, semi-urban and rural areas by having special schemes which could be better tuned to the pattern of their earnings. Trained manpower will be necessary to aggressively market the scheme. Post offices can be roped in through special arrangements to accept premium. There should be some scope for flexibility of payment so that the policy does not lapse if for a year or so a payment has not been made. This could provide an attraction to non-salaried persons.

Saving Schemes for Older Persons

Persons in old age, specially when they are not working, and who have more or less fulfilled their family responsibilities of marriage of children and of educating them, look for opportunities to invest their money received on retirement or from sale of asset, in instruments which are secure, have liquidity and give reasonable returns on a regular basis to meet their monthly expenses. They also consider the savings on tax if the accruals from the amount invested is large enough to attract income tax. Saving schemes in post office, RBI Relief Bonds, Infrastructure Saving Bonds and Banks have been popular among all classes, particularly the old. In the 1990s, these saving instruments gave high returns, usually over 10 per cent, apart from tax reliefs. RBI Relief Bonds, for instance, was a very popular saving instrument, as the interest was totally free of income tax. In the mid–1990s, it used to fetch a tax free interest of 10 per cent. The interest could be taken half yearly or it could be compounded so that the principal and full interest could be received on maturity. The duration of the bond was five years, which was considered a margin safe enough for foreseeing one's pattern of expenses. With the government's decision to soften interest rates on saving instruments and to reduce its own liabilities on borrowings, the rate of interest on Relief Bonds was progressively reduced and in 2003, it fetched an interest of only 6.5 per cent. The new central government voted to power in 2004 has discontinued it.

The softening of interest rates in medium term saving schemes as a measure of economic reforms introduced by the central government have eroded the earnings of senior citizens, specially persons who are not entitled to pension, but have to depend on interest from their savings. The Finance Minister, in his 2003 budget speech, announced the decision to set up a Varistha Pension Bima Yojana Scheme (VPBYS) to be operated by the Life Insurance Corporation of India (LIC). The scheme guaranteed a return of 9 per cent per annum. The central government will pay to the LIC the difference between the guaranteed return and the return which actually accrued to the LIC. Persons who crossed the age of 55 years were eligible to apply. When the scheme was first mooted, the upper age limit was fixed at 79 years. This was later changed on demand by a large number of senior citizens who were aged 80 years or over, and wanted a steady return. The scheme had a lock in period of 15 years, and thus provided protection against any future fall in interest rates. It also meant that the option to exit from the scheme was available at the end of 15 years. On the death of the policy holder, the nominee gets the amount that was initially deposited. Persons applying for the scheme had to deposit the entire sum as a single premium. The minimum amount of deposit was Rs.33,338, and the maximum Rs.288,885. Depending on the deposit, the minimum amount of monthly pension payable is Rs. 250 and the maximum Rs. 2000. The pension payment could be taken on a monthly, quarterly, or half yearly basis. While the monthly payment fetches a return of 9 per cent, the yield goes up to 9.38 per cent if the payment is taken annually, as the interest is compounded on a monthly basis. Loan can be taken at the end of three years at an interest of 10.5 per cent. The maximum ceiling for the loan was 75 per cent of the purchase price. The pension paid to the holder is taxable. The net return to the person from the amount invested will depend on the total amount of interest received from different schemes which qualify for deductions and the total taxable income of the assessee after deducting the rebates permissible for senior citizens.

After the new government was installed at the Centre in 2004, VPBYS was discontinued in the sense that no fresh applications could be made. The Government of India launched a new scheme in August 2004 for persons over 60 years of age (55 years and above in case of voluntary retirees) operated by post offices under the title Senior Citizens Savings Scheme,

2004. The maximum amount of deposit in the name of a single person is Rs. 15 lakhs. The tenure of investment is five years, extendable to three more years. The minimum lock in period is one year. It can be encashed thereafter after some deductions. Joint accounts are permitted with only spouse. The annual rate of interest is 9 per cent payable quarterly on a non-cumulative basis. The current scheme fetches the same rate of interest as the discontinued Varishtha Pension Bima Yojana Scheme. The amount that can be invested in the current scheme is also higher. One can also open a separate account for each deposit depending on the funds that become available, subject to the ceiling of Rs. 15 lakhs. It does not, however, permit loans to be taken. The interest is non-cumulative, whether it is taken on a quarterly, half-yearly or annual basis. The duration of the scheme which has a maturity period of five years (extendable by three years) indicates that the government is unwilling to commit itself to a 9 per cent interest beyond this period. It is operating the scheme under postal savings unlike the earlier scheme which was entrusted to LIC, with the government guaranteeing the deficit if the returns to LIC were below 9 per cent.

Post office has always offered a unique opportunity of saving by all categories of persons, including those from the lower and middle income groups. In 2004–05, there were 155,669 post offices of which 89 per cent were in rural areas. On an average, a post office serves an area of 21 sq km and a population of about 6600 persons. Savings bank facilities are provided by about 154,000 post offices. Such facilities are in a sense, the oldest and largest surviving banking institution in the country. It started a life insurance scheme in 1884, initially for postal employees, which was later extend to employees of Central and State governments, military personnel, local bodies, government aided institutions and public sector undertakings. The Postal Department introduced in 1995 postal life insurance for the rural population (Department of Posts, 2005). The post office has for several decades delivered a friendly, trustworthy and reliable network of savings schemes even in the remote and backward areas of the country to the self-employed, farmers and wage earners. Illiterate persons for the first time got access to a pass book which could give them the current balance. Easy access to post offices has been a major attraction. Many women in rural areas were able to save through the post office. Urban women, too, have found the post office as a useful savings institution.

A number of medium term saving schemes have been popular among older persons. Among these are national savings certificates, Kisan Vikas Patras, recurring deposit scheme, monthly income scheme and the normal saving bank account (which fetches a slightly higher rate of interest than nationalized banks). Interest accruing from these schemes was earlier free of income tax up to a certain limit, inclusive of interest from other schemes where, too, tax deduction was permitted. Retired persons who want a monthly income to defray their household expenses find the postal monthly income scheme particularly attractive. It currently offers an annual interest of 8 per cent. In the past, it fetched a higher rate of interest of 9 per cent. The interest is not compoundable. The tenure of the account is six years. On maturity, it fetches a bonus of 10 per cent on the principal, thus giving it a higher effective yield. The maximum amount that can be invested by a person is Rs. 3 lakhs on a single account and Rs. 6 lakhs in a joint account. Accounts can be opened subject to the ceiling as and when funds become available. The account has a lock in period of one year. It permits liquidity in the sense that it can be encashed after one year. If the account is encashed between one and three years, a penalty is charged on the principal. After three years it can be encashed without any loss, but no bonus is given.

The Finance Minister, in his budged speech on 28 Februrary 2005, has announced some reforms in investment options and tax deductions. Deduction under Section 80L will not now be available. Instead, a new section has been inserted under which investments in savings schemes up to Rs. one lakh is allowed a deduction from gross total income. In the case of senior citizens, Rs. 1,85,000 of net income has been exempted from tax.

Mutual Funds and Equity Investments

Mutual funds as a source of investment became popular with the setting up of the Unit Trust of India. Soon banks, insurance companies and finance companies began to offer such funds, promising higher returns. The Post Office, too, retails some mutual funds and bonds. Mutual funds publicize that with professional financial experts they are in a far better position than individual investors who have neither the time nor the financial expertise to deal with the volatile equity market, monitoring the up and down movements of shares, and deciding on investment options. The clientele are mainly educated classes in urban areas looking for relatively safe investments which can give them a higher return by pooling the investments on a variety of stocks. Initially, mutual funds offered pre-determined dividends which were higher than returns from banks or postal savings. Some mutual fund schemes had no fixed tenure. Due to the fluctuating nature of the stock market, mutual funds realized that they were paying out more to the unit holders than the returns from investments they were making from the fund. Pre-determined returns from funds were eased out. In the new mutual funds floated, a floating rate is offered. They promise, however, better returns than savings banks and post-offices, through market savvy advertisements and attractive fund titles. For the investor in mutual funds the risk of lower returns is there because of the market risks involved. Some investors in mutual funds have, in fact, lost heavily due to the lowering of the net asset value compared to the purchase price. They got back less than the amount they invested. Several mutual funds have not given any returns to investors for a number of years.

Mutual funds advertised through electronic, print and other media are required to inform the applicant to see the offer document and assess the market risks involved in investing in mutual funds. Guidelines have been issued which the companies offering mutual funds are required to comply with.

The government, in order to increase the size of the financial market and draw investors to mutual funds, have given some tax concessions. Newspapers, magazines and the electronic media are busy providing glamour to investments in equity and mutual funds, highlighting the stocks that are giving handsome returns but failing to mention the stocks that have sunk. Senior citizens who have never invested in stocks are ill-advised to invest on the basis of what the tax consultant/

broker recommends. Old citizens will have virtually little time or opportunity to make good their losses. A regular pre-determined interest will give them peace of mind rather than grappling with the volatility of the market, monitoring the movement of stocks, and the highs and lows that goes with market determined investments.

Summing Up

Transfer of resources from children and own assets of production, which have been the prevalent pattern, are proving inadequate for income security in old age. Informal networks are no longer sufficient to meet financial needs in the twilight years. People in their working life (duration about 40 years) have to think early enough to invest on long-term saving instruments and/or build capital assets or businesses to generate income in old age when they are no longer working. Income security in old age comes from prudent use of savings and investments in the working life of a person. Earners must plan for retirement, develop the attitude to save early enough and make accumulation from the savings (interest, dividends, insurance, contribution to pension fund, and other options) for security in old age. For workers in central and state governments, autonomous bodies funded by the government, public sector undertakings and workers in organized sector establishments, retirement benefits by the employer, including pensions, provide income security. These are handsome for workers where the government is the employer, but become inadequate for workers in industrial establishments covered by the Employees Provident Fund and Miscellaneous Provisions Act, 1952, though here, too, the government makes a modest contribution towards pension of workers.

Financial security in old age of workers in the unorganized sector (93 per cent of the workers) has remained virtually unattended. The bulk have uncertain incomes. To a large extent, problems of income security of informal sector workers in old age arise from the nature of their work. Most workers do not have regular and sufficient earnings which can help them save for old age. A major lacunae is absence of institutional structures which can enable such persons with small and irregular earnings to save through various saving instruments specially designed for them.

It is important to look at the extent, nature and pattern of employment of workers to assess their capacity to save. Work participation rate in the Indian population, particularly for males, is fairly high. However, only 14 per cent of the workers in 1999–2000 were in regular salaried employment, 53 per cent were in self employment and 33 per cent in casual employment. About one-fourth of the Indian population in 1999–2000 was below the poverty line. Only 7 per cent of employment is in the organized sector. It has remained static and is likely to be so with the current emphasis on outsourcing and on technology-oriented production methods which reduce manpower.

Right to work with adequate remuneration has to be the goal in the informal sector and holds the key to social security in old age. This will imply the formulation and implementation of employment policies which enhance the quality and quantity of employment, create job opportunities, and fetch better earnings. The manpower asset base of the poor needs considerable strengthening.

OASIS has proposed a pension scheme to be financed through thrift and self help by accumulating savings in the working life of the person through a modest contribution. The scheme also speaks of integrating a micro-credit facility into the pension system whereby individuals can have access to loans against their personal savings for short-term needs.

For workers in the organized sector, benefits of provident fund have been made available since 1952 through the Employees' Provident Fund and Miscellaneous Provisions Act, 1952. It provides a lump sum on superannuation. The scheme currently covers workers drawing wages up to Rs. 6500 per month. On 31 March 2004, the number of establishments covered was 370,386 and the number of members 401 lakhs. In 2003–04, provident fund contribution rose to Rs. 12,356 crores. Partial withdrawals by workers from provident fund accounts is a major problem due to which a worker gets a lower sum at the time of superannuation/resignation. Even though EPFO allows transfer of accounts when a person takes up another job, members prefer to withdraw the amount instead of its transfer. Suggestions have been made to make rules to reduce the incidence of partial withdrawal, and also to get better returns from EPF investments as that will act as an incentive. The provisions of EPF should be extended to self-employed workers.

The EPF Act also provides a pension scheme for workers. Entitlement to pension accrues from a minimum of 10 years of contributory service, and is payable on attaining the age of 58. years. In 2003–04, the number of members in the Employees' Pension Fund was 281 lakhs, and the number of pensioners 17,58,841. The state should contribute a much larger sum for the employees' pension scheme as the current rate is too low.

In view of the much longer life expectancy, and the falling interest rates, government pensions provide good income security in old age. They cannot be nibbled at except at the time of superannuation when a decision has to be made to commute a portion of the pension. The Fourth and Fifth Central Pay Commissions have enhanced pension benefits for government employees. Due to an increase in the number of pensioners, the expenditure on pensions has shown a rapid rise, and has become unsustainable. It increased from Rs. 3272 crores in 1990–91 to Rs. 22,410 crores in 2001–02. The Eleventh Finance Commission commented that in the states, pension payments have been the fastest growing item. The Reserve Bank of India, in its report on state finances 2002–03, has drawn attention to the sharp rise in pension payments. The Ministry of Finance has launched a new pension scheme for fresh entrants to central government from 1 January 2004, based on contributions by the employee and the government (employer). Statutory Pension Funds will operate the scheme. The law is yet to be enacted.

For the general population, a Public Provident Fund was started in 1968–69 as a long-term saving instrument, and was meant to attract self-employed persons in business, professions, consultancy and other services with incomes at middle and higher levels to meet financial needs in old age. Deposits in PPF can vary between Rs. 100 and Rs. 70,000, and has to be paid from taxable income. The minimum tenure of the account is 15 years. PPF provides a tax incentive to the investor. It gives a predetermined, administered assured rate of interest which is tax free. PPF has not been publicized well enough as an incentive for old age security, and has been used primarily for tax saving. Some disincentives for premature withdrawal may be introduced. A bonus may be provided for persons who do not make any withdrawal for at least 15 years. PPF should be promoted throughout the country in rural, semi-urban and urban areas. The accounting system should be so designed as to facilitate deposits in any selected post office or branch of the State Bank of India, and to get the pass book filled up for an up to date account of transactions.

Insurance companies, too, offer long-term saving schemes which not only cover risk of life and disability, but also provide a lump sum amount at the end of the tenure; some also have a provision for partial encashment at the middle of the tenure to incur expenses for marriage, education and other needs. Insurance schemes are particularly useful for those who do not have an employer related pension scheme. Some insurance policies provide for annuities. With the private sector entering the insurance business, a variety of options are being offered, whether in the payment of premiums, the tenure of the scheme, or pay back benefits. Tax incentives have been provided to encourage people to invest in insurance. Insurance companies generally cater to the educated middle class with fairly stable earnings. It would be necessary to promote insurance business in towns, rural and semi-urban areas as a long-term saving instrument for old age. Some flexibility is necessary, particularly in the matter of payment of premiums, in tune with the variable earning patterns, a characteristic feature of self-employment. Mutual funds, too, offer retirement benefit plans. Present policies do not generally guarantee returns. Investments in mutual funds are subject to market risks.

Transfer of resources by the state to partly meet the needs of destitute old persons provides a safety net to such persons. State governments are providing old age pensions as a public assistance measure to those who are without any means of support. From 1995, the central government is providing assistance to the states at the rate of Rs. 75 per person getting the pension. The rate of pension usually varies between Rs. 100 and Rs. 250 per month. States are known to have altered the pension rate and the number of pensions sanctioned, at times on financial grounds, but also on grounds such as electoral compulsions. Some states have started, in addition, pension schemes for specific categories of informal sector workers. Individual and family income below which a person will be entitled, have been prescribed. Domicile requirements need to be fulfilled to entitle a person for pension. Central and state governments also provide pensions for freedom fighters. Under the Annapurna scheme, started by the central government in 2000, 10 kg of foodgrains are provided free of cost through the public distribution system to destitute persons not receiving old age pensions. A complementary scheme (*Antodaya Anna Yojana*) provides subsidized foodgrains every month to persons below the poverty line. Programmes implemented by the public distribution system often suffer from poor implementation, particularly where matters of relief are concerned. Even the old age pension schemes, which are operating for nearly four decades, continue to face implementation problems arising from wrong selection of beneficiaries, fake sanctions and irregular payments.

Resources from extra-familial organizations like old age homes, supported by state government organizations and non-governmental organizations, provide a succour to persons who have no family to support them. The number of such homes have shown a big increase.

The capacity to plan for old age and to save, accumulate and make investments which will be useful in old age cannot be left solely to the initiative of individual earners. The state must also step in a big way to provide income security to different income categories, particularly persons in the lower income groups. It has to formulate policies for stepping up economic development and provide enough income on a sustained basis for all categories of workers. It must also generate revenues to formulate social security measures. The state will also need to create a climate in which both the state and the market can play a complementary role for catering to the needs of older persons. Incentives have to be provided to families, particularly from low and middle income groups, to invest in saving schemes. Regulatory mechanisms have to be set up for a safe and secure investment of earners, specially if these are for a longer period.

3

Health Security

Healthy ageing is a major concern in old age for all classes of people, particularly the poor who need a good physical and mental status to be able to continue to earn, and also to keep down the costs of medical treatment. Without good health, the surviving years in the last stage of the life cycle could end up as a burden to the person himself, his family and society instead of being a productive resource which can play varied social and economic roles. It is true that with age there is a likelihood of general impairment of abilities, mainly through degenerative non-communicable diseases. The prevalence rate of morbidity is also higher among the older population. Healthy ageing has become an important goal of social policy, and has been stated as such particularly in the developed countries which are experiencing growing numbers of old persons. Developed countries spend a significant amount on healthcare of the old, because of the multiple nature of morbidity, extended periods of treatment, longer periods of hospital care, more expensive diagnostic investigation, treatment and rehabilitative procedures, and medicines.

Life Expectancy

Life expectancy is a good summative indicator of the state of health of older persons. It is independent of the age structure of the population which makes it particularly useful for time series data. People are living longer despite the poor state of public health services in the country. At the start of the twentieth century (1901–10), the expectation of life at birth was only about 23 years. In 1941–50, it was still quite low, only about 32 years. In 1995–99, it rose to 61.7 years and is likely to rise further in the coming years. Even persons at age 60 have a longer life expectancy. Significant gains in life expectancy have been made due to advances in medical science resulting in better diagnostic facilities, treatment procedures and drugs, better availability of doctors and paramedical manpower through expansion of medical education and training facilities, increased accessibility and use of healthcare facilities, both public and private, for routine as well as specialist treatment, spread of education and health consciousness, and improvements in standard of living.

Life expectancy has gone up in India even in the older age groups. Table 3.1, which gives the data from 1901–10 to 1995–99 by sex, shows that females have a higher life expectancy at age 60 years and at age 70 years. The gap in life

Table 3.1: Expectation of life at age 60 years and age 70 years by sex, India, 1901–11 to 1995–99

Period	Age 60 years				Age 70 years			
	Male	Female	Person	F-M	Male	Female	Person	F-M
1901–11	10.0	10.1	N.A.*	0.1	5.8	6.0	N.A.	0.2
1911–21	10.7	11.7	N.A.	1.0	5.8	6.2	N.A.	0.4
1921–31	10.2	10.8	N.A.	0.6	6.0	6.4	N.A.	0.4
1931–41	12.6	13.7	N.A.	1.1	6.3	6.8	N.A.	0.5
1941–51	10.1	11.3	N.A.	1.2	6.8	7.3	N.A.	0.5
1951–61	11.8	13.0	N.A.	1.2	7.6	8.0	N.A.	0.4
1961–71	13.6	13.8	N.A.	0.2	8.6	8.9	N.A.	0.3
1970–75	13.4	14.3	13.8	0.9	8.6	9.2	8.9	0.6
1976–80	14.1	15.9	15.0	1.8	9.6	10.9	10.2	1.3
1981–85	14.6	16.4	15.4	1.8	9.7	11.0	10.2	1.3
1986–90	14.7	16.1	15.4	1.4	9.4	10.1	9.9	0.7
1991–95	15.3	17.1	16.2	1.8	10.0	11.0	10.6	1.0
1995–99	15.7	17.7	16.7	2.0	10.3	11.6	11.0	1.3

*N.A.= Not available.
Source: Registrar General, India.

expectancy between males and females has increased. In 1995–99, the gender gap at age 60 was 2.0 years; at age 70, it was 1.3 years. Males at age 60 years are expected to live 15.7 years, and females 17.7 years. At age 70, the expectation of life is 10.3 years for males and 11.6 years for females. Figure 3.1 gives the trend. Between 1970–75 and 1995–99, the average increase in expectation of life at age 60 per annum has been 0.09 years for

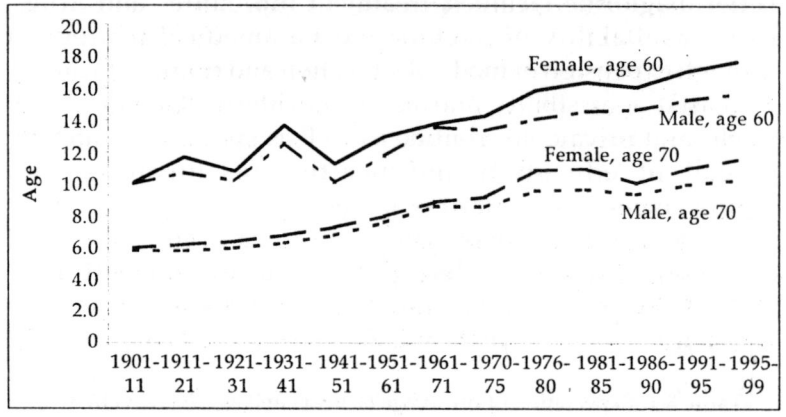

Figure 3.1: Expectation of life at age 60 years and age 70 years by sex, India, 1901–10 to 1995–99

males and 0.14 for females. Life expectancy is expected to rise further. The challenge, therefore, before older persons is to live this life free of morbidity and disability, or to reduce it to as compressed a period as possible as the goal is not only to add years to life, but add life to years. In developed countries, where the ageing are a large segment of the population individual, market, and state responses help keep the preventive, curative, and rehabilitative health needs of older persons as a major public issue. Political parties make health services of older persons a major election issue. In India, the matter is still to get a priority in the political agenda.

There are inequities in availability and use of healthcare in rural and urban areas, which affect the life span of people at all age segments, including older persons. The rural areas are disadvantaged. Table 3.2 which gives the data on expectation of life at age 60 years and at age 70 years in rural and urban areas from 1970–75 to 1995–99, shows that there continues to be a gap in life expectancy between rural and urban areas. In

1995–99, it was 2.2 years at age 60 years, and 1.9 years at age 70 years. Between 1970–75 and 1995–99, the percentage gain at age 60 was 20.7 in rural areas, and 17.8 in urban areas. At age 70 years, the gain in life expectancy was 25.6 per cent in rural areas and 17.6 per cent in urban areas.

Table 3.2: Expectation of life at age 60 years and age 70 years in rural and urban areas, India, 1970–75 to 1995–99

Period	Age 60 years			Age 70 years		
	Rural	Urban	U-R	Rural	Urban	U-R
1970–75	13.5	15.7	2.2	8.6	10.8	2.2
1976–80	14.7	16.2	1.5	10.1	11.0	0.9
1981–85	15.1	16.9	1.8	9.9	11.6	1.7
1986–90	15.3	16.2	0.9	9.7	10.5	0.8
1991–95	15.9	17.7	1.8	10.3	11.9	1.6
1995–99	16.3	18.5	2.2	10.8	12.7	1.9

Source: Registrar General, India.

At age 60 years, a person in rural areas in 1995–99 is expected to live more than 16 years, and in urban areas more than 18 years. At age 70 years, life expectancy is about 11 years in rural areas and about 13 years in urban areas. The average annual increase in expectation of life at age 60 years between 1970–75 and 1995–99 has been 0.11 years for both rural and urban areas. This is the added human resource that has become available in both rural and urban areas, and needs to be utilized.

There is inter-state variation in expectation of life at age 60. Table 3.3 gives the data for 1970–75 and 1995–99. In 1970–75, no state had a life expectancy at age 60 years of more than 16.3 years. In 1995–99, eight states fall in this category, with Punjab topping the list at 20.4 years, followed by Kerala and Haryana. The range in expectation of life at age 60 years for 16 states in 1995–99 is 5.6 years (lowest in Assam — 14.8 years and highest in Punjab — 20.4 years) In 1970–75, it was 4.9 years (lowest in Orissa — 11.4 years and highest in Punjab 16.3 years). Figure 3.2 gives the expectation of life at age 60 years in states in 1995–99.

Table 3.3: Expectation of life at age 60 years in 1970–75 and in
1995–99 in states

Range	1970–75	1995–99
11.0–12.9	Orissa (11.4) Assam (11.6) Andhra Pradesh (12.8) Tamil Nadu (12.8)	
13.0–14.9	Uttar Pradesh (13.6) Gujarat (13.8) INDIA (13.8) Himachal Pradesh (14.2) Maharashtra (14.3) Madhya Pradesh (14.3) Rajasthan (14.6)	Assam (14.8) Madhya Pradesh (14.8)
15.0–16.9	Bihar (15.1) West Bengal (15.1) Karnataka (15.8) Kerala (15.8) Haryana (16.0) Punjab (16.3)	Orissa (15.4) Tamil Nadu (15.8) Gujarat (15.9) Uttar Pradesh (15.9) West Bengal (16.1) Rajasthan (16.2) Bihar (16.6) Karnataka (16.6) INDIA (16.7) Andhra Pradesh (16.8)
17.0–18.9		Maharashtra (16.9) Himachal Pradesh (17.4) Haryana (18.9)
19.0 and above		Kerala (19.7) Punjab (20.4)

Note: Data for 16 bigger states given here. Figures for Bihar and West Bengal
refer to the period 1981–85 as figures for 1970–75 were not available.
In each category, states have been arranged in ascending order.
Source: Registrar General, India.

The extent of increase in life expectancy at age 60 years in
a state between 1970–75 and 1995–99 (a period of two and a
half decades) is given in Table 3.4. In two states, the gains have
been less than one year.

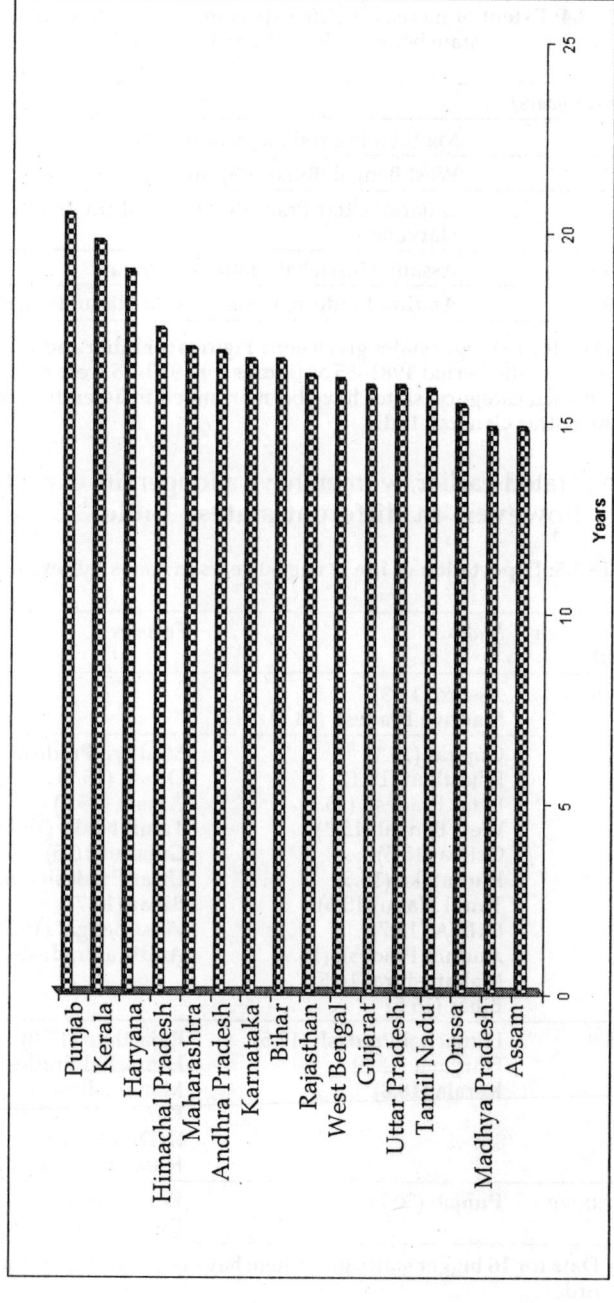

Figure 3.2: Expectation of life at age 60 years in states, 1995–99

Table 3.4: Extent of increase in life expectancy at age 60 years in each
state between 1970–75 and 1991–95

Increase (in years)	State
< 1.0	Madhya Pradesh, Karnataka
1.0 – 1.9	West Bengal, Bihar, Rajasthan
2.0 – 2.9	Gujarat, Uttar Pradesh, Maharashtra, INDIA, Haryana
3.0 – 3.9	Assam, Himachal Pradesh, Kerala
4.0 – 4.9	Andhra Pradesh, Orissa, Tamil Nadu, Punjab

Note: Data for 16 bigger states given here. Figures for Bihar and West Bengal
refer to the period 1981–85 as figures for 1970–75 were not available.
In each category, states have been arranged in ascending order.
Source: Registrar General, India.

As stated earlier, women have a longer life expectancy. It
varies, however, in different states. Table 3.5 gives the

Table 3.5: Expectation of life at age 60 years in states by sex, 1995–99

Life expectation (in years)	Males	Females
Below 15	Assam (14.3) Madhya Pradesh (14.6)	
15.0–16.9	Gujarat (15.1) Rajasthan (15.1) Uttar Pradesh (15.1) West Bengal (15.3) Orissa (15.3) . Karnataka (15.5) Tamil Nadu (15.6) INDIA (15.7) Andhra Pradesh (15.9) Maharashtra (16.5) Bihar (16.5)	Madhya Pradesh (15.1) Orissa (15.2) Assam (15.3) Tamil Nadu (16.1) Gujarat (16.5) Uttar Pradesh (16.5) Bihar (16.7) West Bengal (16.7) Andhra Pradesh (16.8)
17.0–18.9	Himachal Pradesh (17.5) Haryana (18.3) Kerala (18.8)	Rajasthan (17.0) Himachal Pradesh (17.2) Maharashtra (17.3) Karnataka (17.6) INDIA (17.7) Haryana (19.4)
19.0 & above	Punjab (20.7)	Kerala (20.6) Punjab (21.4)

Note: Data for 16 bigger states given here have been arranged in ascending
order.
Source: Registrar General, India.

expectation of life at age 60 years by sex in different states in 1995–99. In the case of both males and females, Punjab has the highest life expectancy at age 60. Inter-state difference in life expectancy at age 60 years is quite large. Assam has the lowest life expectancy for males. It is less than that of Punjab by 6.4 years. In the case of females, Madhya Pradesh has the lowest life expectancy. At age 60 years it is lower than that of Punjab by 6.3 years. In all the states, except Himachal Pradesh and Orissa, females have a higher life expectancy than males. In some states, it is more than 2 years.

Expectation of life at age 70 years by sex in the 16 bigger states is given in Table 3.6. All states have at age 70 years an

Table 3.6: Expectation of life at age 70 years in states by sex, 1995–99

Life expecta-tion (in years)	*Males*	*Females*	*Person*
Below 10.0	Gujarat (9.3) Assam (9.4) Rajasthan (9.4) Uttar Pradesh (9.4) Madhya Pradesh (9.6)	Madhya Pradesh (8.9) Orissa (9.5) Assam (9.8) Gujarat (9.8) Tamil Nadu (9.8)	Madhya Pradesh (9.2) Assam (9.6) Gujarat (9.6) Orissa (9.8)
10.0–10.9	Karnataka (10.0) Orissa (10.0) Tamil Nadu (10.2) West Bengal (10.3) INDIA (10.3)	Uttar Pradesh (10.2) Rajasthan (10.2) Himachal Pradesh (10.4) Andhra Pradesh (10.7) West Bengal (10.7) Maharashtra (10.7)	West Bengal (10.0) Rajasthan (10.0) Uttar Pradesh (10.0) Tamil Nadu (10.0) Karnataka (10.7) Maharashtra (10.9)
11.0–11.9	Maharashtra (11.0) Andhra Pradesh (11.1) Bihar (11.3) Himachal Pradesh (11.8)	Karnataka (11.1) Bihar (11.4) INDIA (11.6)	INDIA (11.0) Himachal Pradesh (11.2) Bihar (11.4) Andhra Pradesh (11.4)
12.0–12.9	Haryana (12.1)	Haryana (12.6)	Haryana (12.3)
13.0 & above	Kerala (13.4) Punjab (15.0)	Kerala (13.2) Punjab (14.7)	Kerala (13.3) Punjab (14.4)

Note: States have been arranged in ascending order.
Source: Registrar General, India.

expectation of life of 9 years or more. Punjab has the highest life expectancy at age 70 years among both males and females. Gujarat has the lowest expectation of life at age 70 years among males, and Madhya Pradesh among females. The data broadly indicates the length of geriatric care needs of persons of this age group.

Expectation of life at age 60 in different states in 1995–99 is higher in urban areas than in rural areas due to better availability and accessibility of medical facilities, higher educational levels and better health consciousness. The data given in Table 3.7 for 16 bigger states shows that in rural areas,

Table 3.7: Expectation of life at age 60 in rural and urban areas
in states, 1995–99

Range	Rural	Urban
13.0–14.9	Madhya Pradesh (14.4) Assam (14.5) Orissa (14.9)	
15.0–16.9	West Bengal (15.0) Rajasthan (15.2) Tamil Nadu (15.3) Uttar Pradesh (15.3) Gujarat(15.7) Maharashtra (16.2) Bihar (16.2) INDIA (16.3) Karnataka (16.4) Andhra Pradesh (16.8)	Andhra Pradesh (15.9) Gujarat (16.0) Himachal Pradesh (16.7)
17.0–18.9	Himachal Pradesh (17.7) Haryana (18.8)	Karnataka (17.1) Rajasthan (17.3) Madhya Pradesh (17.3) Uttar Pradesh (17.6) Tamil Nadu (17.7) INDIA (18.5) Assam (18.7)
19.0 and above	Kerala (19.5) Punjab (20.2)	West Bengal (19.0) Orissa (19.1) Bihar (19.3) Maharashtra (19.3) Kerala (20.3) Punjab (20.7) Haryana (21.0)

Note: Data for 16 bigger states given here have been arranged in ascending
            order.
Source: Registrar General, India.

the range is 5.8 years (minimum 14.4 years in Madhya Pradesh, and maximum 20.2 years in Punjab). In urban areas, the range is 5.1 years (minimum 15.9 years in Andhra Pradesh and maximum 21.0 years in Haryana). Only in Punjab life expectancy in rural areas at age 60 is over 20 years. In urban areas, three states have a life expectancy at age 60 of over 20 years. Himachal Pradesh and Andhra Pradesh have a higher life expectancy at age 60 in rural areas. In the other states, urban life expectancy is higher. In three states (Assam, Orissa and West Bengal), urban life expectancy is higher by more than 3 years.

Mortality

Distribution of deaths by age group indicates broadly the health status of the nation. There should ideally be a much higher percentage of deaths in the older age groups, particularly after 60 years, and a very small percentage in the younger age groups. Table 3.8, which gives the figures from 1991 to 2001, indicates a progressive shift in the percentage of deaths in different age cohorts. In 2001, 40.1 per cent of deaths were in the age group 60 years and above, as compared to 32.1 per cent in 1991. The percentage of deaths in age group less than 5 years is declining. As the health scene improves, the percentage of early childhood deaths will decline still further,

Table 3.8: Percentage distribution of deaths by broad age groups, India, 1991 to 2001

Year	Age group (in years)				
	0–4	5–14	15–59	60 & above	Total
1991	35.2	5.0	27.7	32.1	100.0
1993	32.7	4.6	27.3	35.5	100.0
1995	31.3	5.4	25.9	37.4	100.0
1997	29.1	4.5	28.8	37.5	100.0
1999	27.7	4.1	30.0	38.2	100.0
2001	26.5	4.1	29.3	40.1	100.0

Source: Registrar General, India.

and the percentage of deaths in older age groups will increase, indicating that people will be living a longer life span. In the age group 60 years and above, there is not only a larger incidence of deaths. There is also a shift to the older age groups. The percentage in the age group 70 years and above was 24.4 in 2001, as compared to 15.7 in the age group 60–69 years.

There is inter-state variation in the percentage of total deaths in the age group 60 years and above. Table 3.9 shows

Table 3.9: Deaths of persons aged 60 years and above as a percentage of total deaths by sex in states, 2000

Per-centage	Male	Female	Person
20–29		Assam (26.7)	
30–39	Rajasthan (33.7) Madhya Pradesh (34.6) Assam (35.1) Uttar Pradesh (36.1) Gujarat (36.8) Bihar (36.9) Haryana (38.0) Karnataka (38.0) Orissa (38.5) INDIA (39.7)	Uttar Pradesh (30.9) Madhya Pradesh (31.2) Rajasthan (31.9) Bihar (36.9) Haryana (38.5) INDIA (39.4)	Assam (31.1) Rajasthan (32.7) Madhya Pradesh (32.8) Uttar Pradesh (33.6) Bihar (37.0) Haryana (38.2) Orissa (39.5) INDIA (39.5) Gujarat (39.9)
40–49	Andhra Pradesh (40.6) West Bengal (46.2) Tamil Nadu (46.9) Punjab (48.1) Maharashtra (48.9) Himachal Pradesh (49.7)	Orissa (40.5) Gujarat (43.5) Karnataka (44.9) Andhra Pradesh (47.6) West Bengal (47.8) Tamil Nadu (48.3) Punjab (49.5)	Karnataka (40.8) Andhra Pradesh (43.7) West Bengal (46.9) Tamil Nadu (47.6) Punjab (48.9) Maharashtra (49.9)
50–59		Maharashtra (51.4) Himachal Pradesh (58.0)	Himachal Pradesh (54.3)
60 & above	Kerala (65.3)	Kerala (73.9)	Kerala (69.1)

Source: Registrar General, India.

that seven-tenths of the total deaths in Kerala in 2000 were of persons aged 60 years and above. This is in striking contrast to

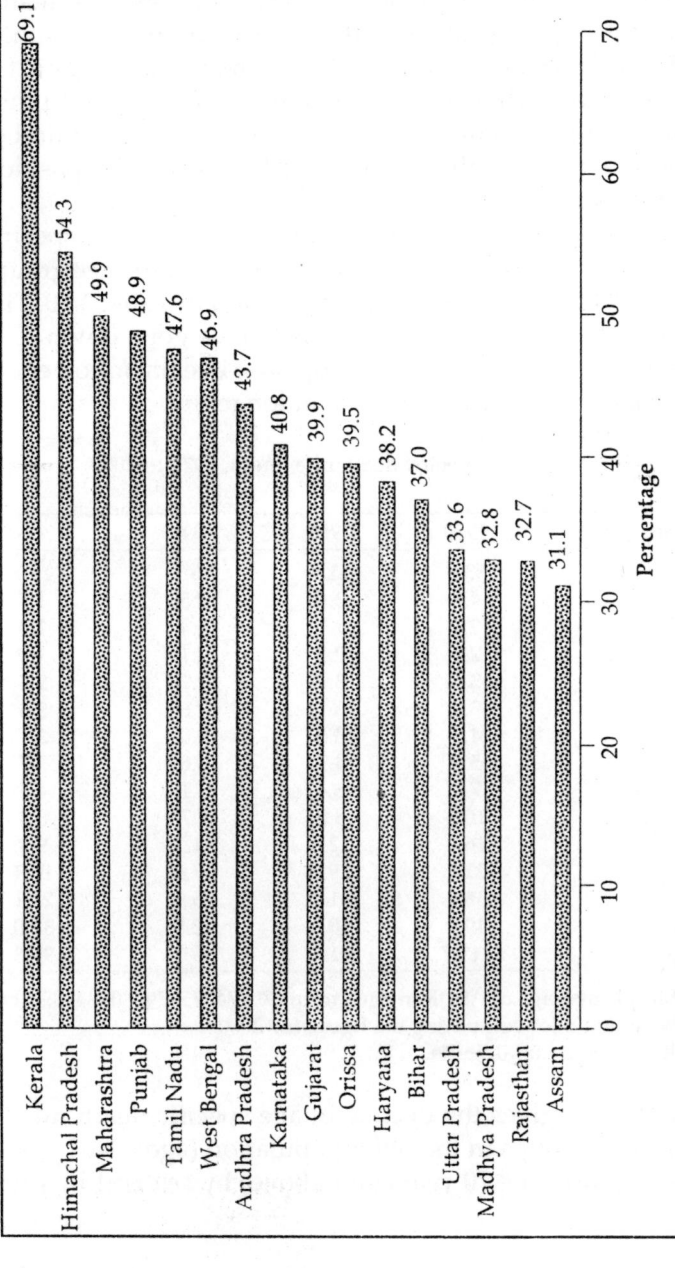

Figure 3.3: Deaths of persons aged 60 years and above as a percentage of total number of deaths in states, 2000

the situation in Assam, Madhya Pradesh, Uttar Pradesh and Rajasthan which have less than half the percentage of deaths in the age group 60 years and above, as compared to Kerala. Thus, from the point of survival for a longer life, Kerala is far better equipped than the other states. There is a higher percentage of female deaths over 60 years in a larger number of states than male deaths. Figure 3.3 gives the relative position in different states.

The age specific death rate (number of deaths in a specific age group per 1000 mid-year population in the same age group) between 1970 and 2000 in India is indicated in Table 3.10. The data show that age specific death rates have gone down. The decline is far greater in the age group 60–64 years, followed by 65–69 years indicating an increase in longevity.

Table 3.10: Age specific death rate, India, 1970 to 2000

Age (in years)	1970	1980	1990	2000
0–4	53.0	41.8	26.3	19.5
5–9	4.8	3.6	2.5	1.7
10–14	2.1	1.7	1.4	1.3
15–19	2.9	2.5	2.1	1.9
20–24	3.6	3.0	2.7	2.4
25–29	3.9	3.1	2.6	2.8
30–34	4.5	3.5	3.0	3.1
35–39	5.1	4.7	3.6	3.7
40–44	7.3	6.4	5.1	4.5
45–49	10.5	8.5	7.7	6.8
50–54	16.0	12.6	11.2	9.9
55–59	22.2	19.2	17.8	16.3
60–64	38.2	31.2	25.9	23.1
65–69	49.0	50.0	42.5	38.0
70 & above	111.7	91.6	85.1	99.8

Note: Simple average of ASDR in age groups 70–74, 75–79, 80–84, 85+ has been taken for computing the figure for 2000.
Source: Registrar General, India.

Table 3.11 gives the decline in age specific death rate in different sub-groups in the older population (age 60–64 years, age 65–69 years, age 70 years and above) by sex and by rural and urban residence. The largest decline in all the categories has been in the age group 60–64 years. Rural areas have a higher age specific death rate than urban areas in all the age groups over 60 years. Males, too, have a higher age specific death rate than females in all the age groups over 60 years.

Table 3.11: Age specific death rate of older persons by sex and
rural-urban residence, India, 1970 and 2000

Characteristic		Year	Age (in years)		
			60–64	65–69	70 & above
Residence	Rural	1970	39.3	50.9	115.8
		2000	23.7	38.8	100.8
		% decline	39.7	24.4	12.9
	Urban	1970	34.1	41.4	97.1
		2000	21.0	35.6	96.1
		% decline	38.4	16.3	1.0
Sex	Male	1970	42.7	53.6	117.1
		2000	26.6	44.2	107.5
		% decline	37.7	17.5	8.9
	Female	1970	31.4	41.5	104.0
		2000	19.7	32.3	92.8
		% decline	37.3	22.2	10.8

Note: Simple average of age groups 70–74, 75–79, 80–84, 85+ has been taken for computing the figure for 70 years and above in 2000.
Source: Registrar General, India.

Age specific death rates (ASDR) in 2000 in states of persons aged 60 years and above by sex, given in Table 3.12, shows that among the 16 bigger states, none has an ASDR below 40 for males; however, seven states have an ASDR below 40 for females. This indicates a lower age specific mortality for females in these states. In the case of males, the state with the lowest ASDR in 2000 was Punjab (44.3) while that with the highest ASDR was Assam (64.5), giving an inter-state range of 20.2. In the case of females, Himachal Pradesh had the lowest ASDR of 35.1. The highest female ASDR was in Orissa (51.1), giving an inter-state range of 16.0 — a lower range than in the case of males.

Table 3.12: Age specific death rate of persons 60 years and above
by sex in states, 2000

ASDR	Males	Females	Person
<40		Himachal Pradesh (35.1) Haryana (35.6) Karnataka (36.3) Gujarat (36.5) Rajasthan (37.1) Punjab (38.0) Kerala (39.5)	
40–44	Punjab (44.3)	Tamil Nadu (40.1) Maharashtra (40.2) INDIA (42.3) West Bengal (42.3) Andhra Pradesh (44.3) Uttar Pradesh (44.2) Madhya Pradesh (44.6)	Haryana (40.3) Gujarat (40.6) Punjab (41.2) Rajasthan (42.4) Himachal Pradesh (42.8) Karnataka (42.5) Tamil Nadu (44.6)
45–49	Haryana (45.1) Gujarat (45.4) Rajasthan (48.7) Bihar (49.4) Tamil Nadu (49.4) Karnataka (49.5)	Assam (48.7) Bihar (49.7)	Kerala (45.9) Maharashtra (47.2) INDIA (47.3) West Bengal (48.2) Andhra Pradesh (48.6) Bihar (49.5) Uttar Pradesh (49.5)
50–54	Himachal Pradesh (50.2) INDIA (52.6) Kerala (53.7) Andhra Pradesh (53.7) Uttar Pradesh (54.6) West Bengal (54.7)	Orissa (51.1)	Madhya Pradesh (50.9) Assam (57.1) Orissa (53.3)
55 & above	Maharashtra (55.1) Orissa (55.6) Madhya Pradesh (57.7) Assam (64.5)		

Note: Data for 16 bigger states given here.
Source: Registrar General, India.

The difference between male and female age specific
death rates (ASDR) in the age group 60 years and above in

2000 in each state shows that males had a higher ASDR in all states. Himachal Pradesh had the largest gender difference (15.1), followed by Maharashtra (14.9), Kerala (14.2) and Karnataka (13.2), Ten states had a difference of more than 10.

Age specific death rate of persons aged 60 years and above in 2000 by rural and urban residence, given in Table 3.13, shows that in rural areas, the lowest ASDR was in Haryana (40.3) and the highest in Assam (58.2), giving an inter-state range of 17.9. In urban areas, the lowest ASDR was in Rajasthan (39.0) and the highest in Madhya Pradesh (49.9), giving an inter-state range of 10.9. The difference between rural and urban ASDR in the age group 60 years and above in a state shows that in two states (Himachal Pradesh and Kerala) urban ASDR was higher than rural ASDR. In the other states, rural ASDR was higher. In Orissa, the difference was 13.6 points, followed by Maharashtra (11.1 points), Assam (9.7 points) and West Bengal (8.2 points).

Table 3.13: Age specific death rate of persons aged 60 years and above by residence in states, 2000

ASDR	Rural	Urban
35–39		Rajasthan (39.0)
		Maharashtra (39.7)
40–44	Haryana (40.3)	Gujarat (40.1)
	Gujarat (40.7)	Haryana (40.2)
	Punjab (41.2)	Karnataka (40.6)
	Himachal Pradesh (42.7)	Tamil Nadu (40.6)
	Rajasthan (43.1)	Punjab (40.9)
	Karnataka (43.3)	Orissa (40.9)
		West Bengal (42.5)
		INDIA (43.6)
		Himachal Pradesh (44.9)
45–49	Kerala (45.8)	Andhra Pradesh (46.3)
	Tamil Nadu (46.4)	Kerala (46.3)
	INDIA (48.3)	Bihar (47.1)
	Andhra Pradesh (49.1)	Assam (48.5)
	Uttar Pradesh (49.6)	Uttar Pradesh (48.8)
	Bihar (49.8)	Madhya Pradesh (49.9)
50 & above	West Bengal (50.7)	
	Maharashtra (50.8)	
	Madhya Pradesh (51.1)	
	Orissa (54.5)	
	Assam (58.2)	

Source: **Registrar General, India.**

Cause of Death

The annual survey on causes of death in rural areas by the Registrar General, India provides data on deaths from diseases in different age groups. Table 3.14 gives the broad distribution by major causes of death categorized by the International Classification of Diseases (Tenth Revision), in the age group 60 years and above. The data were collected from 2059 sample villages in 1997, and the same number in 1998, spread over 23 states and 3 union territories. Figures show that the largest percentage of ailments was due to diseases of the respiratory system (pneumonia, bronchitis, asthma, etc.), followed by diseases of the circulatory system (heart diseases etc.). Other major causes were cerebral apoplexy, infectious and parasitic diseases, and cancer.

The Survey further reported on specific diseases which were the leading causes of deaths of persons over 60 years. Results from the 1997 and 1998 surveys indicate the following incidence:

1. *Bronchitis and asthma:* 79.2 per cent of the total deaths in the country from this disease in 1997, and 82.6 per cent in 1998, were of persons aged 60 years and above.
2. *Ischaemic heart disease (heart attack):* 58.0 per cent of the total deaths in the country from the disease in 1997 and 61 per cent in 1998, were of persons aged 60 years and above.
3. *Cerebral apoplexy (paralytic strokes):* 76.8 per cent of the total deaths in the country from the disease in 1997, and 77.9 per cent in 1998, were of persons aged 60 years and above.
4. *Cancer:* 45.8 per cent of the total deaths in the country from this disease in 1997, and 45.3 per cent in 1998, were of persons aged 60 years and above.
5. *Tuberculosis of the lungs:* 32.4 per cent of the total deaths in the country from this disease in 1997, and the same percentage in 1998, were of persons aged 60 years and above.
6. *Anaemia:* 43.8 per cent of the total deaths in the country

Table 3.14: Percentage distribution of deaths in age group 60 years
and above in rural areas by probable cause of death,
India, 1997 and 1998

Probable cause of death	1997			1998		
	Male	Female	Total	Male	Female	Total
Infectious and parasitic diseases (diarrhoeal diseases, tuberculosis, typhoid etc.)	6.8	5.0	6.0	7.2	5.4	6.4
Viral infection (measles, malaria etc.)	1.9	2.4	2.2	1.1	1.3	1.2
Neoplasm (cancer)	4.3	3.8	4.1	3.8	3.9	3.9
Diseases of the blood and blood forming organs (anaemia etc.)	2.4	3.5	2.9	2.7	3.7	3.1
Metabolic diseases (diabetes etc.)	1.4	1.4	1.4	1.4	1.4	1.4
Mental and behavioural disorders	0.2	0.3	0.2	0.4	0.4	0.4
Inflammatory diseases of central nervous system (cerebral apoplexy)	7.9	7.5	7.7	7.7	7.4	7.5
Diseases of circulatory system (heart diseases)	15.3	12.5	14.1	15.3	13.3	14.4
Diseases of respiratory system (pneumonia, bronchitis, asthma etc.)	21.0	19.4	20.3	23.3	21.2	22.4
Diseases of digestive system	1.9	1.3	1.6	1.9	1.4	1.7
Diseases of genitourinary system	1.4	0.8	1.2	1.6	1.0	1.3
Symptoms, signs and abnormal clinical findings not elsewhere mentioned	31.8	38.9	34.9	29.6	36.6	32.8
Injuries, poisoning and other consequences	0.3	0.4	0.4	0.2	0.4	0.3
External causes of mortality (vehicular accidents)	1.0	0.6	0.8	0.8	0.4	0.6
Other external causes of accidental injuries (Falls, drowning, etc.)	0.4	0.4	0.4	0.5	0.4	0.5
Venomous animal contact etc. (snake bite/scorpion bite, exposure to excessive heat and cold, natural calamities, suicide etc.)	2.1	1.4	1.8	2.3	2.0	2.1
Total	100.0	100.0	100.0	100.0	100.0	100.0

Source: Survey of Causes of Death (Rural), 1997,1998.

from this disease in 1997, and 45.3 per cent in 1998, were of persons aged 60 years and above.

7. *Diabetes:* 64.7 per cent of the total deaths in the country from this disease in 1997, and 65.9 per cent in 1998, were of persons aged 60 years and above.

8. *Acute abdominal disease:* 30.3 per cent of the total deaths in the country from this disease in 1997, and 38.0 per cent in 1998, were of persons aged 60 years and above.

9. *Uraemia:* 54.5 per cent of the total deaths from this disease in 1997 and 55.9 per cent in 1998, were of persons aged 60 years and above.

10. *Peptic or gastric ulcer:* 42.8 per cent of the total deaths from this disease in 1997 and 47.5 per cent in 1998, were of persons aged 60 years and above.

11. *Whooping cough:* 28.1 per cent of the total deaths from this disease in 1997 and 67.3 per cent in 1998, were of persons aged 60 years and above.

Morbidity

Incidence of case fatality from some of the diseases, which affect older age groups, has been given in the earlier paragraphs. The disease profile of older persons has a much wider spectrum which may not lead to death but can cause acute suffering and pain. They are often the outcome of hard work not backed by adequate food and nutrition, bad environmental sanitation and hygiene, poor housing, hardly any access to basic amenities of living, and poor availability as well as use of health services. Even though morbidity data by gender are not available, most health experts believe that even though women live longer, they have a higher incidence of morbidity, though not always disclosed in surveys based on lay reporting because of socio-cultural inhibitions (such as not reporting their ailments, unless very obvious and painful), and other factors such as not having visited medical practitioners for diagnosing ailments. An important feature of morbidity among the old is that it is often of a multiple kind. There is a far heavier load of non-communicable degenerative diseases. There is also a higher prevalence rate among the elderly of cardio-vascular diseases, musculo-skeletal disorders, diabetes, cancer, gastro-intestinal problems, neuro-vascular problems, dyspepsia, prostate disorders, urinary incontinence, osteoporosis and tuberculosis. A higher incidence of dementia and psychiatric morbidity (particularly depression) has also been reported. Physical disability, particularly after age 70, arises from visual impairment, hearing impairment, mobility problems and ill-health. Many of these ailments are of a chronic nature, require long-time treatment, high costs, and accessible and affordable facilities of secondary and tertiary care. Old persons who have multiple chronic illness, who live alone, are homebound, and are poor and widowed, are more severely disadvantaged, more so if they happen to be women, are illiterate and resident in rural areas. In the developed countries, the healthcare system, both public and private, has grown in response to the changing demographic structure of the population. Health insurance, often subsidized by the state, allows access to healthcare. In India, unfortunately, services are poorly developed, particularly where the public healthcare system is concerned. Long distances of government hospitals, absence of transport facilities and escort, and poverty prevent the elderly from receiving timely help. As a result, illnesses, particularly in rural areas and in large segments of urban slums where the disadvantaged live, are not properly diagnosed and remain untreated for long periods causing pain and suffering. This phenomenon affects their longevity and causes impairment.

Some micro-studies have reported on ailments which primarily affect older persons. The presence of coronary heart disease has been found to be higher in the older age groups. Studies among different ethnic groups in countries where Indians have settled have shown that Indians have a larger prevalence rate of coronary artery disease. (Enas, Garg et al., 1996; Bahl, Prabhakaran et al., 2001). A community-based survey of coronary heart disease in Delhi covering 13,723 adults of age 25–64 years in 1985–86 showed that the prevalence rate increased with age. It was 6 per cent in the age group 45–64 years and 9 per cent in the age group 55–64 years. The prevalence rate was more in the case of both males and females of a higher socio-economic class (Chadha et al., 1990). A review of prevalence of coronary heart disease has indicated that urban areas have a much higher prevalence rate than rural areas (Shah and Prabhakar, 1997).

Prevalence of strokes (cerebro-vascular disease), estimated to be about 200 per 100,000 persons, has a larger prevalence rate after the age of 50 years. Rehabilitation of persons who survive the stroke with varying degrees of disability puts a heavy stress on the family and society in terms of both costs and care arrangements. Hyper-tension, high blood sugar, low concentration of normal hemoglobin, and tobacco use are important risk factors. They need to be monitored and controlled (Dalal, 1997).

Hypertension has a high prevalence rate among the elderly and is estimated to be about twenty times the prevalence in the general population. Females have been found to have a higher prevalence rate than males. The incidence is also higher in urban areas as compared to rural areas (Shah and Prabhakar, 1997).

Diabetes has been identified as a major health problem in the country. It has been referred to as a silent killer as it could potentially create complications in the functioning of other organs. India has reportedly the largest number of diabetes patients in the world. Some experts have described the incidence as reaching epidemic proportions. One estimate has given the prevalence rate at 12.1 per cent (Pradeepa and Mohan, 2002). Genetic factors and life style factors have been identified as the major causes. Obesity, unhealthy food habits (high intake of calorie rich foods), physical inactivity, lack of exercise and high stress are important risk factors. Prevalence rates have been found to be similar in both males and females. Some studies have found a higher prevalence rate among the urban elderly (Shah and Prabhakar, 1997). There is a large percentage of undetected cases. The direct and indirect costs of outpatient treatment of a person with diabetes is quite expensive and often beyond the reach of the poor. An ORG survey covering 5516 diabetes patients across 22 states in the country found that the mean age of diabetes getting detected was 45 years. On an average, patients were found suffering from the disease for the last eight years. Patients do not monitor the status of diabetes regularly. Prevention of diabetes can best be done by controlling the life style factors – healthy diets, increase in physical activity and exercise, meditation, lowering of stress and weight reduction.

There is also a large incidence of mental morbidity among the elderly, estimated at 89 per 1000 persons. Affective disorders, particularly depression, dementia and delusional disorders comprise the main forms of mental morbidity. Apart from genetic pre-disposition, bio-psychosocial factors play an important contributory role. The risk of psychiatric morbidity rises with the age of the elderly. It is seldom an isolated event. Incidence of co-morbidity is common (Rao, 1997).

Tuberculosis is a major health problem among all segments of the population and has persisted despite the national programme for control of tuberculosis. Persons are exposed to infections, particularly in conditions of poverty, overcrowding, malnutrition, and poor housing. Surveys have shown that most persons do not take the full course of treatment and stop taking medicines when they start feeling better. The incidence of tuberculosis has been found to be high among the aged as compared to other segments of the population (Dey, 1997). The National Family Health Survey, 1998–99 reported a prevalence rate of tuberculosis at 1374 per 100,000 persons aged 60 years and above (IIPS, 2000).

Lower immunity among older persons makes them vulnerable, particularly to diseases like pneumonia, urinary tract infections, endocarditis, pressure sores, infectious diarrhoea, septicemia, meningitis and arthritis (Dey, 1997). They have also been found to be more susceptible to renal and prostatic disorders, gastro-intestinal diseases and ulcers. One of the commonest problems of the elderly is constipation (Natarajan, 1997). The prevalence of asthma has also been found to be high. The National Family Health Survey reported a prevalence rate of 10,375 per 100,000 persons aged 60 years and above. It was higher among males, and among the rural population (IIPS, 2000).

The National Sample Survey in its 52nd Round (July 1995 to June 1996) reported on the incidence of morbidity in four broad age groups by sex in rural and urban areas of the country. The survey is based on the ailment as reported by the person. The ailments were categorized as acute (ailment less than 30 days) or chronic (ailment lasting 30 days or more). The findings given in Table 3.15 show that older persons have a much higher degree of morbidity, both acute (ailment less than 30 days) and chronic (ailment lasting 30 days or more). The difference by gender and by type of residence is small. Females aged 60 years and above tend to have a slightly higher degree of morbidity in both rural and urban areas.

Table 3.15: Percentage of persons reporting ailment during the last 15 days by age, sex and type of ailment in rural and urban areas, India, 1995–96

Type of ailment	Sex	Rural					Urban				
		0–14	15–39	40–59	60+	Total	0–14	15–39	40–59	60+	Total
Acute ailment (less than 30 days)	Male	4.6	2.7	4.2	9.5	4.1	5.1	2.8	3.6	6.5	3.9
	Female	4.3	3.6	4.8	9.0	4.4	4.7	3.7	4.2	7.3	4.3
	Person	4.5	3.2	4.5	9.3	4.2	4.9	3.2	3.9	6.9	4.1
Chronic ailment (30 days or more)	Male	0.3	0.8	2.2	8.6	1.3	0.3	0.7	2.4	8.5	1.3
	Female	0.3	0.9	2.7	7.3	1.4	0.3	0.9	3.1	9.4	1.5
	Person	0.3	0.9	2.4	8.0	1.3	0.3	0.8	2.7	8.9	1.4
Any ailment	Male	5.0	3.5	6.4	17.8	5.4	5.4	3.5	6.1	14.8	5.1
	Female	4.5	4.5	7.5	16.1	5.7	4.9	4.5	7.3	16.6	5.8
	Person	4.8	4.0	6.9	17.0	5.5	5.2	4.0	6.6	15.7	5.4

Source: NSSO 52nd Round, 1995–96, *Morbidity and Treatment of Ailments.*

The prevalence of long duration (chronic) ailment per 100,000 persons by age and sex in rural and urban areas is given in Table 3.16. Persons aged 60 years and above have a much higher prevalence rate of chronic ailment.

Table 3.16: Prevalence of long duration (chronic) ailment per 100,000 by age and sex in rural and urban areas, India, 1995–96

Age (in years)	Rural			Urban		
	Male	Female	Person	Male	Female	Person
0–14	345	272	311	292	280	286
15–39	779	942	860	693	893	788
40–59	2171	2691	2425	2434	3094	2739
60+	8624	7344	7978	8507	9356	8940
Total	1278	1372	1324	1251	1529	1384

Source: NSSO, 52nd round, 1995–96, Morbidity and Treatment of Ailments.

Empirical micro-studies in different parts of the country, too, have reported that persons aged 60 years and above have higher rates of morbidity than the other age groups. The incidence of chronic disease episodes was also higher (Duggal and Amin, 1997; George, Shah and Nandraj, 1997).

NSSO also reported on different types of chronic diseases by gender in rural and urban areas. The data given in Table 3.17 shows that nearly half the population has a chronic disease. Urban females tend to have a higher percentage of chronic disease as compared to urban males. In rural areas there is hardly any gender difference. Most old persons tend to suffer from the problem of pain and swelling in joints, blood pressure and coughs in both rural and urban areas. The prevalence of blood pressure, heart disease and diabetes in urban areas is almost twice that in rural areas. Some empirical studies conduced in rural areas have found a high prevalence rate of chronic morbidity among both males and females.

Table 3.17: Percentage of persons aged 60 years and above reporting chronic disease by type, sex and residence, 1995–96

Chronic disease	Rural			Urban		
	Male	Female	Total	Male	Female	Total
Joints	36.31	40.45	38.40	28.54	39.25	34.01
Blood Pressure (high/low)	10.79	10.47	10.64	20.02	25.09	25.56
Cough	24.99	19.53	22.24	17.86	14.19	15.98
Heart disease	3.39	2.66	3.03	6.83	5.31	6.06
Diabetes	3.62	2.82	3.22	8.53	6.58	7.54
Piles	3.29	1.61	2.44	3.22	1.83	2.51
Urinary problem	3.85	2.27	3.06	4.92	2.41	3.65
Cancer	0.20	0.31	0.25	0.18	0.39	0.29
Any type	52.67	51.41	52.03	52.82	56.03	54.46

Source: NSSO, 52nd Round 1995–96, The Aged in India.

Old persons who have a higher prevalence rate of morbidity are expected to report for out-patient treatment in larger numbers. The NSSO survey has reported that this is not the case. The percentage distribution of persons seeking out-patient treatment during the last 15 days by age and sex, given in Table 3.18, shows that a smaller percentage of old persons

Table 3.18: Per 1000 distribution of out-patient treatment during last 15 days by age and sex in rural and urban areas, India, 1995–96

Age (in years)	Rural			Urban		
	Male	Female	Total	Male	Female	Total
0–14	183	147	330	169	140	309
15–39	134	159	293	144	181	325
40–59	101	110	211	113	112	225
60 & above	89	76	166	67	74	141
Total	507	493	1000	493	507	1000

Source: NSSO 52nd Round, 1995–96, Morbidity and Treatment of Ailments.

as compared to other age groups report for out-patient treatment. The main factors which deter use of out-patient facilities are costs, distance, absence of escort, problem of transportation, and the general feeling that such ailments are

an outcome of the process of ageing. There is also an attitudinal
problem. Ailments in old age are believed to be an outcome of
the ageing process, and that nothing much can be done. The
myth needs to be systematically attacked.

When old persons get seriously affected by their ailment,
they are taken to a medical facility. The pattern of utilization
of hospital care by different age groups has shown that older
persons have a disproportionately larger share. The duration
of hospital stay is also longer. The NSSO survey, 1995–96
reported on the number of persons per 1000 by age group who
were hospitalized during the last 365 days. The data in Table
3.19 shows a larger incidence of old patients in rural and urban
areas, among both males and females. More males aged 60
years and above tend to be hospitalized than females aged 60
years and above, may be because of gender bias. Urban areas
show a higher incidence of persons aged 60 years and above
who were hospitalized, probably because of greater availability
of secondary and tertiary care facilities.

Table 3.19: Number of persons hospitalized during the last 365 days
per 1000 persons by age and sex in rural and urban areas,
India, 1995–96

Age (in years)	Rural			Urban		
	Male	Female	Total	Male	Female	Total
0–14	9	6	7	15	10	12
15–39	11	14	12	14	19	17
40–59	22	19	21	31	30	31
60+	47	28	38	75	57	66
Total	14	13	13	20	20	20

Source: NSSO 52nd Round 1995–96, *Morbidity and Treatment of Ailments.*

Disability

A key concern in old age is a life free of disability as long as
one lives. With a life expectancy of 15 to 17 years at age 60
years, old persons strongly desire a functional capacity for
autonomous living. They hope that visual, hearing, speech,
mobility, incontinence, amnesia and other such problems

would not appear in their life and, even if it occurs in some cases, it would be compressed to a very small part of the life span over age 60 years.

NSSO, in its 52nd Round conducted in 1995–96, reported on disability by gender in rural and urban areas. These are based on lay reporting and subjective assessment, and indicate the degree of functional impairment which would count it as a disability. Some persons, however, consider a decline in functional capacity as a sign of old age, and did not report it as a disability. Table 3.20, which gives the data on disability among persons aged 60 years and above, shows that visual disability is more common. The prevalence is larger among females than males in both rural and urban areas. In the case of other types of disability, too, the same trends are discernible. Rural persons over age 60 years have a higher prevalence rate of disability than urban persons over age 60, may be because they have poorer access to medical care facilities.

Table 3.20: Percentage of persons aged 60 years and above having disability by type, sex and residence, 1995–96

Type of disability	Rural			Urban		
	Male	Female	Total	Male	Female	Total
Visual	24.89	29.13	27.03	22.55	26.02	24.32
Hearing	13.94	15.61	14.78	11.08	13.18	12.16
Locomotor	10.67	11.54	11.11	7.96	9.37	8.68
Speech	3.20	3.76	3.49	2.93	3.44	3.19
Amnesia/ Senility	9.55	11.34	10.46	6.08	7.98	7.05
Any disability	38.00	42.46	40.25	33.29	36.70	35.03

Source: NSSO, 52nd Round 1995–96 *The Aged in India.*

The prevalence of disability varies in different states. The NSSO survey reported the prevalence of disability among persons aged 60 years and above in 16 states by type of disability, as well as any type of disability. Table 3.21 gives the disability by any type. In rural areas, Haryana had the lowest percentage with any type of disability (32.16 per cent), and Andhra Pradesh the highest (47.44 per cent). In urban areas, Bihar had the lowest percentage (30.52 per cent) and Gujarat the highest (40.02 per cent).

Table 3.21: Percentage of persons 60 years and above with any disability in rural and urban areas in states, 1995–96

Percentage with any disability	
Rural	*Urban*
Andhra Pradesh (47.44)	Gujarat (40.02)
West Bengal (46.14)	West Bengal (39.88)
Himachal Pradesh (45.24)	Haryana (39.21)
Maharashtra (44.16)	Madhya Pradesh (36.12)
Gujarat (43.07)	Orissa (35.91)
Uttar Pradesh (41.71)	Maharashtra (35.77)
Orissa (40.99)	Uttar Pradesh (35.75)
Kerala (39.68)	Andhra Pradesh (34.73)
Madhya Pradesh (38.00)	Assam (34.26)
Punjab (37.92)	Punjab (34.02)
Tamil Nadu (37.91)	Rajasthan (36.61)
Rajasthan (37.33)	Kerala (32.13)
Bihar (35.06)	Karnataka (32.06)
Assam (34.89)	Tamil Nadu (31.48)
Karnataka (33.13)	Himachal Pradesh (30.96)
Haryana (32.16)	Bihar (30.52)

Notes: States are arranged in descending order.
Source: NSSO 52nd Round, 1995–96, *The Aged in India.*

Some micro-studies on ailments affecting the elderly indicates their disability profile. An ICMR study on the health of the elderly (aged 60 years and above) at a Primary Health Care Centre near Madurai in 1984–88, covering 1910 respondents, showed that 88 per cent had visual handicap, 40 per cent had locomotor problems, 8.2 per cent had a hearing problem, 18.7 per cent had neurological problems, 17.4 per cent had respiratory problems, 13.3 per cent had dermatological problems, 9.9 per cent had gastro-intestinal problems, 8.1 per cent had psychiatric problems, 3.5 per cent had genito urinary problems. Cases of oncological problems and diabetes were also found. The findings showed that in terms of clinical diagnoses, 76.5 per cent had 2 to 3 clinical diagnoses of ailments, while 16.5 per cent had 4 or more. Single diagnosis was found in only 6.8 per cent. The study concluded that multiple diagnoses are a common clinical experience in geriatric medicine (Rao, 1990).

A study was conducted in the geriatric clinic at the All India Institute of Medical Sciences, New Delhi, on 612 ambulatory elderly to find out their functional assessments and to detect functional disabilities. Data showed that nearly two-thirds of the patients were males. This could be reflective of gender bias in seeking medical care. The study also found that 34.3 per cent had visual impairment, 24.5 per cent had hearing impairment, 3.6 per cent had arm function impairment, and 4.6 per cent had leg function impairment. Most of these impairments were of persons from lower socio-economic category (44.0 per cent). This was followed by the middle income group (33.3 per cent) and high income group (22.7 per cent). Urinary incontinence was found in 18.3 per cent, depression in 23.0 per cent, and impaired ADL (Activities of Daily Living) in 5.9 per cent. Cognitive impairment was noticed in 5.7 per cent, the incidence being higher in persons of lower socio-economic category. A group of 50 persons specially investigated for locomotor problems showed that 40 per cent had spine problems, 32 per cent had lower limb problems and 28 per cent had upper limb problems (Khetarpal et al, 1996). It needs to be noted, however, that the socio-economic profile of patients at AIIMS is different from the patients in most public and private sector hospitals.

The national survey of blindness in India conducted in 1986–89 estimated about 12 million blind persons in the entire population. The number with blindness in one eye was 7.12 million persons, and with low vision 28.56 million. The prevalence rate was far higher in the age group 60–69 years, and 70 years and above. Age related cataract was the single most common cause of blindness. Rural persons and women had a higher prevalence rate (Mohan, 1989). A subsequent study estimated the number of blind persons in India to be 18.7 million of which 9.5 million were due to cataract and about 3 million due to refractive error. The projections were based on a survey done on blind persons in Andhra Pradesh. The study also found a higher prevalence rate among women, and in the rural population. Prevalence of blindness was very high in the older age groups. The prevalence rate was 9.16 per cent among males and 12.78 per cent among females in the age group 60–69 years. In the age group 70 years and above, the prevalence rates were 16.83 and 25.53, respectively. The study suggested that in view of the huge backlog, there should be a large augmentation of eye care infrastructure, particularly for treatment of cataract (the more important cause) and refractive error (Dandona et al., 2001). Other epidemiological micro studies have also found a higher prevalence rate of blindness among the old, and among females (Sharma and Prasad, 1962).

A rapid assessment survey of cataract blindness in seven states in 1998, covering 28,055 persons aged 50 years and above, reported a blindness prevalence rate (<6/60 in the better eye) to be 12.4 per cent in the age group 60–69 years, and 26.2 per cent in the age group 70 years and above. Cataract was found to be the commonest cause of low vision and blindness. The prevalence of cataract was 43.3 per cent among persons 50 years and above, which increased with age. It was as high as 63 per cent in the age group 70 years and above. The researchers estimated that 11.9 million people (vision <6/60 in the better eye) were in urgent need of cataract surgery in the country (Bachani, Murthy and Gupta, 2000).

Some of the factors responsible for the high case load is the growth of numbers of persons over age 60 due to increase in life expectancy and the absence of affordable facilities in large parts of the country. Blind persons become economically, socially and functionally dependent on others. There is a substantial reduction in work output of persons handicapped by cataract which also affects the quality of their life. They need help for their daily life activities. They become marginalized, lonely and depressed, and become helpless because of their inability to contribute to family life. Factors compounding the sufferings of loss of functional ability of blind/nearly blind persons are poverty, ignorance, lack of escorts to a hospital facility and distance. Persons most affected are those in backward rural areas where health facilities are very poor. A large number are ignorant about the seriousness of the problem, which could mean not being treated at all, or coming too late for surgery. Some studies have reported that females attending eye camps had a more serious visual handicap, an outcome of the inhibiting social and economic environment (Angra et al., 1997). Compliance rates on surgical advice have been found to be poor. A survey conducted on patients attending eye camps in Haryana and Western Uttar Pradesh showed there was little gender bias in attending the camps for treatment. The study suggested that children and spouse were the main motivating factors in attending the camps. It also found that the elderly did not venture far from their residence for surgical facilities. Also, females received attention rather late. The study suggested that cataract surgical services should be integrated at the Primary Health Centres (PHC) and Community Health Centres (CHC). A mechanism of screening for cataract blind needs to be instituted. This will particularly benefit females who come for surgery rather late (Gupta et al., 1996). For persons in remote rural areas, eye camps offer a solution. Unfortunately, from a few camps, infections have been reported which have led to loss of eyesight. These need to be conducted in a more efficient manner.

Hearing impairment is also related to age. A multi-centric study on hearing impairment carried out by the Indian Council of Medical Research reported a prevalence rate of 10.7 per cent in rural areas and 6.8 per cent in urban areas in the general population (ICMR, 1983). The prevalence rate was much higher in the older age groups. Most studies have not reported any significant difference in hearing impairment of males and females. There are very few facilities in India for treating loss of hearing, particulary in rural areas. The impairment is largely untreated and ignored, and is rationalized as a symptom of the process of ageing. A very small percentage is able to acquire hearing aids. For persons living alone, loss of hearing is a very serious disadvantage as it affects daily living, and can cause accidents. It reduces the ability to communicate, and leads to isolation and marginalization in the family and in the community (Kacker, 1997).

Very few older persons, even in the lower and middle class, ever visit a dentist. Difficulties of chewing food adds to their nutritional problems. Dental services and dental prosthetic aids are not only expensive. They are virtually inaccessible in rural areas. Even in urban areas, they are beyond the means of most people.

Malnutrition

Adequate nutrition holds the key to good health in old age. Within the household in many families, the old are nutritionally more disadvantaged as compared to children and working males. Malnutrition among the elderly has been a matter of concern as it affects their health status and could accentuate to degenerative diseases. Dietary intake is often not nutritionally balanced, specially so in the case of disadvantaged sections, and is usually caused by poverty and lack of information on food requirements in old age. Many families do not take cognizance of the food restrictions to be observed in the case of older persons and the special diets that need to be prepared to help in digestion, absorption of food and recuperation from illness. Poor dentition is an added cause. Old persons nutritionally at greater risk are the poor, illiterate, the widowed (particularly women), living alone, having physical ailments, mentally depressed and recently bereaved.

Review of a series of research studies on nutritional status of the elderly found that the nutrients least adequately supplied in the diets of Indian elderly are calcium, iron, vitamin A, riboflavin and niacin, along with energy deficits. Inadequate consumption of cereals, pulses, fruits, vegetables, milk and milk products may be a contributing factor to these deficiencies. A high prevalence of iron deficiency anaemia has also been reported among the Indian elderly (Wadhwa et al., 1997). The National Family Health Survey, 1998-99 reported that half the women aged 35-49 years were anaemic. The percentage was higher in rural areas, among the illiterate population, and among Scheduled Tribes and Scheduled Castes (IIPS, 2000). The deficiency is likely to be carried over to the older age groups.

Reports from the National Nutrition Monitoring Bureau have shown a large percentage of persons above 60 years with body mass index less than 18.5 (chronic energy deficiency). A micro study conducted at the All India Institute of Medical Sciences on patients attending the geriatric clinic showed that 50 per cent of elderly males and 36 per cent of elderly females had deficits in calories, 42 per cent of elderly males and 16 per cent of elderly females had deficit in proteins, 51 per cent of elderly males and 57 per cent of elderly females had deficit in calcium, 69 per cent of elderly males and 50 per cent of elderly females had deficit in iron, 33 per cent of elderly males and 27 per cent of elderly females had deficit in riboflavin (Srivastava et al., 1996). There is thus need to improve the nutrient status through proper meals and medicines.

Nutritional needs in old age will have to be disseminated widely, specially targeting families which have old persons. Multi-media packages will help families to know about planning of diets which do not cost much, but are tasty and nutritious. Families must be made aware of the foods to avoid and the foods to be consumed.

Providers of Healthcare for the Old

Healthcare services in India are mainly provided by the:

1. Public sector (centre, state, local authorities and public sector undertakings).
2. Private sector, ranging from independent practitioners to corporate entities running large multi-speciality hospitals. There are also unqualified practitioners who dispense treatments in urban slums and rural backward areas.
3. Non-governmental sector, including voluntary organizations and health cooperatives.

Public Sector

Public sector healthcare in rural areas in the country comprises mainly of the primary healthcare network, the foundations of which were laid by the Health Survey and Development Committee (1946). It is operated by state governments, with assistance from the central government for some public health programmes, as are indicated in the five year development plans. The rural public health network has the following set up: (i) A sub-centre for a population of 5000 in the plains (3,000 in hilly and tribal areas). The sub-centre is manned by a multi-purpose male worker and a multi-purpose female worker (ANM). It is assisted by a village health guide for attending to minor ailments, and keeping track of communicable and other diseases. (ii) A Primary Health Centre (PHC) for a population of 30,000 in the plains (20,000 in hilly and tribal areas). The PHC acts as a referral point for 6 sub-centres. It is manned by a medical officer (M.O.), supported by 6 para-medical and 8 administrative staff. A PHC provides 4 to 6 beds for patients. (iii) A Community Health Centre for a population of 120,000 in the plains (80,000 in hilly and areas). The CHC acts as a referral center for four PHCs. It has four medical specialists, 11 paramedical personnel and 10 other staff members. The CHC is a 30 bed patient care unit with an operation theatre, X-ray, labour room and laboratory facilities. It provides both indoor and outdoor facilities. On 31 March 2003, there were 138,368 Sub-centres, 22,936 Primary Health Centres (PHC) and 3,076 Community Health Centres in the country. On an average, there were 6.04 Sub-centres per PHC, and 7.46 PHCs per CHC. There was a shortfall of 8,127 Sub-centres (6.1 per cent of the required strength), 1666 PHCs (7.5 per cent of the required strength) and 2541 CHCs (45.5 per cent of the required strength). (MOHFW, 2004).

The rural primary healthcare network caters to the entire population, including the old. The four medical specialist posts in a CHC are a surgeon, a physician, a pediatrician and a gynaecologist/obstetrician. There is no specialist in geriatrics. Doctors and paramedical staff in a PHC do not have an orientation in geriatric care.

The functioning of the primary healthcare network, even for general healthcare, has drawn a lot of criticism. There are shortfalls in the institutional framework, particularly in the setting up of Community Health Centres, which is far below the norm. There is also a big shortfall in the appointment of medical, paramedical and other staff, and in supply of equipments and medicines. The buildings are in a bad shape and are often unclean. The PHC/CHC is not only characterized by low budgetary provisions. It also has poor reach of outlying areas due to long distance and inconvenient locations. Due to bad roads and poor transportation, it requires a long time to reach the centre. The quality of services offered is very unsatisfactory. Patients have to put up with a long waiting period. They have also to contend with absence of doctors. Very little time is given to the patient. Poor and irregular supply of medicines, pilferages, unfriendly attitude, poor motivation and insensitivity to complaints and grievances of patients are big deficiencies. Doctors have been found to be concerned more with private practice and attend to patients as per their own convenience.

A study on the aged in rural Karnataka makes more explicit the poor medical facilities available in public sector institutions. Due to bad roads and poor transportation facility, access was rendered difficult. The aged had to wait for days so that some person in the household could take them to the nearby hospital or dispensary. Public hospitals, which are expected to give free or subsidized medicines, generally do not provide the same. Corrupt practices in hospitals affect the quality of care provided. Patients are expected to tip the doctors and para-medical staff to get the treatment or prescription. The study observed: " The practice in government hospitals is that the patients pay the staff and get the facilities, including beds in hospital wards. If one fails to pay, he will simply be told to wait or go to some hospital for the service. On payment, the patients get immediate attention from the staff, including quick scheduling for operation, ward facility, and good care and attention......... .The equipments in the government hospitals are not only old fashioned, but also do not work" (Gurumurthy, 1998). The situation stated above more or less illustrates the treatment meted out to the old in most public sector run hospitals/dispensaries in other states.

The NSSO Survey on morbidity and treatments in 1995–96 found that in rural areas only 6 per cent of the total number of patients for non-hospitalized treatment went to a PHC/CHC, and 11 per cent to a public hospital. The percentage availing public healthcare facilities for non-hospitalized treatment was found to have declined from 26 in 1986–87 to 19 in 1995–96. This has meant more problems for the rural old as it means more costs. In urban areas, primary healthcare is provided by health posts. Local authorities also provide some dispensaries for primary health. Because of the rising costs of medical care and the unsatisfactory fiscal position of states, there has been little public sector expansion to cater to the needs of the population. No reforms have been carried out to tone up the health administration in rural areas. The system has descended into a state which can very well carry the label of a virtually non-functional health service for the rural poor. They have no alternative but to depend on quacks who proliferate in rural areas and urban slums. Their ailments continue.

The secondary and tertiary levels of healthcare are provided by the public sector at block/taluq/district and city level. These are, again, far less compared to the need. The quality of services is unsatisfactory. After meeting the requirements of enhanced pay and pension of government and quasi-government employees, there is little money for upgrading and expansion of health facilities and supply of medicines. The quality of services is unsatisfactory.

Public sector hospitals have now started charging for surgical and diagnostic facilities, particularly in the case of World Bank aided projects. Patients are expected to buy most of the medicines. Ailment of older persons gets the lowest priority, specially in view of the rising costs of medical treatment.

Local authorities in urban areas provide mainly primary and, to some extent, secondary care facilities. They cater mainly to the poorer sections of society. Medical dispensaries/hospitals often suffer from shortage of doctors and paramedical personnel, medicines, accessories and diagnostic equipment. The maintenance, upkeep and standards of service of local authority hospitals/dispensaries are unsatisfactory. Several such outfits have witnessed a decline in number of patients due to poor services. Due to paucity of funds, some have become non-functional.

Facilities for treatment of degenerative diseases in public sector hospitals, which afflict the old the most and require repeat visits, are far too short of their demand. Given the fiscal health of the states and the growing population of old persons, the gap between demand and supply is increasing rapidly. Affordable healthcare will not be possible for a very large number of persons unless suitable institutional arrangements are made, the public sector steps in, and strong initiatives are taken in this regard.

Unfortunately, the government, instead of embarking on a large increase of secondary and tertiary care facilities and upgrading the quality of services to cater to a growing number of older persons at an affordable cost, is shying away from this responsibility. For its own superannuated employees, it has empanelled private sector hospitals/diagnostic centres for reimbursing the costs of treatment, re-emphasising the statement that retirees from government are the most favoured segment, whatever the expenditure. For the huge majority of the elderly, there is no alternative but to pay the high costs of private medical treatment. Persons in rural areas will continue to suffer the most as the location of private sector hospitals is based on the potential profile of the paying client, which means the urban centres. The device adopted by some state governments of giving subsidized land in cities so that health services will be provided free or at subsidized rates, has not worked because of poor enforcement. Doctors, as a group, are an important lobby and influence decision making in government to protect and promote their interests.

Private Sector

The private sector in healthcare has played an important role, mainly through services run by individual practitioners and hospitals/dispensaries. The 1980s witnessed the beginning of a new era in the organization of medical care. Rapid growth in private nursing homes/hospitals began to emerge, often promoted as a business enterprise with huge capital costs. Hospital industry beginning from the 1990s is regarded as a favourite investment sector and is expanding fast. Many hospitals are drawing an increasing number of clients from abroad. Medical tourism is being promoted, advertising availability of top class medical standards at third world prices. Some state governments are promoting medical cities with 'state of the art' facilities for location of super-specialty hospitals, pathological laboratories and private medical colleges. High cost super specialty medical care has grown mainly to take care of life style diseases of middle and upper income groups who find public sector hospitals overcrowded and lacking in 'latest techniques' of medical care. The growth in number of persons over 60 years from the better off sections of society have provided an expanding clientele. Large private sector hospitals and nursing homes publicize their services through overt and covert means in print and electronic media to attract clients who are either rich enough to pay, or have arrangements with insurance companies and employers. Public relations exercises by big private sector hospitals are a part of the marketing technique. Ministers are called to inaugurate functions organized by private hospitals who routinely declare that private hospitals as a part of their social responsibility should treat the poor either free or at a very affordable rate, and then forget about it. Beneficiaries of Central Government Health Scheme, retirees from public sector undertakings and autonomous bodies funded by government provide an important clientele to private hospitals/diagnostic centres which have now been empanelled.

A large number of elderly, who have no insurance or post-retirement benefits of healthcare, are forced to pay for expensive diagnostic investigations, escalating costs of medicines, surgery and nursing care for ailments either by borrowing, taking loan or selling assets. Even the healthcare insurance companies provide only for hospitalization expenses. Non-hospitalization expenses can be very large, particularly for chronic ailments, which primarily affect the old. A couple can end up paying Rs. 5000 to Rs. 15,000 annually for routine non-hospitalized treatment.

Private nursing homes and hospitals are perceived to provide better treatment mainly because of better marketing, a far lesser amount of time for availing the service, and a show of attentiveness. There are, however, reports of excess billing, over-prescription of expensive drugs, uncalled for repeat visits, non-essential tests and specialist consultations, and an increase in more than necessary bed occupancy by a patient. There are also allegations of unethical practices. Media accounts indicate some doctors (including those in the public sector), have an informal network with pathological laboratories, diagnostic centres and hospitals for making referrals for which they get a commission.

The private sector in medical care is not governed by perfect market conditions where competition ensures lowering of costs. The patient is not fully aware of the product that is being offered, and its outcome. Even within the private sector, for the same surgical facilities, costs vary considerably, depending not only on the surgeon's reputation but also the type of comfort that is provided, the aura of being treated in a state-of-the-art medical centre and the publicity of the facility through a variety of public relations devices.

Non-governmental Providers of Healthcare for the Elderly

Non-governmental organizations have provided healthcare, mainly at the micro-level. NGO activity has been in existence, even before independence, motivated primarily by humanitarianism and charity to provide relief for the disadvantaged. Religious organizations, primarily the church, sponsored and executed a large number of projects. It received a fillip in the 1970s, when health professionals, who were socially motivated, visualized a number of initiatives in the conceptualization and delivery of healthcare. They viewed the NGO sector as being complementary to the public sector by giving affordable professional care, providing competition to the costlier private care, and replacing professional medical care as against quacks who were dispensing treatment because of their easier access and low costs. Several NGO initiatives adopted a much wider perspective than just curative care, and pioneered the pursuit of health goals in a developmental perspective, with involvement from the community. It trained local people in preventive healthcare. Non-governmental organizations have reached out to disadvantaged groups in urban slums, and backward rural areas. The initiatives are mainly home grown and community based, with strong leadership and commitment, and flexibility to local demands.

NGOs usually do not provide health services free of cost, except in cases of dire need. They generally hold the view that the key to a good health delivery system depends on convenience of access, right approach, quality of treatment and affordable cost. A graduated user charge is levied, usually at a subsidized rate, while ensuring at the same time that no one is left untreated because of poverty. The reasons for levying some charge to the user have been well stated: "(a) Whatever is given free is not seen by people to have a value; (b) It creates a 'feudal' relationship of donor-recipient, reinforcing 'patriarch; (c) It generates a dependency among beneficiaries, and, therefore, makes the latter complacent; (d) It acts as a barrier to people's participation" (Jesani, Duggal and Gupte, 1996).

NGOs raise a portion of maintenance expenses from user charges and from other funding sources. They usually depend on government grants and donations to upgrade facilities and for expansion. The funding sources of NGOs show a wide variety, and come from both national and international NGOs, religious bodies, civil organizations, and bilateral and multilateral development agencies. They also raise funds from special events and sponsorships, direct mail appeals, donations from salary under pay-roll giving scheme, greeting cards, legacies, and various other arrangements. Most grants are tied to projects and are for a specified period. Few NGOs have an untied funding source, which would give them autonomous decision-making powers for activities rather than be driven by the donor's perceptions. Long-term financial security remains a problem. NGOs will need to look at this issue in a more professional manner by building reserves and having regular source of income.

NGOs provide healthcare to the elderly, as for any other client. They generally do not provide the specialization required for geriatric care, nor do they have the clinical services or networking with hospitals that would be necessary for diagnosing and treating chronic and other diseases of older persons which would require a higher order of tertiary care facilities. Funding for adding geriatric care in secondary and tertiary hospitals is a major problem since the grants are usually for catering to all segments of the population. Geriatric care, including hospitalization, has not been incorporated into the NGO system which is still burdened with treating communicable diseases, and with maternal and child health services.

Some NGOs working for the welfare of the elderly are now sponsoring/executing projects which aim also at providing health services to the old in rural areas and urban slums. HelpAge India runs mobile medical care units, some of which are specially funded by charitable organizations/trusts, thus making healthcare accessible to remote places. It also funds other organizations to provide mobile services, or gives grants to medical centres for upgrading and expansion of services for the old as, for instance, ophthalmic care. In 2002–03, 56 opthalmic projects were supported by HelpAge at a cost of Rs. 291.40 lakhs. Some NGOs working for the elderly organize out-patient services on a small scale for the surrounding community. Professional bodies of doctors at times hold camps for specific ailments which affect the old (diabetes, blood pressure, heart problems, ophthalmic care) either free or at a heavily subsidized cost.

Cataract surgeries, which primarily affect older persons, are funded by several charitable organizations and corporate bodies which also organize camps for such persons resident in rural areas. The government, too, under the National Programme for Control of Blindness which was launched in 1976, assists NGOs engaged in ophthalmic services by way of grants for expansion/upgrading. In some camps, absence of proper sterilization facilities and procedures have caused infections and loss of eye sight, pointing to the need of strict norms for providing such services.

The NGO sector, while it supplements the services provided by the state and takes up new initiatives, is limited by the range of services they can provide. They are often constrained by financial, organizational and manpower services. But they do provide valuable services in a more amiable environment, and are mainly led by the initiative, drive and vision of a few motivated individuals which help them mobilize funds and deliver the services. The government must promote and sustain this sector through grants for meeting capital costs and recurring expenditure for providing affordable not-for-profit health services.

Health Cooperatives

Healthcare cooperatives have grown in India, either as a full time endeavour (as in the case of health cooperatives in Kerala), or as a subsidiary activity of a cooperative whole main function may be production or distribution activities. In the latter case, it functions as an 'add on' activity. Cooperatives often extend healthcare to their members by tying up with an insurance company which has an arrangement with a hospital/group of hospitals which agrees to provide medical treatment as per an agreed schedule of services. At times, the cooperative society directly enters into an agreement with hospitals. Some services are provided free of cost (consultation, some medicines) while for others a subsidized rate is charged (pathological tests, diagnostic procedures, hospital care). Medical services are provided to members who are within accessible limits. The ceiling of medical treatment costs of a family is fixed. An essential requirement in cooperative medical care is that all members of the cooperative join so that all the age groups are covered to make the insurance viable. The problem of adverse selection (persons who are at greater risk of falling ill, as in the case of the old) is thus taken care of. The society undertakes to collect a pre-paid premium from the member and deposit it with the insurance company/hospital. The experience of SEWA, a trade union of self-employed women workers, has been encouraging in providing cooperative healthcare at an affordable cost to its members. Some cooperatives (like the Mallur Health Cooperative in Karnataka) attached itself to an ongoing dairy cooperative. It raised funds by levying a cess per litre of milk produced by members. The Department of Community Medicine, St. John's Medical College, supported the initiative and helped in its operations by giving some services free and some others at a subsidized cost, including referral services at the hospital. Some other categories of producers' cooperatives (sugar cooperatives in Maharashtra, for instance), too, are providing such services.

Health cooperatives in Kerala have a separate identity. They provide healthcare to people at an affordable cost through dispensaries/hospitals, distinct from the public sector and private sector hospitals. Health cooperatives have been in existence in the state since 1969. Hospitals in the cooperative sector cater to district/taluk level clients offering in-patient facilities, laboratories for pathological tests, medicine shops and ambulances. Dispensaries function at the village panchayat level and provide out-patient services. Funding for the cooperatives come partly from pre-paid contributions of members for which they receive some services free of cost or at a subsidized rate as per the schedule of charges agreed upon. Other funding sources are government support for selected items (maintenance and capital cost, some as grant, and the others as loan), donations, endowments, charities, sponsorships and special fund raising events. An evaluation of functioning of cooperative hospitals showed that though they have provided health services at an affordable cost to low and middle income families, and have given concessions to the poor, they face several problems such as attracting good manpower, upgrading of services through appointment of specialists, and technological inputs for diagnosis and treatment. Cooperative healthcare no longer functions in a sheltered environment, and has to compete with the private sector in terms of quality and cost. However, some funding support for selected items would be essential from government as it provides care to the people at a far lower cost than government run services.

The government of Karnataka has recently come forward with the Yeshaswini Health Insurance scheme which has been launched by the Cooperative Department of the state to help 50 lakh farmers who are members of cooperative societies. They are expected to contribute Rs. 5 per person per month, while the state government contributes half this amount. Free treatment can be availed by members at accredited hospitals. The National Insurance Company and the United India Insurance Company are joint ventures in the project.

Health cooperatives cover the elderly as any other member of the family. It is viable only if the entire family comprising all age segments are covered. Otherwise the problem of adverse selection will arise which will be difficult for the cooperative society to sustain as older persons are at a much greater risk of falling ill.

The role of cooperatives in providing healthcare as an 'add on' function needs to be seriously explored. Institutional mechanisms need to be set up to tie with existing hospitals/dispensaries on a networking basis. Strong leadership and commitment from cooperative societies is essential for making available affordable healthcare. Government contribution by way of grant/loan for meeting capital and maintenance costs would help in making the institutions financially viable, as they have to compete with the private sector. The societies should be permitted to raise funds through donations, endowments, sponsorships, charities, etc.

Health Insurance

Health insurance covers only a small segment of the Indian population, mainly in urban areas. Some are individual arrangements with insurance companies while others are based on arrangements made by employers with the insurance companies. Some schemes collect the pre-paid premium (monthly/annually) to provide medical services, some arrange through an agreement with private providers of medical care to give services as per a schedule. Some offer a combination of both. We describe here some of the main schemes which cater to elderly persons as well.

(i) *Central Government Health Scheme:* CGHS covers central government employees and their families. The scheme also covers members and ex-members of Parliament, judges of Supreme Court and High Courts (sitting and retired), accredited journalists, freedom fighters, employees of some semi-autonomous bodies, pensioners of central government and some other categories listed in the scheme. CGHS has its own chain of service providers, some of which are government owned and run. In 2003, CGHS covered 23 cities. Its infrastructure includes 244 allopathic dispensaries, 31 ayurvedic dispensaries/units, 34 homeopathic dispensaries/ units, 9 *unani* dispensaries/units, 2 siddha dispensaries/units, 3 yoga centers, 6 allopathic first aid post, 19 polyclinics, 65 laboratories and 17 dental units, 1 maternity hospital and 2 maternity centres. To augment its facilities, CGHS has recognized 662 private hospitals/diagnostic centers in 18 cities for providing specialized treatment/investigations at agreed rates. Private hospitals recognized by CGHS provide credit facilities to all beneficiaries on production of a valid CGHS card.

Membership of CGHS is compulsory for an employee of the Central Government. Central Government pensioners who opt to be covered by CGHS contribute as per the schedule which classifies the monthly rate of contribution on the basis of the monthly pension. Effective from 1 May 1998, the monthly rate of contribution varies from Rs. 15 per month for persons drawing a pension up to Rs. 1500, to Rs. 150 per month from those drawing pension of Rs. 7501 and above. Despite the different rates of contribution, entitlement to medical services remains the same, except for some difference in accessing directly for specialist consultation, and in use of nursing home/ private ward facilities. CGHS can thus claim that they have provided equity in healthcare for different income levels despite the varying rate of contribution.

Pensioners have been given the option to either pay an annual contribution or to get a permanent CGHS card for life on payment of a lump sum equivalent to a ten year contribution. While the contribution by the employee has been fixed at a differential rate depending on earnings, there is no ceiling on the expenditure to be incurred by the government (who is the employer), unlike the Employees State Insurance Corporation where the contributions of both the employer and the employees have a fixed rate. The total annual receipts out of contributions made by CGHS card holders is not known. Whatever the expenditure, the Government meets the cost from the general revenues, as in the case of pension payments to government employees.

Pensioners/family pensioners can get themselves registered with any dispensary in the cities covered by CGHS, irrespective of whether they are residing in the city or not. Pensioners resident in areas not covered by CGHS are given a fixed medical allowance of Rs. 100 per month for meeting medical expenses that do not require hospitalization.

In 2000–01, the number of CGHS pensioners' cards was 171,746, and the number of beneficiaries 433,491, giving an average of 2.52 beneficiary per pensioner card holder. The number of serving CGHS cardholders in 2000–01 was 813,325, and the number of beneficiaries 34.77 lakhs, giving an average of 4.27 beneficiaries per serving CGHS card holder. Pension card holders are thus 17.4 per cent of the total number of CGHS card holders. Data on dependent parents of cardholders entitled to CGHS facilities are not available. If these are taken into account, the number of persons above 60 years covered by CGHS would be much larger. In 2003–04, the number of CGHS cardholders rose to 10.45 lakhs; the number of CGHS beneficiaries increased to 43.85 lakhs. Information on CGHS pensioner cards in 2003–04 is not available.

CGHS is a heavily subsidized health insurance scheme, and provides comprehensive health security to its members (serving employees and pensioners) for both out-patient and in-patient care. Retired persons represent a high risk category in insurance terms. Disease episodes are likely to be more frequent and chronic, which may require major surgical procedures and diagnostic treatments. There is no ceiling on the cost of treatment from a government hospital. Even for treatment from an empanelled hospital, a liberal ceiling has been provided for each episode. There is no ceiling on the total amount to which a pensioner will be entitled in his life time, including his spouse. CGHS is, therefore, completely different from a private insurance company, where the liability of the insurance company varies with the premium paid. It is an open-ended scheme for treatment (drugs, diagnostic tests, hospitalization, medical accessories and implants for both in patient and out-patient care) after the initial membership amount has been paid. CGHS thus provides a great relief for a retired person and his spouse. Escalating costs of medical care due to new techniques, new procedures and new medicine need not bother him. Private sector medical care centres recognized by CGHS have benefited from being entitled to treatment of CGHS beneficiaries (serving and retired).

CGHS covers all the members of the family of the cardholder, irrespective of the size, at no extra cost. Dependent parents of a serving employee can live away from the family and yet receive medical care at his place of stay. CGHS also covers widows getting family pension. Central government employees, who had retired early with a contributory provident fund benefit, are also entitled.

Increasing budgetary provisions in CGHS are an indication of the growing volume of medical care requirements for both serving and retired employees. The cost of medical care is rising fast as newer drugs, newer diagnostic tests and new surgical procedures enter the market. The number of pensioners is also increasing due to the higher volume of recruitments that took place in the 1960s and 1970s. The volume of expenditure on them is also increasing at a fast pace.

The revised estimate (RE) for CGHS increased from Rs.63.01 crores in 1990–91 to Rs.134.16 crores in 1995–96, Rs.263.50 crores in 2000–01, and Rs.407.14 crores in 2003–04. In other words, in a period of 13 years, RE increased by 546 per cent. For the last few years, expenditure on CGHS has far exceeded the budget estimate. In 2003–04, the B.E. was Rs.290.00 crores, whereas the R.E. was Rs.407.14 crores, an increase of Rs.117.14 crores or 40.4 per cent. In 2002–03, the B.E. was Rs.277.00 crores, while the R.E. was Rs.329.13 crores, an increase of Rs.52.13 crores or 18.8 per cent. The increase from 1998–99 may reflect, to some extent, the higher salary payment to medical manpower of CGHS dispensaries due to the recommendations of the Fifth Central Pay Commission (raising the salary scales of doctors and others). Other reasons are expansion of CGHS facilities, higher cost of medical care and the opening up of entitlement of CGHS beneficiaries to private medical care. Even in the earlier years, expenditure on CGHS exceeded the budget provision. Budget allocation for CGHS has to be seen in the context of the total budget of the health sector where the anticipated expenditure has been lower than the budget provision, some of it due to directives from the Ministry of Finance to reduce expenditure.

As the number of pensioners increases and the expenditure on medical care of CGHS pensioners goes up because of higher costs of treatment, the system will be unsustainable except at the cost of healthcare of the total population which includes a massive population of the elderly who urgently need subsidized secondary and tertiary healthcare facilities through a much larger public sector allocation. Successive governments have ignored the need to set a database on costs of healthcare of CGHS pensioners. It would be necessary, in the first instance, to segregate the cost of medical care (OPD, and hospitalization) for pensioners and others so that the total amount of subsidy paid can be known, and an insurance cost structure worked out accordingly. Expenditure on empanelled private medical care has to be monitored closely as there is a feeling that there is over-use of medical care because it brings in more profits to the hospital/ diagnostic centre. There have been reports of influence peddling by some private hospitals/laboratories/diagnostic centres so that more patients are referred for treatment, and of corrupt practices. It will be necessary to work out the right mix of CGHS as a provider of healthcare services and CGHS as a third party administrator which empanels private healthcare which dispenses services more cheaply than a government set up. The organizational structure of CGHS also needs a radical change. It should be transformed into a corporation to give it greater autonomy and flexibility to improve its efficiency. It should have its own balance sheet of income and expenditure, so that the extent of subsidy provided by the government can be known, and steps taken to reform the system. There has to be a balance between contribution by the members and the extent of benefit that can be availed.

(ii) *Employees' State Insurance Scheme:* For employees in the organized sector working in factories where 10 or more employees are employed in case power is used, and 20 or more employees in case power is not used, health insurance is provided under the provisions of the Employees' State Insurance Act, 1948. It is a compulsory health insurance scheme applicable to all workers drawing wages below Rs.7500 per month. State governments have been enabled by ESIC Act to extend the provisions to new classes of establishments employing 20 or more persons.

The Employees' State Insurance Scheme is administered by the Employees' State Insurance Corporation (ESIC), a statutory body. The Act began its operations in 1952, initially at Kanpur and Delhi. It has progressively extended its coverage and in March 2003, it had in its jurisdiction 687 industrial centres covering 2.54 lakh factories/establishments, and 70 lakh employees. The ESIC infrastructure operates in 25 states and Union Territories. Its infrastructure comprises of 142 hospitals, 43 annexes, 26.849 hospital beds, 1447 dispensaries, 6812 insurance medical officers and 2651 insurance medical practitioners. The number of beneficiaries covered by the scheme was 303.73 lakhs.

The scheme is financed mainly from contributions made by employers and the employees. Contribution made by employers is 4.75 per cent of the wages payable to employees. Contribution from employees is at the rate of 1.75 per cent of the wages payable to an employee. State Governments share expenditure on the provision of medical care, at least to the extent of 12.5 per cent.

From February 1991, medical benefit has been extended to retired insured persons and their spouses on attaining the age of superannuation, on an annual payment of Rs.1200. The number of superannuated members is about 5000. The reason why so few superannuated workers opt for medical services by ESIC despite the low cost of insurance, needs to be ascertained as they get the same medical care benefits as serving employees.

(iii) *Health Financing from Insurance Companies:* A number of insurance companies are offering coverage for healthcare, either as an exclusive policy or with other life insurance policies. In the public sector, the more prominent in the former category is that of Mediclaim offered by the four subsidiaries of the General Insurance Corporation, namely, National Insurance Corporation, Kolkata; New India Assurance Company, Mumbai; Oriental Insurance Company, New Delhi; and United India Insurance Company, Chennai. With the opening up of insurance to the private sector, private insurance companies are offering services similar to Mediclaim, some as a joint sector project with a foreign partner. Some of these policies have been described below. The products and packages change depending on the market conditions. Some polices are no longer taking fresh applications.

Mediclaim covers all age segments of the population, excepting the very old. It covers expenses, limited to the sum assured, for hospitalization/domiciliary hospitalization from a registered hospital as an in-patient. Certain conditions are excluded from the insurance cover such as pre-existing diseases at the time of proposing the insurance; hospitalization/ domiciliary hospitalization incurred during the first 30 days of the commencement of insurance etc. Certain specified diseases have been excluded.

The extent of insurance cover sought in Mediclaim can vary from Rs. 15,000 to Rs. 500,000. The policy can be taken for a year or for a shorter period. Persons aged above 85 years cannot be insured. For persons above 45 years of age who wish to take an insurance policy, medical tests have been prescribed to rule out persons who have some categories of ailments. The

premium schedule depends on the age of proposer. Age groups
have been divided into seven categories, viz., up to age 35
years, age 35–45 years, age 46–55 years, age 56–65 years, age
66–70 years, age 71–75 years and age 76–85 years. The higher
the age of the proposer, the larger is the premium. For instance,
for an insurance cover of Rs. 1 lakh (overall liability) the
insurance premium for a year would be Rs. 2191 if the policy
holder is 56–65 years of age, Rs. 2451 if he is 66–70 years of
age, Rs. 2626 if he is 71–75 years of age, and Rs. 3,250 if he is
76–85 years of age, plus service tax. The cover is only for the
person insured. If the spouse is to be covered, a separate
insurance has to be taken, following the same procedure.
However, a discount of 10 per cent is admissible in this case.
The sum assured under the policy increases by 5 per cent in
respect of each claim free year, subject to a maximum of 10
years. In view of the high-risk category of the very old, it is not
easy to get a medical insurance done, specially if one is over
65 years. Even for persons over 50 years, applicants are required
to give medical history for several ailments such as diabetes,
hypertension, heart disease and a few other diseases, and get
a medical certificate. They are not certain if they will get the
insurance cover unless the person been covered by the
company in the earlier years as well. Insurers follow the policy
of selective exclusion. They exercise the discretion to refuse a
policy to any individual. The policy holder, if he has no claim,
does not get back the premium paid. The payment is terminal
in character.

Earlier, for Mediclaim policies offered by the GIC chain,
insured persons were required first to pay for the expenses
incurred, and then claim reimbursement. This caused problems
as the person had to organize the cash for payment. He would
also not know whether the full amount will be paid, and the
time it would take for reimbursement. Due to competition from
private insurance companies who are promoting Mediclaim
as a cashless transaction for the insured, there has been a change
of procedure. The insured person is issued an identity card
and can get himself treated in a registered hospital/nursing
home as per his entitlement. The insurance company settles

the dues. Third party administrators (TPA) have been appointed by public insurance companies to settle claims with the hospital/nursing home, making it a cashless transaction. TPAs function as insurance intermediaries who administer the health plans of insurance companies. These provide a better service to customers and hopefully can reduce fraudulent claims. The cost on TPA is included in the insurance premium charged. Many clients have expressed dissatisfaction with TPAs as they feel that the objective is to reduce the cost of medical expenditure in an ailment as they work more for the interests of the company than the client. Some feel that there is an unwritten understanding with the empanelled doctors. Several persons in the middle age groups are classified in the high risk category so that the premium can be increased. Such medical reports are treated as confidential (De, 2005).

Some companies offer variants of Mediclaim. The New India Assurance Company offers health plus medical expenses policy which covers persons up to 70 years of age for reimbursement of medical expenses. Pre-existing ailments can be covered after completing four claim free continuous renewals.

The premium paid for Mediclaim by cheque is eligible for income tax benefit by the assessee by way of deduction from gross total income chargeable to tax, subject to a maximum of Rs.15,000 in a year for senior citizens aged 65 years and above (Section 80D), if the amount is paid out of income chargeable to tax. It is also permissible in case the spouse is a senior citizen. Assessees whose parents are senior citizens are also eligible. The tax payer can claim tax benefits for the premium paid for his parents.

Group Mediclaim policy is also available from the GIC stable for coverage of any group/association/corporate body of more than 50 persons. The insured person gets a group discount. Hence the premium paid is lower.

Some private insurance companies are now offering policies similar to Mediclaim. Royal Sundaram, for instance, provides 'cashless treatment' at 65 authorized hospitals in 6 cities, a 24 hours helpline and an ambulance referral facility at no additional cost to the policy holder. The policy can be taken by a person upto 75 years of age. A Health Shield Card is issued to the policy card holder. No payment of medical expenses is required to be made if it is as per entitlement. The policy is thus promoted as a 'hassle free' claim settlement. The expenses are settled by the company directly with the hospital. In case a person wants to go to any hospital other than network hospitals, a person will have to pay the bills and get it reimbursed. The policy holder is entitled to claim income tax benefit under section 80D. In-patient hospitalization has to be for more than 48 hours. Diseases contracted during the first 30 days of inception are excluded. Some other exclusions have also been listed.

The Cholamandalam Health Insurance Cover (Mediclaim) offers similar facilities covering hospitalization, surgical fees, consultancy fees, treatment facilities, medicines and other listed items of expenditure. Pre- and post-hospitalization expenses are also covered. With extra premiums, it covers local ambulance services and hospital daily allowance. A minimum of 24 hours hospitalization is required. Some exclusions have been listed. The maximum insurance age is 74 years. However, the general maximum age of entry is 56. For applicants aged 55 years and above, a medical certificate is required. The range of insurance cover (total insurance liability) varies from Rs.50,000 to Rs.10 lakhs. For a 'hassle free service' private insurance companies charge premiums which are higher than the GIC companies.

Mediclaim policies, whether by public sector undertakings or private insurance companies, have to be taken every year following the same procedure. They are directed mainly to the middle and upper class. While the upper insurable age limit of 75 or 80 years has been prescribed, conditions of medical fitness increase as the age goes up, virtually leaving out many persons. The policy covers only hospitalization (including domiciliary hospitalization) expenses. Older persons who have chronic ailments or sicknesses, which do not require hospitalization, have to get themselves treated on their own.

A policy somewhat similar to Mediclaim is Tertiary Care Insurance offered by New India Assurance, a public sector undertaking, for expenses arising from hospitalization/ domiciliary hospitalization in respect of nine major ailments (nephritis requiring kidney transplantation; cerebral or vascular strokes; open and close heart surgery; malignancy disease; encephalitis; neuro-surgery; total replacement of joints; liver disorder and grievous injury). The policy provides for reimbursement of expenses incurred in a recognized hospital/ nursing home and covers room/boarding expenses, nursing fees, surgical fees, consultancy fees, medicines, investigations, cost of pace maker, dialysis, chemo-therapy, artificial limbs, cost of organs, etc. The ceiling for reimbursement is the sum assured. Some exemptions for claims have been made as, for instance, pre-existing ailment conditions, ailment contracted within the first 30 days of commencement of the policy, etc. The insurance is available to persons between the age of 5 years and 75 years. A rebate of 10 per cent is given if the spouse is also insured. The sum assured is progressively increased by 5 per cent in respect of each claim free year, subject to the maximum accumulation of 50 per cent. The application has to be submitted with specified medical reports and a certificate that the person is free from all the nine major ailments proposed for insurance under this policy.

The sum assured can be from Rs.50,000 to Rs.500,000. The tenure of the policy can be for a year, or for 5 or 10 years. For the annual policy, the upper age limit for joining is between age 71 to 75 years, for the five years policy, the upper age limit is between age 66 to 70 years, and for the 10 years policy, the upper age limit is between age 61 to 65 years. In other words, a person above age 75 years is not insurable for the annual policy, above age 70 years for the five years policy, and above age 65 years for the ten years policy.

The premium paid depends on the sum assured and the age at which the policy is taken. The older the person, the higher is the premium schedule. For instance, for a five years tertiary care insurance policy for an insurance cover of Rs.500,000, persons of age group 66–70 have to pay a premium which is more than twice the premium paid by a person below 40 years. Unlike the premium paid for Mediclaim insurance, the premium paid for tertiary care insurance policy is not eligible for income tax benefit under section 80 D of the Income Tax Act. There is also no return of the money paid as premium, even if no claims have been made. It is thus similar to the Mediclaim policy.

The Jan Arogya Bima Policy is meant to cover the financial liability for hospitalization and domiciliary hospitalization expenses for illnesses contracted. The sum assured is only Rs. 5,000 per person. It thus covers persons of modest income. It has most of the features of the Mediclaim policy in regard to the expenses for which a claim can be made. Pre-existing diseases prior to the date of insurance, and some ailments listed, are not covered. Ailments have to occur after the first 30 days of the date of insurance (except in the case of accidents). Persons from age 5 and upto 70 years can be insured. The policy is issued for one year. The premium rate varies with the age of the person, which has been divided into four groups, viz., up to age 45 years, age 46-55 years, age 56-65 years and age 66-70 years. For persons of age 56-65 years, the annual premium is Rs. 120, while for a person of age 66-70, it is Rs. 140. For the spouse, the rate is the same. The policy is issued for a period of one year and is subject to review if it is to be renewed. Like Mediclaim, in the case of this policy, too, there is no refund, even if no claim for reimbursement has been made.

The Critical Illness Policy offered by the National Insurance Company Limited is meant for individuals between 21 and 65 years of age. The premium for the policy depends on the age of the person, and the sum assured which ranges between Rs. 5 lakhs and Rs. 25 lakhs. The premium is higher for males than females. It is a benefit policy and not a reimbursement cover. Six critical ailments are covered by the policy: (i) Coronary Artery Surgery; (ii) Renal failure; (iii) Stroke; (iv) Multiple sclerosis; (v) Major organ transplant, and (vi) Cancer (malignant). For making a claim, the critical illnesses have to be diagnosed by a registered medical practioner, supported by evidence. The insured person needs to survive for 30 successive days after the diagnosis of critical illness. If the critical illness incepts or manifests itself within the first 90 days of the policy period, no claim is permissible.

Asha Deep II policy of LIC covers the risk of four major ailments: (i) malignant cancer; (ii) paralytic stroke leading to permanent disability, (iii) renal failure of both kidneys; (iv) coronary artery diseases. The policy can be taken by a person in the age group 18 to 50 years for terms of 15, 20 or 25 years. The maximum age at maturity has been fixed at 65 years. Thus no person above 50 years can take the policy. The minimum sum assured under the scheme is Rs.50,000 and the maximum is Rs.3 lakhs. The amount of premium paid varies with the age of the policy holder and the term. If, during the term of the policy, the insured person has been affected by any of the ailments mentioned above, the following benefits are available: (i) Immediate payment of 50 per cent of the sum assured is paid. The benefit is fixed irrespective of the expenses incurred. The policy is thus a benefit plan to take care of medical expenses, and is not a reimbursement, as in the case of Mediclaim; (ii) There is a waiver of subsequent premiums falling due from the policy; (iii) There is also payment of an amount equal to 10 per cent of the sum assured every year commencing from the policy anniversary; (iv) Payment will also be made of the balance of 50 per cent of the sum assured and vested bonuses (on the full sum assured) on the date of maturity or on death of the life assured, which ever is earlier. A lien for a period of one year from the date of inception of the policy has been kept. Asha Deep II is thus different from Mediclaim policies in that the payment is not terminal in character. It has a longer duration. It covers, however, only specific diseases. The person taking the policy can, if there are no claims, get back the amount paid along with the bonuses.

LIC's Jeevan Asha II provides insurance coverage to persons between 18 and 50 years of age. The maximum age at maturity is 65 years. The sum assured can vary from Rs.50,000 to Rs.300,000. The policy tenure can be for a period of 15, 20 or 25 years. Jeevan Asha II is a benefit policy and not reimbursement of expenses incurred. The policy holder will be eligible for 20 per cent or 50 per cent of the sum assured, depending on whether the surgery is categorized as minor or major. The benefit will be paid only once during the term of the policy. However, if the first claim is towards a minor surgical procedure, the policy holder will be eligible for another benefit towards surgical procedure (as specified) during the term of the policy. The policy holder can choose between two types of survival benefits. He can receive 2 per cent of the sum assured at the end of every second year or he may get an enhanced lump sum benefit towards any health emergency at a later date. On maturity, the policy holder will get the sum assured plus additions. Loyalty addition will be paid after deduction of survival benefit/surgical procedures.

While the earlier policies were intended to meet expenses of the insured person at any period of life, the Bhavishya Arogya Insurance Scheme offered by the National Insurance Company is intended to take care at a later period of life by paying premium during the working life of the person. The applicant is required to be in the age group 25 to 55 years. The premium paid varies with the age of entry. The selected age of retirement can be between 55 and 60 years. The maximum total benefit available is Rs.50,000 commencing from the retirement age, and will not exceed Rs.20,000 from any one illness or injury. The scheme does not call for pre-insurance medical examination. Medical expenses are reimbursed subject to the ceiling prescribed for hospitalization/domestic hospitalization. Some exclusion clauses have been specified. Refund of premium on death, or voluntary withdrawal before commencement of risk, is permissible.

The Unit Trust of India offered the Senior Citizens' Unit Plan (SCUP) to take care of medical expenses in old age. Persons in their working life (21 to 55 years) contribute to SCUP. Members will be entitled to a benefit cover of Rs.2.5 lakhs, starting from the age of 58 years. The spouse of the person is also covered under the scheme, without any additional payment. After the age of 61 years, the policy holder (and his spouse) will be eligible for a cover up to Rs.5 lakhs, after adjusting for claims made earlier. The SCUP member can avail of medical treatment from authorized hospitals in different cities. An identity certificate has been issued. No direct payment has to be made by the policy holder. The minimum one time investment varies with age. At age 21 years it is Rs.2500 while at age 55 years it is Rs.38,000. SCUP has been introduced in collaboration with the New India Assurance Company. Members of SCUP, on making a one time investment, will thus have the benefit of medical treatment (self and wife) on completion of 58 years of his age. SCUP covers only hospitalization. There is a limit of Rs.1.50 lakhs per illness. After the commencement of medical benefit cover, bonus at 5 per cent will be added for every claim free year. The bonus will be added to the sum insured for subsequent years. For joining SCUP, no medical examination is necessary. After the age of 61 years, the member may prefer to withdraw the total amount outstanding in his name. The medical benefit will, however, continue as long as he lives. No new members are now being made members of SCUP.

With private insurance companies entering the market, a number of life/endowment insurance policies are being offered with riders on healthcare (ICICI Prudential, SBI Life, Birla Sun Life, Tata AIG, to mention a few). The health riders cover the risks for specified critical illnesses, major surgical procedures and disability. An added premium is charged for these riders. A medical examination is necessary. Rider benefits are not payable to the policy holder during the first six months (or as may be specified in the policy). Some exclusion clauses are also indicated. In case of illnesses specified by the policy, the sum assured in the rider is paid as soon as the disease has been identified, making it a benefit policy rather than reimbursement of expenses. Private insurance companies are aggressively marketing their products with sophisticated publicity and specially trained agents who can market their products. The policies cater to the middle and upper classes.

Peerless General Finance and Investment Company offered for some time free critical illness benefits with a three years multi-protector fixed deposit scheme (Rs.15,000/Rs.25,000/Rs.40,000/Rs.50,000). For a fixed deposit of Rs.50,000 for three years, for instance, the free critical insurance benefit is of Rs.100,000 (only one claim), for the tenure of the certificate. Five critical illnesses have been covered, viz. paralytic stroke, cancer, renal failure, major organ transplant, coronary artery disease. These are diseases which primarily affect the old. Accidental injuries are also covered. The maximum age limit for taking up the scheme is 62 years at age of entry. Diseases which pre-exist are not covered. Some other conditions have also been prescribed. On maturity, the depositor receives 6 per cent as interest, compounded annually. A maturity value of 4 per cent has been added. The company has tied up with IFFCO-TOKIO General Insurance Company for administering the critical illness coverage provided by the scheme.

Health insurance in India covers mainly the organized sector or self-employed persons in the middle and upper income segments. In the case of the Central Government Health Scheme for government employees, it is heavily subsidized by the government. For employees covered by ESIC, workers and employers contribute to its funding. Retired workers covered by ESIC comprise a small number. Workers in most quasi-government undertakings, on retirement, get medical cover either free or at a low cost. Some individuals on their own go for policies which give them coverage in old age. These are available only for ailments which require hospitalization. For non-hospital care, they have to depend on their own.

Most Indians are not insurance minded, not even the middle classes, and certainly not the lower income groups. They have long lived on political promises to get free medical care from the public sector. This is no longer feasible, given the inflationary cost of medical care, with newer medicines and procedures making their entry in the healthcare market. The attitude has to change as health insurance is about risk sharing. Insured persons, unfortunately, feel that if they have not fallen ill and have not taken the medical service for which they have paid, they have suffered a loss, little realizing that it is the risk that is being covered. The policy holders should, in fact, feel better off that they are in good health and did not take recourse to treatment.

Health insurance for the old in India is an unchartered territory. It is a high risk category and can be sustained only if all age groups are covered. There is clearly a case where government has to play a major role in providing health insurance to all persons, including the old, at an affordable cost by subsidizing the cost of the programme. There is an existence for a long time in the developed countries insurance packages which get state subsidy. Persons pay for health insurance throughout their working life, and get benefits in old age as well (subject to a ceiling). Several healthcare packages can be offered with different rates of premium and entitlement. A ceiling on free healthcare to the very poor can be prescribed, above which affordable user charges should be levied, depending on the socio-economic situation. The government cannot rest assured on the fact that it exists only to look after its own retired employees, providing benefits without a ceiling. It has talked about health insurance but has done little to implement it. The National Health Policy, 1983 spoke of the need for health insurance schemes in different states, with the community sharing the cost of services "in keeping with its paying capacity". No progress has, however, been made. The new National Health Policy, 2002 speaks of encouraging private insurance instruments for increasing the scope of secondary and tertiary sector services under private health insurance packages. For the poor, it mentions of a social health insurance scheme 'funded by the government, and with service delivery through the private sector', and visualizes the starting of a pilot scheme. The scheme is yet to make a beginning

The Finance Minister, in his budget speech of 2003, had indicated the starting of a community based universal health insurance scheme in 2003-04. Under the scheme, a premium equivalent of Re. one per day (Rs. 365 in a year) for an individual, Rs. 1.50 per day for a family of five, and Rs. 2 per day for a family of seven, will give the person eligibility for reimbursement of medical expenses upto Rs. 30,000 for treatment in a hospital. The scheme also provides insurance coverage of Rs. 25,000 in case of death due to accident, and compensation due to loss of earning at the rate of Rs. 50 per day, upto a maximum of 15 days. In order to make the scheme affordable to below poverty line families, the government will contribute Rs. 100 per year towards the annual premium. In other words, for every Rs. 365/Rs. 548/Rs. 730 given by a family (depending on number of members covered), the government will contribute Rs. 100. Details on progress of the scheme are not yet known.

Summing Up

Expectation of life at age 60 is a good summative indicator of health status of old persons. During the period 1995–99, the expectation of life at age 60 was 16.7 years, and at age 70 it was 11.0 years. Females have a higher life expectancy than males. In urban areas, too, life expectancy is higher than in rural areas. Among the states, Punjab, Kerala and Haryana have the highest life expectancy at age 60. Distribution of deaths by age group indicates that in 2000, 39.6 per cent of the deaths were at age group 60 years and above. The age specific death rates have come down. In 2000, it was 23.1 in the age group 60–64 years, 38.0 in the age group 65–69 years, and 99.8 in the age group 70 years and above. It was higher among males, and among persons resident in rural areas.

The annual survey of causes of death in rural areas by the Registrar General had indicated that among older persons, the largest percentage of ailments were due to diseases of the respiratory system (pneumonia, bronchitis, asthma etc.), followed by diseases of the circulatory system (heart diseases etc.). Other major causes were paralytic stroke, cancer, tuberculosis, diabetes, acute abdominal diseases, uraemia and ulcer. A higher incidence of dementia, psychiatric morbidity and physical disability have also been reported. Many ailments are multiple in nature, and require long time treatment, higher costs, and facilities of secondary and tertiary care. A survey carried out by NSSO in 1995–96 found a much higher degree of morbidity among the old compared to other age segments in both rural and urban areas. Nearly half the population of persons aged 60 years and above have some chronic disease. However, a rather small percentage can afford treatment. The old also suffer from malnutrition arising from deficiencies in calories, proteins and micro-nutrients. A survey on disability by NSSO in 1995–96 showed 40 per cent of persons aged 60 years and above in rural areas and 35 per cent in urban areas to have some kind of disability. The incidence was higher among females.

Public sector healthcare system is unable to cope with the need for services for the old, the bulk of whom are in the low income category. The quality of care is poor, particularly for the population living in rural areas where health services are very indifferent. Rural poor old do not survive for long because of poor access. Most ailments are untreated or poorly treated, often in the hands of quacks. They are conditioned to treat their ill-health and suffering as matters of destiny. Secondary and tertiary care facilities are unavailable to most, particularly in backward areas. Even where they exist, access is constrained by poor functioning. Grants need to be given to hospitals to constitute a separate Welfare Fund for treating very poor 'patients. Hospices have to be set up for the chronically ill. Outreach services for rural areas, including mobile vans, ambulances and camps have to be a part of the healthcare system. Given the fiscal health of the states and the growing population of older persons, the gap between demand and supply is increasing. NGO activity, though useful, is rather limited and aims mainly at primary healthcare. Some organizations hold camps for cataract surgery, while some extend mobile services for treatment of persons living in remote and backward rural areas and towns, either free or at a subsidized cost. Non-governmental organizations providing healthcare have to be promoted and assisted, with both capital costs and recurring expenditure for extending affordable not-for-profit healthcare services, and complement the efforts of the state.

Training of medical and paramedical personnel in geriatric care needs to be provided. Private sector diagnostic facilities and treatment cost much more, specially since some diseases require a longer period of treatment. Many ailments of the old, therefore, remain untreated or partially treated. The richer segments of the population and government pensioners have benefited from the expansion of hospitals in the private sector. Affordable healthcare will not be possible for a large number of old persons unless suitable institutional arrangements are made. The advances in medical science will thus continue to be beyond the reach of many.

Health insurance covers only a small segment of the Indian population, mainly in urban areas. Some are individual arrangements with insurance companies, while others are based on arrangements made by the employers. Some schemes collect the prepaid premium and themselves provide the services; some have an arrangement through private medical care providers, while some offer a combination of both. The best insurance scheme from the point of view of the client is the Central Government Health Scheme which provides highly subsidized healthcare to its employees, including the pensioners. Workers in the organized sector of industry drawing less than Rs. 7500 per month, and covered by the Employees' State insurance Corporation, get benefits after retirement, on an annual payment of Rs. 1200. However, not many opt for such a scheme. A number of insurance companies offer health coverage to the general public, either as an exclusive policy or as a rider with life insurance policies. Prominent among these are Mediclaim and critical illness policies which cover hospitalization expenses only for the individual insured. Some policies enable persons in their working life to pay premium for coverage of illnesses in old age. With private insurance companies entering the market, a large variety of healthcare options are being offered, including payment of a fixed amount when a critical illness has been identified, rather than as a reimbursement for hospital expenses.

The goal in the coming decades is to add life to the extended years. The concept of healthy ageing has to be promoted. Preventive healthcare has to be the goal. The importance of healthy and nutritious diets, physical exercise, reduction of stress, meditation, yoga, allocation of time for rest and relaxation have to be incorporated in the life style of the elderly. Old persons need to understand and appreciate that diseases do not automatically emerge at a particular age. On the other hand, preventive healthcare and early diagnosis can help the person stay healthy.

The performance of the public sector in providing healthcare has been very poor. The government is shying away from its responsibility of expanding and augmenting the services at primary, secondary and tertiary levels of care. It is not providing enough budget for expanding and upgrading healthcare. Subsidized healthcare has to be provided to the bulk of the population. The government cannot rest assured by the fact that it exists only to look after its own employees and let the public suffer due to paucity of funds. The poor levels of existing healthcare services need drastic reforms in organization, structure and management. The government has, without saying so in an explicit manner, left healthcare to the market forces which affects the poor the most. It has to play a major role in developing comprehensive health insurance packages for both inpatient and outpatient care at an affordable cost by subsidizing the programme. In most countries of the world, including the developed ones, insurance packages provide wide coverage through state subsidy. This has to be the policy for this country as well.

4

Security of Family Care and Shelter

A caring family, and a shelter which is comfortable, safe and secure is needed by all persons, more so by children, women and the elderly. Hindu scriptures ordained that a son owes three types of debts, one of the three being towards his parents/ ancestors, the other two debts being towards teachers/seers (*rishis*), and towards gods (*daiva*). Other religions, too, prescribed moral and religious obligations of sons to look after and care for parents. The prescribed norm for all religious faiths was an age integrated society.

In earlier times, society and economy were interwined. Property and assets of production were jointly owned. Every person was looked after according to needs. The old were not considered a liability or a burden; they were assigned roles consistent with their age and capacity. They were fewer in number and lived for a much shorter period because of lower life expectancy. Norms for the care of the old were reinforced by kinship, caste and village community which gave an unwritten but strong moral sanction of the responsibility of sons to look after their parents. Sons viewed it stigmatic and loss of face if they were seen by their kinship and caste group as uncaring.

Ownership and management of financial assets and property helped to keep the family together and ensure security to the old. Persons who distribute their property or financial assets to their children during their life time become vulnerable. NSSO, in its 52nd Round in 1995–96, investigated the number of persons having financial assets and property by sex in rural and urban areas. It also inquired into the management of these assets, management being defined as 'involvement in making decisions to change the portfolio of assets held, or to convert its form'. It found that nearly half of the aged had financial assets in rural areas; about the same percentage had financial assets in urban areas. Sixty-three per cent of the aged in rural areas owned property; in urban areas, the percentage was 58. Far more aged males than females owned financial assets. The same was true in the case of ownership of property. Conflicts in the family due to incompatible personalities, sharing of household duties or utilization of income prompts the head of the family to divide the assets during his life time even though it means increase of their vulnerability in old age. A micro study in rural Karnataka pointed out that the decision to divide the property was also influenced by economic reasons — the policy of the state government that subsidies, credit and other benefits will be given to farmers with smaller holdings (Gurumurthy, 1998).

Changes in family structure and composition, which became more visible in the second half of the twentieth century, began to make a dent in the traditional living and caring arrangements of older persons. Informal support from children or close family members, which old persons believed as their natural right, ordained by religion, tradition and custom, was getting eroded by a number of circumstances affecting the modern family. Its size, composition and structure were also under stress. To a large extent, these were influenced by social and economic circumstances facing the family which affected their ability to cope with the problems of care, and that too for a longer period.

In the past, stability of the family arose from the low rate of migration and the joint holding of property. Changes in sources of livelihood of earning members have meant that the family is no longer the unit of production and sustenance. Employment opportunities outside the family are providing some degree of autonomy in decision making and in migration to other places. Career ambitions of women, and employment outside the home, has meant less time for care giving when parents/grandparents are not physically capable of looking after themselves. Families are, thus, increasingly splitting into households, depending on the location of jobs.

Change in technology and modes of production for improving productivity in agriculture and allied activities, and in the new job opportunities that are available, has meant that the oral tradition of knowledge and knowhow in production and economic activities has become less relevant, and sons need to look to lateral sources of information. Decision making powers are thus shifting to the younger generation.

Demographic transition has meant that there are fewer children in the family to take care of older members. The number of persons aged 60 years and above (notional age for retirement) per 1000 persons in the working age group 15–59 years has shown an increase. Caring for the old has meant more responsibility for one or two sons to look after old parents, and for a much longer life span. In some cases, disability and infirmity of old parents are likely to cause a greater stress on care givers.

Throughout the world, females have been the primary care givers, more so in the case of developing countries where care in the family has been the predominant pattern. Table 4.1 gives the ratio of care receivers to care givers (females aged 15–54 years) in India. Two age groups of care receivers have been chosen, viz., persons aged 65 years and above, and persons aged 70 years and above. These are average figures but give the trends. The data shows that the number of care receivers per 1000 care givers will increase in the coming decades. Figure 4.1 gives the pattern in graphic form.

Table 4.1: Number of care receivers (persons aged 65 years and above/persons aged 70 years and above) per 1000 care givers (females aged 15–49 years), India, 1961 to 2050

Ratio	1961	1971	1981	1991	2001	2010	2020	2030	2040	2050
(65+/15–49) *1000	134	152	163	171	195	224	276	367	481	615
(70+/15–49) *1000	86	94	101	106	117	137	167	229	314	410

Source: **Based on Census of India; UN World Population Prospects, the 2002** Revision.

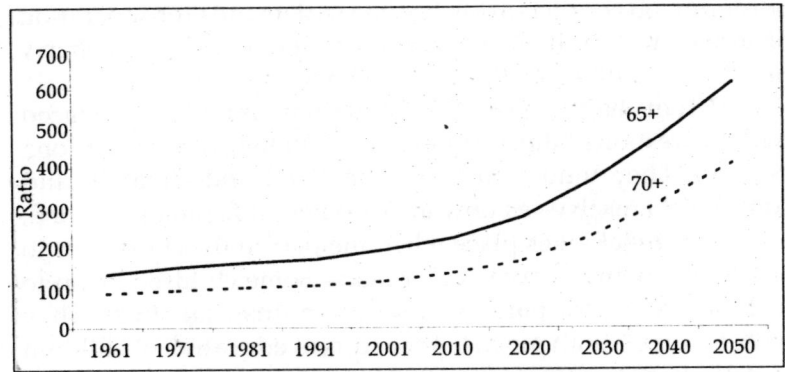

Figure 4.1: Number of care receivers (persons aged 65+/70+) per 1000 care givers (females aged 15–49 years), India, 1961 to 2050

Increase in urban rents and shortage of accommodation has made it difficult for large families to live together. Space has become a problem. As a value, sharing of space among family members is declining. Privacy is becoming important. Space for children is often accorded a higher priority than space for parents. Some families have found a more convenient arrangement by which parents look after the traditional dwellings and some family assets, as children migrate and provide remittances to sustain their financial needs.

A transition from family values to individual values and perpetuation of self is becoming apparent due to the impact of education, urbanization and industrialization, and exposure to western life styles. Difference in inter-generation values, attitudes and modes of social behaviour and levels of education can cause embarrassment in interaction of parents with the social circle of friends and acquaintances of children, specially in the case of those who are ambitious and would like to achieve through adopting a different life style. The social circle of children may not blend with the life style of their parents. Children and families are thus not fully integrated even when there is co-residence. Incompatible personalities of mother-in-law and daughter-in-law, and strong differences in attitude towards family norms and traditions lead to conflicts and tensions and adversely affects cordial living. There is less time spent on family interactions. Inter-generation disagreements, bordering on conflicts arise, leading to demands for separation of assets and split in the family, specially when property prices/value of agricultural land shoot up.

Parents begin to feel that children do not like to be faced with the responsibilities of looking after older parents for long periods. They tend to feel marginalized and isolated, and consider themselves as unwanted. When ill-feeling is created, a sense of relief takes place when the person dies or moves to an old age home or some other place. Some children begin to feel that caring for parents can cause a financial stress. They have to put up with much higher costs of education of children and their entertainment which has to be traded off with expenses on care of parents. Assuring parents of the same standard of living as the sons are often seen as competing propositions by the son and his immediate family.

At times, problems arise because older persons are not inclined to go through a slow process of transition which implies role modification and role adjustments. These are natural processes of family dynamics. Parents who are able to adjust find their stay in the family as more meaningful and less stressful.

Most vulnerable in terms of family care and shelter are single widowed females, handicapped females, deserted females and single unmarried persons, as very few people now are willing to take care of relatives other than immediate family members. Their problems are further aggravated when they have no assets, and no sources of income. Also vulnerable are the old living in very poor households, for whom caring for an extra dependant means further stress on their depleted resources. Some sons find themselves helpless because of unemployment, physical handicaps and loss of livelihood. Poverty tends to become an important factor when family resources are very fragile.

Some sons would like to forget the love, care, attention of parents during their growing years and the investments they have made on their education in the hope that in their twilight years they would be taken care of. They would like to ascribe the role of parents as duty towards their children, a one way traffic. They do not consider duties towards parents as their filial obligation. To an extent, this is a reflection of the child-centered way in which parents bring up children, without instilling the values of integration of roles and responsibilities between different generations. Some sons would like to avoid the botheration to look after parents for long periods.

Several patterns have emerged in the care taken by sons of their parents, even when they have the means. If parents have more than one son, they are seen to share the responsibility by rotating them between the sons, even if it means that they do not have a fixed abode. Another arrangement is that one son looks after one parent, while the other son looks after the other, by turn, without bothering about their feelings and the psycho-social anxiety it creates when parents in old age are made to live separately. If the sons are located in the same house owned by parents but have separate households, they would still like the parents to make their own arrangements, or take turns in providing meals. In either of the above arrangements, there is little intra-family interaction; parents become isolated and lonely. If the parents do not own a house, and the living arrangements become humiliating and intolerant, they would be forced to opt for old age homes, not a very happy alternative in the twilight of their lives. Migrant sons living abroad, if they are unable to bring the parents to live with them for financial reasons, visa restrictions, temporary period of stay or excessive costs of healthcare, but are conscious of their responsibilities, make arrangements in old age homes in India on payment of maintenance and other expenses. In a growing number of cases, daughters provide emotional support and act as a watchdog, if the sons deviate from the responsibility, or have migrated to some other country but do not send remittances. In some cases, a widowed parent is accommodated in the daughter's household when it is nuclear in character, and the son-in-law agrees to such an arrangement because his parents are in the native village and do not plan to come to stay with him. Such an arrangement cuts across different income segments; it does, however, create tensions as the arrangement is against the social norm, and the widowed parent treats co-residence as the last resort.

Despite the changing social structure, which has made family care vulnerable for some parents, family bonds in India are still quite strong. A large number of families are often guided by their own values and sentiments. Old persons, who are physically capable, continue to be economically active, play a role in social, religious and family matters, and do a wide variety of household chores. A large number continue to share expenditure in running the household. Working women find it useful when old parents living with them share household responsibilities. There is thus a two way transfer of supportive roles, a reciprocal relationship. The National Sample Survey, in its 52nd Round conducted in 1995–96 on the profile of older persons, found that more than three-fourths persons aged 60 years and above in both rural and urban areas made a contribution in performing household chores (NSSO, 1998). Some empirical studies have shown that when sons migrate to another place for work, they often leave their wives and children in the protective custody of their parents (Gulati, 1998).

The National Sample Survey, 1995–96 has indicated the living arrangements of persons aged 60 years and above in rural and urban areas. The data given in Table 4.2 shows that

Table 4.2: Per 1000 distribution of persons aged 60 years and above by type of living arrangements in rural and urban areas, India, 1995–96

Type of living arrangement	Rural			Urban		
	Male	*Female*	*Person*	*Male*	*Female*	*Person*
Living alone	25	61	43	30	60	45
Living with spouse only	137	77	107	103	57	80
Living with spouse and other members	613	313	462	648	297	469
Living without spouse but with children	179	481	331	178	512	349
Living without spouse but with other relations	34	55	44	30	59	45
Living without spouse with non-relations	4	4	4	5	6	6
Not recorded	8	10	9	6	9	8
Total	1000	1000	1000	1000	1000	1000

Source: NSSO: The Aged in India, 52nd Round, July 1995 to June 1996.

the two predominant categories of living arrangements of older persons are 'living with spouse and other members', followed by 'living without spouse but with children'. A number of micro-studies have also reported residence of older persons with their children as the predominant form (Dandekar, 1996; Gurumurthy, 1998). Almost the same percentage of old persons in both rural and urban areas live with spouse/without spouse and other members. More females than males live without spouse because a larger percentage have a widowed status. About 4 per cent persons in rural areas and about the same percentage in urban areas live alone, which includes those in old age homes. The 2001 census too, reported that about 4 per cent old persons lived alone; also more females than males lived alone. A study in rural Maharashtra in the early 1990s, for instance, indicated that 4 per cent of elderly males and 14 per cent of elderly females were living alone. A large percentage of persons who lived alone moved to an old age home when they were unable to maintain themselves. Of the 541 inmates interviewed in 19 old age homes (rural and urban), 36 per cent reported that they were living alone before moving to the home (Dandekar, 1996). Surprisingly, more women than men live alone in both rural and urban areas.The NSSO survey found that Tamil Nadu had a rather high frequency in this category, followed by Andhra Pradesh. Another survey covering about 1600 elderly persons in rural Tamil Nadu in the 1970s found 16 per cent living alone (7 per cent male elderly and 24 per cent female elderly). They were mostly widowed or divorced (Nair, 1980). More women lived alone as they were widowed or had children who lived away because of inability to adjust with the son's family, making her feel unwanted, and a liability. About 11 per cent in rural areas and 8 per cent in urban areas live with their spouse. Other micro-studies conducted in rural areas, too, have indicated a growing number of aged persons living alone or with spouse only (Dandekar, 1996; Gurumurthy, 1998; Panda, 1998). The percentages living with spouse were 17 per cent in the case of male elderly, and 10 in the case of female elderly. Some are childless. A small percentage are unmarrried. A study of 541 inmates of old age homes in Maharashtra indicated that 51 per cent had no children. Living alone or with spouse has a different context in rural areas as compared to urban areas. In rural areas, family members/extended family members are often in the same village/adjacent village, and help is often received at times of need. The caste and kin groups keep social interaction alive. If the categories 'living alone' and 'living with spouse' are taken together, the NSSO survey has shown that about 15 per cent aged persons in rural areas and 12.5 per cent in urban areas are living by themselves. About four per cent of old persons live with non-relations, who are known to them. They usually contribute to the households where they live in cash or kind. A micro-study in rural Karnataka found that a living arrangement with non-relations arose because of absence of family members, quarrels with sons/daughters, or because they were needed in the family where they were staying, indicating a mutual benefit (Gurumurthy, 1998).

The inter-state variations in persons aged 60 years and above living alone or with spouse in rural and urban areas is given in Table 4.3. The data shows that Jammu and Kashmir has the lowest percentage of such persons in both rural and urban areas, while Tamil Nadu has the highest percentage.

Since children are, normatively, the main source of support of elderly persons, NSSO investigated the number of living sons and daughters of persons aged 60 years and above. Table 4.4 gives the position. More than half the number of elderly persons have 4 or more children. It would be worth investigating whether presence of more children could lead to better care due to shared responsibility, and better options on the part of the parents. Some researchers have indicated that having a smaller number of children permits the elderly to provide for their education and training so that they can earn better and have the means to support their parents (Dandekar, 1996; Gurumurthy, 1998). Only about 6 per cent elderly persons in rural and urban areas have no surviving child. They have to be on their own in old age, or depend on other family members. Persons who have surviving children but have no sons have often to sustain on their own savings and assets in old age.

Some micro studies have shown that a small percentage of widowed mothers or fathers live with their married or widowed daughters even though this is not the social norm (Dandekar, 1996; Gulati, 1998; Gurumurthi, 1998; Nair, 1980; Panda, 1998).

Table 4.3: Per 1000 distribution of persons aged 60 years and above living either alone or with only spouse in rural and urban areas in states, 1995–96.

Rural/ Urban	Per 1000 distribution of persons aged 60+ living alone or with only spouse				
	< 50	50–99	100–149	150–199	200 & above
Rural	Jammu & Kashmir (36)	Assam (59) Haryana (75)	Kerala (102) Karnataka (106) Punjab (116) West Bengal (118) Uttar Pradesh. (128) Bihar (131) Madhya Pradesh (133)	INDIA (150) Rajasthan (153) Orissa (160) Himachal Pradesh (166) Gujarat (168) Maharashtra (185)	Andhra Pradesh (234) Tamil Nadu (312)
Urban	Jammu & Kashmir (43)	Assam (70) Bihar (73) Kerala (75) West Bengal (76) Karnataka (89) Himachal Pradesh (94)	Gujarat (106) Orissa (112) Madhya Pradesh (117)- Mahara shtra (118) Andhra Pradesh (147) INDIA (125) Uttar Pradesh (148)	Punjab (166) Rajasthan (168) Haryana (184) Tamil Nadu (197)	

Source: NSSO: The Aged in India, 52nd Round, July 1995 to June 1996.

Table 4.4: Per 1000 distribution of persons aged 60 years and above by surviving children, India, 1995–96

Rural/Urban	Number of living sons and daughters							
	None	1	2	3	4	5	6 & others	Total
Rural	58	71	113	173	173	168	243	1000
Urban	59	79	112	179	181	157	232	1000

Source : NSSO: The Aged in India, 52nd Round, July 1995 to June 1996.

Security of Shelter

The concept of shelter goes far beyond a roof and four walls to provide protection against adverse climatic conditions. It implies the availability of good ventilation, proper circulation of air and sunshine, absence of insanitary, unhealthy and polluting conditions, and access to basic community and social services. Housing includes, in addition to dwelling rooms, provision of kitchen, toilet facilities, electricity, safe drinking water, and sewerage and drainage connections. Shelter thus holds the key to a secure physical and social environment in which normal household activities can be efficiently carried out.

Ownership of a dwelling confers socio-economic status to the person, and assurance of a safe and secure living in old age. It is considered a big achievement and requires organizing and managing the financial and manpower resources required, but also blessings of divine powers. Construction of the house is associated with the performance of a number of rituals at all stages, from selection of a plot to a house warming ceremony.

Separate data on housing situation of the elderly is not available. The general picture is given by census authorities. The data in Table 4.5 shows that in rural areas, 94 per cent houses were owned. In urban areas, the percentage of households owning houses increased from 46 per cent in 1961 to 67 per cent in 2001. Ownership of a house does not imply that the older person and/or his spouse would continue to occupy the same space as he did in his active years. They often have to make way for other members of the family.

Table 4.5: Distribution per 1000 households by tenure status,
India, 1961 to 2001

Year	Rural		Urban	
	Owned	*Rented*	*Owned*	*Rented*
1961	936	64	462	538
1971	938	62	471	529
1981	930	70	535	465
1991	945	40	631	341
2001	944	36	668	285

Note: In 1991, a new category of 'others' was added. This category has not been included here. The category includes households who live in rent free accommodation or in houses where ownership either of the land or the structure does not belong to the household. In the 2001 census, 21 households in rural areas and 41 households in urban areas per 1000 households belonged to this category.

Source: Census of India, 1991, 2001.

The 2001 census has assessed the quality of housing in rural and urban areas for residential use. It found that the quality of 50.4 per cent households was good (45 per cent in rural areas, 64.2 per cent in urban areas), 44.1 per cent were livable (48.7 per cent in rural areas and 32.2 per cent in urban areas), and 5.6 per cent were dilapidated (6.3 per cent in rural areas, and 3.6 per cent in urban areas). About half the households lived in permanent houses (41.1 per cent in rural areas and 79.3 per cent in urban areas), 30 per cent in semi permanent houses (35.7 per cent in rural areas and 15.4 per cent in urban areas), and 18.1 per cent in temporary houses (23.1 per cent in rural areas and 5.2 per cent in urban areas).

The 2001 census data also showed that about 40 per cent of the households in rural areas and 35 per cent in urban areas lived in only one room (Table 4.6). Shortage of space influences the living arrangements of old persons. All household activities including cooking of food, washing clothes, cleaning the room, leisure time activities, entertaining visitors and resting are carried out in a single room, or by using an adjacent open space, if any. When household chores are being carried out, the old have to move out, which causes discomfort. About 30 per cent of the households in rural areas and about the same percentage in urban areas lived in two rooms. The intra-household distribution of living space and the comfort associated with it generally indicate a higher preference to young persons, and the neglect of old persons. Sons virtually decide on the allocation of space, rationalizing that the old need lesser space and can share the room with others. Old persons, specially widows, are often relegated to the rear portion of the house where the living conditions are poorer; it also virtually isolates them from interaction with visitors. Very few households are even aware of the type of accommodation that older persons need to stay healthy, to be free from noise and boisterous behaviour of children, and some degree of privacy for sleep and rest.

Table 4.6: Number of rooms per household, India, 2001

Resi- dence	Number of rooms per household							
	No exclusive room	1	2	3	4	5	6 & above	Total
Rural	3.4	39.8	30.2	13.3	7.0	2.8	3.6	100.00
Urban	2.3	35.1	29.5	17.1	8.7	3.3	4.0	100.00
Total	3.1	38.5	30.0	14.3	7.5	2.9	3.7	100.00

Source: Census of India, 2001.

More pertinent to shared accommodation by members of the household, would be the number of persons per room, information on which has been provided by the National Family Health Survey, 1998–99. The data shows that 62.5 per cent households have less than 3 persons per room (60.2 per cent in rural areas and 68.6 per cent in urban areas), 23.1 per cent households have 3 to 4 members per room (24.4 per cent in rural areas and 19.5 per cent in urban areas), and 14.2 per cent households have 5 or more persons per living room (15.2 per cent in rural areas and 11.8 per cent in urban areas). Over-crowding, shortage of space, lack of privacy affect the health and well-being of members, which falls disproportionately higher in the case of old persons.

Old persons are adversely affected if public utilities like electricity, drinking water and toilet are not available within the house or are not adjacent to it. The 2001 census reported that only 43.5 per cent rural households in India had electricity as a source of lighting. In some states, the situation is far worse. Bihar had only 5.1 per cent rural households with electricity, Jharkhand 10 per cent, Orissa 19.4 per cent, Uttar Pradesh 19.8 per cent and West Bengal 20.3 per cent. Urban households were better off with 87.6 per cent households in India having electricity as a source of lighting. Absence of electricity at night poses a danger to the movement of older persons, specially if they have disabilities.

Drinking water within the premises (tap, hand pump/ well etc.) was available to 28.7 per cent rural households in India, as reported by the 2001 census. For 51.8 per cent rural households, the source was near the premises, and for 19.5 per cent it was away from the premises. Here, too, there was considerable inter-state variation. In Orissa, for instance, only 13.7 per cent rural households had a source of drinking water within the premises, while Madhya Pradesh had 14 per cent rural households with such a facility. Punjab, on the other hand, had 82 per cent rural households with a source of drinking water within the premises. Urban households were better placed. For the country as a whole, 65.4 per cent urban households had a source of drinking water within the premises, 25.2 per cent near the premises, and 9.4 per cent away from the premises. If the source of drinking water is a well, or has to be fetched from outside, difficulty is faced by old persons, specially if they have physical impairments, weakness and pains. They have to depend on other persons for availing this basic facility.

The situation in regard to latrine facilities continues to be very poor. For the country as a whole, the 2001 census reported that 78.1 per cent rural households and 26.3 per cent urban households had no latrine within the house. The situation is far worse in some states: 94.8 per cent rural households in Chhattisgarh, 96.1 per cent rural households in Himachal Pradesh, 92.3 per cent rural households in Orissa reported no latrine within the house. The aged may need to use the toilet at night, and if they have some disability, the problems of use are far worse. The old have to depend on the open space in farms/pasturelands to defecate which are normally used at dawn and at dusk.

Only 22.8 per cent rural households and 70.4 per cent urban households were reported by the 2001 census as having bathroom facilities within the house. Here, too, there is a large inter-state difference. In some states, among rural households, the percentage was less than 10 (Chhattisgarh 3.1 per cent, Jharkhand 4.1 per cent, Orissa 4.3 per cent, Bihar 6.1 per cent, Assam 7.9 per cent and West Bengal 9.4 per cent). At the other end were Punjab and Kerala which reported 62.4 per cent and 56.5 per cent, respectively, with this facility.

Having a place to stay is a valuable asset in old age. Persons need to plan for a house in their working life, specially if there is no ancestral property where they can live. The government has come forward with loans and subsidies for housing for the rural poor. In urban areas, housing schemes are being offered, both by public and private sectors across all income segments. Low interest rates, payment by instalments over a number of years and tax reliefs have provided incentive for persons to invest in housing. Provident Fund Schemes allow the subscribers to take a loan/partial withdrawal for constructing/paying instalments for housing.

In western countries, homes are being specially designed for the elderly which contain features both within and outside the home, taking into consideration safety and comfort aspects. Old couples who have a home prefer to dispose them off and move to such complexes. Layouts are designed to prevent accidents from falls, and to provide barrier free access to shopping centres, community centres, parks and other services. These are yet to make their presence felt in India.

Changing family structures in India have meant that the market for housing of older persons who are reasonably well off is expanding. Some persons who have the means do not wish to stay in old age homes. They would rather prefer housing which gives them a better life style, while providing a safe and secure environment, and gives opportunities of interaction with persons of the same socio-economic class. Retirement benefits and loans in easy instalments make available the financial resources to invest in housing, depending on one's needs. At times, sons, too, make a contribution. The private sector is coming up with various alternative housing programmes specially designed for the elderly. 'Pay and stay' homes are being offered to old persons living by themselves who find that even when they have homes of their own, house keeping is a big problem when they become too old, and have to depend on others for repairs and other problems of maintenance. They often feel that their present stay is lonely, domestic help is scarce and insecure, and there is little assistance at times of crises. Retirement villages/abodes/resorts/complexes have been developed with specially designed apartments for persons to 'age with grace'. They offer apartments with one/two/three bedrooms/studios, at some distance from the metropolitan areas so that a quiet environment in more spacious surroundings can be provided. The cost becomes affordable because of the low cost of land. Land developers publicize secure and safe living with architectural designs suitable for old persons, inter-communication facilities foolproof security, barrier free access to lobbies/elevators/parks/community space, emergency care, ambulance, medical facilities, meditation, physical fitness centres, shopping conveniences, recreation facilities and community kitchens. The residents are expected to pay for the maintenance charges. Non-resident Indians settled abroad look at such complexes as an alternative for accommodating their parents. The clientele of such complexes are usually educated, and have retired from senior positions in business or profession. Companionship and interaction among persons of the same class are an added incentive. While younger persons can come and stay as guests of owner members, there are restrictions in passing the membership so that the complex continues to retain its character of an abode for senior citizens.

The LIC Housing Finance Limited has floated a subsidiary company to build community apartments for the elderly in suburbs near metropolitan cities, after making an assessment of the market for homes for the elderly. Persons who have retired or are retiring can take on lease apartments which will be valid till the resident's death. The apartments, fully furnished, will have a tie up with hospitals, recreation centres and other facilities. The complex takes care of security concerns. Occupants can outsource meals from the community kitchen or cook them individually at home. LIC Care Homes is developing a ten acre land in Bangalore for elderly persons and has plans for similar projects in other cities. Other construction companies are also planning similar projects. The homes usually start from Rs. 3 lakhs onwards.

In the past, families did not desert the elders. Persons who needed shelter in old age homes were childless couples/ widows or widowers without any means of support. A number of old age homes were built by charitable organizations, mainly Christian missionaries, for persons who were relatively destitute. Places of worship/Ashrams/*matths* were able to look after the few persons who needed this type of help, with support from religious endowments, charitable trusts and offerings. In the current scenario, elderly persons in low, middle and even upper income segments, who find that their stay with their children is unwelcome, or who are too old to live on their own, seek an alternative in old age homes. The number of such homes is on the rise. A directory of old age homes compiled by CEWA in 1982 located 229 organizations in the country. Most agencies provided the services free of cost. In 1994–95, HelpAge India compiled a nationwide survey of old age homes. It found the number to be 354. A subsequent survey by HelpAge India in 2002 listed 965 homes, which reflects a growth in demand for such homes.

The Ministry of Social Justice and Empowerment has prepared a scheme to assist *panchayati raj* institutions/self-help groups/voluntary organizations for a one time financial grant for construction of old age homes/day care centres. The scheme, started in 1997, has provided assistance for construction/extensions of 88 old age homes/day care centres, mobile health services and recreation facilities in different parts of the country. State governments/local authorities have also given grants for the construction and maintenance of old age homes. They run some of these institutions.

Some homes are free and cater mainly to persons from the lower income group. Several old age homes also take in chronically ill, disabled and infirm elders. Some provide for both free and paying residents on a self supporting basis. Some middle and upper class persons prefer to pay and stay in old age homes with better facilities as they do not like their stay to be based on charity. A few homes have come up which offer air conditioning, single or double room accommodation, medical and other facilities, which are fully charged. Children resident abroad but are unable to provide care because of personal circumstances and job related uncertainties, opt for such facilities as a better alternative. At times, older persons sell their property and, with the proceeds, pay for services in such homes. Residents in old age homes get physical care, but they feel starved emotionally. They have to rebuild relationships with fellow inmates. Researchers have commented that it is only because of acute necessity (financial need, no one to look after, domestic squabbles, total neglect by children, acute shortage of accommodation), persons opt for old age homes as no one likes to leave his or her home, away from family and community to live in an institution. About one-fifth of the homes are purely for women. On an average, less than 50 persons stay in a home. These have single/ double/dormitory type of accommodation. Some homes have a capacity above 100.

Some homes are located in premises which were already existing, either donated to them or taken on rent. The location of an old age home is often decided by the main sponsor who takes the initiative to form an organization after an assessment of its need, scout for a site which can be made available through an endowment or through donations, and organizes the financial and manpower resources needed for constructing the home and running it. Several homes are in old structures. The homes have to adjust their activities according to the existing accommodation. Homes which are newly constructed have better facilities. The standards of services in the homes vary, as also the quality of care provided. Very few have trained manpower. Some services to the residents are outsourced. A number of homes have developed a schedule of activities in which residents, to the extent they can, participate as it gives them a healthy way to occupy their time. It would be important for organizations like HelpAge to prepare manuals giving different types of layouts of old age homes from which a choice could be made. The manual should also indicate the facilities they should provide, accommodation needed for different activities, equipments required, and the minimum norms to be observed. Training of manpower to manage and run old age homes is an urgent need to improve the quality of services.

Day care centres for old persons are an important need as they give them the opportunity to meet and interact with other persons of the same age, gossip, share experiences and memories, and help to shape their outlook in life. A number of activities are built round these day care centres as, for instance, reading room and recreation facilities, meditation and physical fitness programmes, hobby centres, talks by professionals and medical facilities. Some centres also provide services for the community at large through senior volunteers who wish to serve the community through activities such as coaching classes for children from the low income group, adult literacy classes, medical assistance and craft training.

Some old age homes provide a variety of facilities. For instance, Vishranti in Chennai, apart from providing free services for the old such as residential facilities, also has an infirmary block, a temporary shelter for run away women, a home for children from broken or abusive families, a hospice for dying destitutes and a medical care unit with 18 beds for elderly patients discharged from hospital who still need care. It also provides a short stay home for elders whose families are away on vacation or on some emergency visit on the basis of payments to be made for intermediate or a longer term care.

Organizations like HelpAge India provide grants for construction, training of manpower and upgrading of facilities. They raise funds through charities and special events. They also mobilize resources for the inmates of the homes through

'Adopt a Granny Programme' under which individuals sponsor the basic needs of many old persons. In 2003–04, Rs. 1036 lakhs were spent by HelpAge on the programme covering 16,875 grannies (HelpAge, 2004).

The distribution of old age homes is very uneven. The southern states have the largest number. The 2002 Directory by HelpAge India showed that of the 971 homes, 53 per cent were in the four southern states (Kerala 182, Tamil Nadu 132, Andhra Pradesh 116, Karnataka 86). The western states had 25 per cent old age homes (Maharashtra 135, Gujarat 80, Goa 25). Goa, which has 112,273 persons aged 70 years and above (2001 census) has the same number of old age homes as Uttar Pradesh which has 6,690,334 persons aged 70 years and above. Bihar which has 2,042,428 persons aged 70 years and above (2001 census) has only two homes and Rajasthan which has 1,466,124 persons aged 70 years and above has only seven. Almost all the old age homes are located in the cities where the problem is more acute and visible.

A study of 19 old age homes by Dandekar spread over rural and urban areas of Maharashtra observed that they were " useful institutions badly needed for the homeless, helpless or childless". It added "old age homes catered to the needs of the majority of inmates; at least they were better living in them than outside". The study found that a large number of homes were located in places which had sufficient land. Most residents lived free. Those, who could, paid partly or fully for their upkeep. Most rooms had a shared accommodation for 3 to 5 persons. Some also had a dormitory type of accommodation. Eighty per cent of the inmates came from urban areas. Forty-three per cent came to the home by themselves, while 26 per cent were brought by unrelated persons. Twenty-one per cent were brought by son/daughter/daughter -in -law/son-in-law/ brother/sister/nephews. The inmates helped according to their capacity in the daily routine of cleaning vegetables, cooking, serving food, washing their own utensils, keeping the premises clean and other sundry work. The homes had a dining room, kitchen, place for meditation, library, reading room, recreation room and garden where they could keep themselves busy. In several places, outing activities were also provided, often with the help of volunteers. The homes also provided some rudimentary medical facilities. Doctors visited the homes at fixed hours. In case of serious illness, they were shifted to a hospital. Some institutions have an arrangement with local hospitals which reserve a few beds for the inmates. Several homes expected the inmates to deposit a lump sum with the home for use in an emergency. Some homes run supplementary institutions within its premises or nearby (children's homes, schools, hostels). Interactions with them livened the atmosphere. Some institutions, to supplement their income, ran convalescent homes and physio-therapy centres which could be used on payment of a fee. Visits by relatives (including sons/daughters) or by inmates to the relative's home helped in relieving the tension and the feeling of unwantedness. These were, however, rather infrequent. No relatives visited the inmates in 37 per cent cases; in the case of 17 per cent, relatives visited very rarely. About 27 per cent were visited once a quarter. The study found that four-fifths of the inmates liked the old age home. The rest continued to live there because they had no where else to go to (Dandekar, 1996). Old age homes in Maharashtra were better off than that in many northern states because of the old tradition of welfare work. In several parts, the quality of services was not satisfactory. Evaluation studies sponsored by the Ministry of Social Welfare in the northern states found the situation to vary from one home to the other.

Protection of Life

Old persons living in urban areas are vulnerable to assault, mainly for purposes of robbery. The National Crime Records Bureau has compiled information on the number of persons by age group who were victims of murder and culpable homicide. The data shows that in 2001, 8.96 per cent of the victims of murder and 8.30 per cent of the victims of culpable homicide not amounting to murder were of the age group over

50 years (data on persons aged 60 years and above was not separately available). In this age group, there were 238 female victims of murder for every 1000 male victims, and 260 female victims of culpable homicide not amounting to murder for every 1000 male victims (NCRB, 2003).

Fear stalks the life of older persons living alone or as a couple, specially at night. Media reports indicate that murderous assaults on older persons who live alone or with spouse usually take place in their homes, and are often carried out by domestic servants or maintenance persons, masons, carpenters, painters, labourers, vendors and others who, for some reason, have had access to the house or visit it on some pretext. Old persons living in group housing colonies with boundary walls and security personnel are safer. In the bigger metropolitan cities, police personnel have been asked to specially identify old persons and check their safety. Their vulnerability, nonetheless, continues because of poor police patrolling. Residents' Welfare Associations have also been advised to keep a check by appointing their own security personnel. The police have prepared guidelines for the safety of older persons. Among these are: securing all doors and windows before retiring for the day; installing magic eye, door chain or electronic devices to identity the visitor; checking the visitor before opening the door; fixing grills in windows, verandahs; varying the daily routine outside the home; not keeping valuables at home or, when absolutely necessary, to keep them away from the sight of servants; preventing hawkers, vendors, strangers for entering into the house; getting domestic servants verified from the police. Some NGOs have set up a hotline to comfort such persons or visit them to check on the security. They have also tied up with the local police. Volunteers are also asked to keep a vigil.

Old persons who own property in prime areas, and whose children are settled abroad, are subjected to pressure tactics by property dealers who want to buy them at a price far lower than the market rate, and rebuild the area as residential flats or as a commercial centre. Property dealers employ local toughs to identify such areas. Old persons living in such houses need protection from the police.

Tenancy laws in most states affect older persons, depending on whether the person is an owner or a tenant. Those who own the property are forced to put up with very low rents on premises given earlier. Even when they have no other place to stay, and wish to settle down, evictions become virtually impossible. Those who live as tenants, however, tend to benefit as they pay rents far lower than the market price. The maintenance of such homes is, however, poor. Owners use a variety of means to ask the old tenants to vacate and, when persuasion fails, coercive tactics are used. At times, the owner agrees to pay a negotiated price to the tenant to vacate. Tenancy laws in states need modification so as to be fair to all segments of the population.

Older persons have not only to be careful inside the house. Outside, too, accidents occur, some fatal while others leave the victims disabled for life. The National Crime Records Bureau compiles information on accidental deaths by age due to natural causes (natural calamities, cold and exposure, starvation/thirst etc.) and unnatural causes. In 2000, the number of accidental deaths of persons aged 60 years and above by natural causes was 2,914 which was 16.87 per cent of the total number of such deaths. The number of accidental deaths of persons aged 60 years and above by unnatural causes was 20,540 which was 8.61 per cent of the total number of such deaths. There were 339 female deaths due to unnatural causes for every 1000 male deaths.

Table 4.7 gives the number of accidental deaths by unnatural causes among persons aged 60 years and above in 2000. The data shows that traffic accidents caused 39.26 per cent of the deaths. Other important causes were drowning, falls, fire, sudden deaths and poisoning.

Table 4.7: Number of accidental deaths by unnatural causes among persons aged 60 years and above, India, 2000

Cause	Age 60+			Total (all ages)			% of persons 60+ by each cause		
	Male	Female	Total	Male	Female	Total	Male	Female	Total
Collapse of structure	120	76	196	1,544	689	2,233	7.77	11.03	8.78
Drowning	1,143	568	1,711	15,320	6,676	21,996	7.46	8.51	7.7
Electrocution	212	54	266	4,728	935	5,663	4.48	5.78	4.70
Explosion	9	8	17	506	219	725	1.78	3.65	2.34
Falls	558	144	702	5,878	1,209	7,087	9.49	11.91	9.91
Factory/Machine Accidents	12	4	16	528	97	625	2.27	4.12	2.56
Fire	488	739	1,227	7,531	17,936	25,467	6.48	4.12	4.82
Fire arms	133	7	140	2,311	323	2,634	5.76	2.17	5.32
Sudden deaths	1,901	484	2,385	11,462	2,462	13,924	16.59	19.66	17.13
Killed by animals	62	20	82	527	142	669	11.76	14.08	12.26
Mines or quarry disaster	15	2	17	361	106	467	4.16	1.89	3.64
Poisoning	842	443	1,285	14,889	8,506	23,395	5.66	5.21	5.49
Stampede	3	4	7	27	23	50	11.11	17.39	14.00
Suffocation	81	22	103	718	263	981	11.28	8.37	10.50
Traffic accidents	6,421	1,643	8,064	81,866	16,172	98,038	7.84	10.16	8.23
Other causes	1,952	510	2,462	14,611	4,909	19,520	13.36	10.39	12.61
Cause not known	1,387	471	1,858	11,040	4,003	15,043	12.56	11.77	12.35
Total	15,339	5,199	20,538	173,847	64,670	238,517	8.82	8.04	8.61

Source: Accidental Deaths & Suicides in India, 2000.

Suicides

Deaths due to suicides among older persons have become a cause of concern. Suicidal deaths among persons aged 60 years and above have increased from 6,381 in 1996 to 8,493 deaths in 2000, a growth of 33.1 per cent (Table 4.8). In the total population, suicidal deaths during the same period increased by 23.1 per cent. Males far outnumber females in suicidal deaths in old age. In 2000, the number of suicidal deaths of females aged 60 years and above for every 1000 male suicidal deaths aged 60 years and above was 434. In the total population, the ratio was 645.

Social Security for the Old

Table 4.8: Number of suicides of persons aged 60 years and above by sex, India, 1996 to 2000

Year	Suicides Age 60+			No. of female suicides per 1000 male suicides	Suicides All ages			No. of female suicides per 1000 male suicides	% of persons 60+ committing suicide to total number committing suicides		
	Male	Female	Total		Male	Female	Total		Male	Female	Total
1996	4,288	2,093	6,381	788	51,206	37,035	88,241	723	8.37	5.65	7.23
1997	4,754	2,207	6,961	464	56,281	39,548	95,829	703	8.45	5.58	7.26
1998	4,958	2,585	7,543	521	61,686	43,027	104,713	698	8.04	6.01	7.20
1999	5,378	2,546	7,924	473	65,488	45,099	110,587	689	8.21	5.65	7.16
2000	5,921	2,572	8,493	434	66,032	42,561	108,593	645	8.97	6.04	7.82

Source: National Crime Records Bureau.

The causes of suicidal deaths of persons aged 60 years and above in 2000 indicated that illness was the predominant cause (39.02 per cent). This was followed by family problems (14.48 per cent). The main method adopted by males aged 60 years and above in committing suicide was poisoning (37.49 per cent), hanging (27.88 per cent), drowning (6.46 per cent) and fire/self-immolation (4.76 per cent). In the case of females, the main means adopted were poisoning (32.58 per cent), hanging (17.49 per cent), drowning (12.67 per cent) and fire/self-immolation (14.23 per cent) (NCRB, 2002).

Abuse

Older persons are at times abused in India, within the four walls of the house. Its prevalence is grossly under-reported. Abuse of parents or close aged relatives is not socio-culturally acceptable. It is often regarded by the victim as an intra-family matter, a private affair not to be discussed with others as the dignity and respect of the family (*izzat*) is at stake. They consider the family as sacred, whose dignity should be preserved at all costs. Due to socio-cultural, emotional and psychological barriers, parents would not like to make their condition known, as they would not like their children to suffer from loss of status. Abuse is at times highlighted by the media when it takes a morbid form. The elderly refer to it as a form of ill-treatment. They are also not sure whether reporting abuse will help them in any way; it may even cause further deterioration in relationships. When persons are old and infirm and have very little contacts with medical personnel, neighbours and relatives, they do not know how to open up the matter, or how to articulate the forms of abuse. Neighbours and relatives are discreet not to ask as it may look like probing into intra-family affairs. Friends and acquaintances may also not be able to provide an alternative as there are no support services, not even access to legal remedy. More women than men are abused, specially if the person is a widow, and there is no one to protest. Gender, illiteracy and absence of financial resources make her totally dependent on her son and daughter-in-law, and their attitude. They are tied to the family for emotional reasons, rationalizing the behaviour of their children, believing that such a treatment is a matter of destiny, or that there must have been some lapses in the upbringing of their son which has made him hostile, and/or entirely submissive to the daughter-in-law's attitude. They would not like to brooch the subject with relatives and acquaintances for moving to an old age home because they consider it a loss of dignity for the family.

Abuse takes various forms. A more prevalent form of abuse is neglect. Essential needs of older persons are not met, or are treated in a casual manner. These may relate to confining the person to the home, not helping him to go out and interact with neighbours and friends, or to consult with a doctor. Neglect may also relate to intra-household matters such as personal hygiene and cleanliness, changing clothes, giving proper diets, provision of a quiet resting place and making available essential accessories such as glasses, hearing aids, a walking stick or a wheel chair. While some of these actions could be deliberate, they could also arise from poverty, ignorance and lack of time.

A not so uncommon method is psychological or mental abuse of older persons which causes them stress, lowers their dignity and self worth, and is extremely disturbing. It may express itself in various ways such as veiled or direct insulting behaviour, harsh language, yelling, imitating or making fun, passing caustic remarks, humiliating conduct and treatment, conveying to old person constantly that they are a burden to the family and are causing too many problems, totally ignoring them in inter-personal contacts within the family, with restraining contacts with relatives and neighbours, and socially isolating them. Such action often leads to depression, anxiety, confusion, loneliness, withdrawal and behavioural distortions. In its extreme forms, it can be more devastating than physical abuse.

Another form of abuse, though less frequent, is physical in character. It normally implies non-accidental use of force through single or repetitive acts in order to torment the person. It could result in hurting or injuring the older person, hitting the person, handling the person roughly, causing pain or temporary impairment, causing fear, or physically restraining movement. It could also imply the deliberate use of medication to keep the person quiet.

Persons who have moveable or immoveable assets become vulnerable to financial abuse. In middle and upper class households, where the value of property is large, old persons are asked to divide the property among the children, or sell it and distribute the proceeds, giving the assurance that the parents will be looked after. When parents do not comply, various methods are used such as neglect, threats, harassment, taunts, caustic remarks and abusive conduct to compel the person to divide the property. When parents find life unbearable because of maltreatment by children, they may ask the son to look for his own accommodation. Some children refuse to leave the house. Sons decide on the space they want to occupy, relegating to older parents cramped rooms which have little comfort. Retirement benefits are at times taken away by a son to buy a house in his name, assuring the person of care and comfort. There are also instances of unauthorized or fraudulent use of the person's money, property or other financial resources, forging of signatures, abuse of power of attorney, disposal of property or cash using deceit, trickery or force, pressurizing the person to make a will in their favour, or change the will or other legal documents. Various methods are used to restrain access or control by the elder person of his moveable or immoveable property. Older persons with liquid assets become vulnerable to commercial fraud. Investment of money is often solicited through various incentives without indicating the risks involved. Evidence of fraud through telemarketing is also on the rise.

Researches on abuse in old age reported from developed countries, where it emerged as an important social problem in the 1980s, have indicated that the main perpetrators are family members, including adult children and their spouses, and to some extent the spouse and relatives. Some perpetrators of financial abuse are neighbours or professional persons who win the trust of those with investible funds, and make them invest in schemes which are risky, and often cause loss.

Abuse at times finds expression in abandonment by close relatives. Older persons admitted to hospitals, even after getting well, are not visited by relatives to take them home. A wrong address of the patient is given to avoid tracing out their place of stay. The discharged patient is sent to a destitute home/old age home by the local authority/social welfare directorate. Cases of older persons being deliberately abandoned in fairs, railway stations or in places of pilgrimage have been reported. Deserted wives are also a vulnerable category in their old age. Other persons at risk of abandonment are the poor, the disabled, the sick and infirm, childless persons, persons living alone with no contact by their children, and displaced persons. Some old persons without any means of subsistence are forced to beg.

A severely abused category is that of widows who often find it extremely difficult to continue in the household after the death of her husband. Illiteracy, ignorance of dealing with the outside world, absence of support from persons who could help them for a fair deal and socio-cultural inhibitions about asserting her rights, compounds the problem. Pressures, snide remarks, poor treatment and social isolation force the widow

to leave her husband's residence because she becomes an extra
dependent in the household. It is also done to divest the widow
from the use of the husband's property by the husband's
relatives. In some states, particularly Bengal, a socio-religious
context was institutionalized to send widows to pilgrimage
centres, particularly Varanasi, Vrindaban, Mathura and
Nawadwip where they were forced to live on a pittance by
performing some religious rituals in temples out of funds
donated by well-to-do Bengalis and others. An impression was
often created as if the widow herself opted for this kind of life
devoted to service of the Lord. She thus became 'invisible' in
the social relationships of the deceased husband's family/
parental family, and was soon forgotten.

There are no specific laws to deal with abuse of older
persons in India. Older women have now been covered by the
legislation on domestic violence enacted in 2005. The general
legislation applicable to all persons seems to be inadequate
for older males. Word of mouth from neighbours often helps
to identify situations of gross abuse. In some developed
countries, mandatory reporting of abuse of older persons exists,
but this has not been effective because of problems of resources
and skilled manpower. Helplines have been set up in some
countries by NGOs. They can provide assistance only if
legislation and social welfare services come to their aid to stop
abuse by the family and close relatives.

There is need to generate public awareness of the
emerging problem of adult abuse through research and
dissemination. Men, too, need to be covered. Existing
legislations need to be amended through specific clauses to
deal with the problem. Counselling of both the family members
and the abused adult is an important preventive measure.
NGOs can help by energizing community efforts to end the
isolation of older persons, and provide them day care services
and the support networks for both the older person and their
families. In some countries, specialized NGOs exist to handle
problems of abuse of older persons. Medical and nursing
personnel are oriented to identify abuse. Approach to problems
of abuse of older persons through the human rights approach

may not, at this stage, be the starting point to tackle the situation, particularly when seen in the context of absence of alternative support services and the ground reality of a large number of families which are themselves victims of poverty and find it difficult to meet the needs of an extra dependent.

Summing Up

Changing norms have made a dent on the traditional living arrangements of the old. Most vulnerable in terms of family care and shelter are the widowed, the deserted, and single persons. However, family values in India are still quite strong. A survey carried out by NSSO in 1995–96 showed that the two predominant categories of living arrangements of older persons are 'living with spouse and other members' and 'living without spouse but with other children'. Less than 5 per cent old persons in rural and urban areas live alone, while about 11 per cent in rural areas and about 8 per cent in urban areas live with spouse.

Separate data on housing arrangements for the elderly is not available. General census data on housing shows that in 2001 about 3 per cent had no exclusive room, 38.5 per cent had one room, 30 per cent had two rooms, and the rest had three or more rooms. The intra-household distribution of living space shows a greater preference to young persons. Old persons are adversely affected if public utilities like water, toilet and electricity are not available within the house or are not located adjacent to it. The 2001 census reported that in rural areas 43.5 per cent households had electricity, and 21.9 per cent had toilet (latrine) facility within the house. In urban areas, the percentages were 87.6 and 73.7, respectively. Drinking water was available within the premises to 28.7 per cent rural households and 65.4 per cent urban households.

Housing becomes a valuable asset in old age. Persons have to plan for their housing in their working life. Public and private sector housing development agencies are offering houses in the primary market across all income segments. Low interest rates, payment by instalments, and tax reliefs have provided incentive to persons to invest while they are still working. Special housing schemes are being floated for older persons. Retirement villages are being developed. Pay and stay homes are under offer. Apartment complexes for the elderly are coming up. Some prefer to stay in old age homes which offer services either free of cost or at subsidized rates. Some are run on the basis of no profit no loss basis.

Old persons living in urban areas are vulnerable to crime. Figures from the National Crime Records Bureau show that in 2001, nearly 9 per cent of victims of murder and nearly 8 per cent of victims of culpable homicide not amounting to murder are from persons aged 50 years and above. Old persons have been advised by the police to adopt precautions to reduce their vulnerability. About 9 per cent of accidental deaths are of persons aged 60 years and above. Traffic accidents are a major cause. About 8 per cent of suicides are from persons aged 60 years and above. Male suicides outnumber female suicides. The predominant cause of suicide was illness.

Abuse of older persons is on the increase. They are often regarded by the victims themselves as ill-treatment. The incidence is grossly under-reported as it is considered as an intra-family matter, not to be communicated to outsiders so that the dignity of the family can be maintained. This attitude perpetuates its recurrence. There is an urgent need to generate public awareness of the emerging problem of abuse and to initiate steps to alleviate the problem.

5

Policy for Older Persons

The previous text has stated that informal care by children is no longer sufficient to meet the financial, health and other needs of older persons who now have a longer life span after the age of 60 years. The financial burden is often beyond the means of children, particularly expensive medical care, as public health services do not function satisfactorily in most parts of the country. The psycho-social and emotional needs of older persons are also an important factor so that they do not feel marginalized and helpless. Policy makers have, therefore, been thinking of how to lighten the coping responsibilities of families through various interventions.

Legislative Policy

Prior to 1947, the main social response towards meeting the needs of older persons, who had no family to support them, was in the form of old age homes/*ashrams* run by charitable institutions, many of which were promoted by religious organizations. The state had virtually no role, except for relief granted at times of natural calamities, like famines. The Constitution of India realized the need for action by the State to provide relief to older persons without any means of support. It stated in Article 41, a Directive Principle, that the State shall, within the limits of economic capacity and development, make an effective provision for securing the right to public assistance in case of old age. The Constitution also placed social security in the Concurrent List, indicating thereby that both the central and state governments have responsibilities in this regard.

Two central legislations were passed to legitimize the right of older persons to seek financial support from their children through legal means. Section 125 (d) incorporated into the Criminal Procedure Code in 1973, made it incumbent for a person having sufficient means to maintain his parents without any means of support, through a monthly allowance. The order can be passed by a first class magistrate on the basis of an application indicating such neglect. The Hindu Adoptions and Maintenance Act, 1956 recognizes the obligation of a person following Hindu, Jain, Sikh, Buddhist religions to maintain his aged or infirm parent. Section 20 of the Act states that a person during his or her life time is bound to maintain his or her aged or infirm parent if the parent is unable to maintain himself or herself out of his or her own earnings or other property. Persons other than Hindus (viz. Muslims, Christians, Parsis, Jews) have to take recourse to Cr. P.C. for maintenance rights. Thus, while the state recognized its responsibility for public assistance to old persons, it also made legal the responsibility of children to pay for the maintenance of their parents.

A point raised was whether daughters (including married daughters) having their own incomes could be asked to provide maintenance to the parents, if applied for under Cr. P.C. The Supreme Court, in its 1987 judgement, stated that the pronoun 'his' used in Section 125 of Cr. P.C. includes both a male and a female. It elaborated:

"We are unable to accept the contention of the appellant that a married daughter has no obligation to maintain her parents even if they are unable to maintain themselves. It has been rightly pointed out by the High Court that a daughter after her marriage does not cease to be a daughter of the father or mother. It has been earlier noticed that it is the moral obligation of the children to maintain their parents. In case the contention of the appellant that the daughter has no liability whatsoever to maintain her parents is accepted, in that case, parents having no son but only daughters and unable to maintain themselves, would go destitute, if the daughters even though they have sufficient means refuse to maintain their parents". The judgment added: "The purpose of such enactment is to enforce social obligation and we do not think why the daughters should be excluded from such obligation to maintain their parents". The Court also stated that before ordering maintenance it has to satisfy itself that the daughter has sufficient means of her own independently of the means or income of her husband, and that the father or the mother, as the case may be, is unable to maintain himself/or herself (AIR 1987, Supreme Court, 1100, Dr. Vijaya Manohar Arbak *Vs* Kashirao Rajaram Sawai).

States have also been contemplating the passing of separate legislation for providing maintenance by children/ grandchildren to parents and dependents. Himachal Pradesh enacted its own Act in 2001 (Himachal Pradesh Maintenance of Parents and Dependents Act) appointing a Tribunal to order the maintenance. The Act states under section 3(i): "any person who is unable to maintain himself and having income below the level laid down for persons living below the poverty line, and is resident in the state of Himachal Pradesh, can apply to the Tribunal for an order". Assessment of needs of the person applying for maintenance takes into account basic physical needs (shelter, food and clothing), and medical costs. Maharashtra introduced a Bill in 1997. This has not yet been enacted for political reasons. Since social security is in the con-current list it would be desirable for the Central Government to enact a legislation in this regard for providing maintenance by children/grandchildren to parents. It should be applicable to all communities, like the provision in the Cr.P.C.

Several countries are now enacting separate Acts to legalize responsibility of children to take care of dependent parents, thereby legitimizing their filial duties ordained by customs and traditions. Singapore, for instance, has created a Tribunal for implementation of the Singapore Maintenance of Parents Act, 1996 making it legally obligatory for children to · maintain dependent parents.

Some commentators feel that a legal remedy for enforcing the moral responsibility of children to take care of the financial needs of their parents is more of the nature of a provision which can be taken resort to as a last measure. The son knows that a legal remedy is open to the parent. He also knows that it is a time honoured social tradition to look after one's parents, and the law only requires him to fulfil it. He also understands that it is equally undignified and a fall from social disgrace if he is to be sued for maintenance. Most parents, however, even when they feel neglected, are sad and agonized about it, and suffer in silence, think it undignified to approach the court for the right to maintenance as that would amount to taking a private matter into the public domain. Even when maintenance has been granted, sons may become more hostile to the parents as a result of the legal remedy and invent excuses for interruptions in payment. The only remedy is that courts have to be approached again, which is not an easy matter.

Parents recognize that law is not the best way to promote filial devotion. It can, however, be made to act if responsibility is found wanting. It provides a legal social safety net, accepted by tradition. A pro-active society would, through voluntary organizations or other forms of negotiation, try to bring in some form of mediation rather than seek redressal by approaching the courts.

Events Leading to National Policy

Even though the Constitution of India included social security in the Concurrent List, for almost three and a half decades after independence, the central government did not have any programmes for the well being of the elderly. State governments, however, responded to destitution among older persons by starting the scheme of old age pensions, a public assistance programme, details of which have been given in the chapter on financial security. This was the first major initiative to meet as best as possible the constitutional directive of public assistance. The scheme was, however, implemented through an administrative order. It was not a statutory right. It did not, therefore, make it incumbent upon the state to grant such a pension. It was its sole discretion to either sanction a pension or discontinue it. It was not treated as an entitlement but as a charitable endeavour by politicians to display munificence to gain electoral mileage. It did not act on Article 41 of the Constitution in letter and spirit to secure the right of old person to public assistance in case of old age.

The Planning Commission showed a dithering role and indecisiveness in allocating central plan funds. The Third Five Years Plan (1961-62 to 1965-66) recognized the need of older persons without any means of support for plan outlay but suggested that voluntary organizations and local bodies could provide the assistance. It suggested the setting up of Funds in the states for relief and assistance. An outlay of Rs. 2 crores was made for social assistance which included the elderly, but no schemes were framed; the amount remained unutilized. The Fourth and Fifth Five Years Plans did not provide any outlays. The Planning Commission, in fact, showed a negative attitude in making allocations for the elderly. Permission was not given to the states to budget old age pensions in the state plan on the ground that plan funds are meant only for development purposes, whereas allocations for old age pensions are not an investment as they did not provide any returns. The states were naturally very much restrained both in regard to amount of pensions that could be provided and the number of pensions to be sanctioned, as non-plan budgets had little elasticity. The Finance Commissions set up to make allocations under the non-plan head to states allowed devolution to the states on account of old age assistance, and indicated the criteria on the basis of which allocations were to be made. The states continued to urge the Planning Commission to permit old age pensions as a plan scheme. This was ultimately conceded.

For almost three and half decades since independence, the Union Ministry of Social Welfare performed a rather passive role. Even in response to Parliament Questions, it continued to reiterate that care of the elderly was a major problem of developed societies, while in India the family continued to discharge its responsibility towards old persons with care and affection. In different forums of the United Nations when the problems of the elderly were discussed, the Government of India took no initiative in supporting the cause, dwelling on the social norm in Indian society, rather than be guided by the reality on the ground.

The United Nations had been advocating for a long time the need for social security in old age. It foresaw the demographic changes leading to increase in percentage of the elderly population and the growing inability of families to cope with such responsibilities. The General Assembly adopted in December 1948 the Universal Declaration of Human Rights, and in 1966 the International Covenant on Economic, Social and Cultural Rights urging the states to honour the right to social security in old age and to an adequate standard of living. The International Labour Organization also adopted several Conventions concerning minimum standards of social security. Important among them being Convention No. 102 in 1952, Convention No. 128 in 1967 and Convention No. 157 in 1982.

The climate for positive thinking by central government on the elderly began to take shape in the 1980s. An international event of vital importance to the cause of old persons was the decision of the United Nations to convene the World Assembly on Ageing in 1982, in order to provide a forum to launch "an international action programme aimed at guaranteeing economic and social security to older persons, as well as opportunities to contribute to national development." The action was prompted by the rapid ageing of populations throughout the world. The Assembly brought into focus the multi-sectoral character of ageing issues, and not just humanitarian welfare. It brought out the stark reality of the demographic transition resulting in growing numbers of elderly in the population, and their proportion to the total population, projecting the huge efforts that would be needed. It emphasized that older persons were also an asset, and not just a liability. Both before and after the World Assembly on Ageing, there were a number of regional and international seminars and conferences, and advocacy material, which emphasized the importance of looking at the elderly from a long-term policy perspective. It led to a growing consciousness in India at the decision making level to have a policy formulated, covering not just welfare but other segments as well. The International Plan of Action for Ageing, adopted by the World Assembly in 1982, led to some serious thinking in India at different forums on ageing concerns. Non-governmental organizations which were coming up in different parts of the country on ageing issues began to urge the government to formulate a policy, keeping in view the multi-sectoral nature of an ageing population. The media and public figures began to voice their concern on ageing issues and suggested interventions to promote coordinated action. Research on ageing, primarily conducted by university Departments of Social Work, several of which were sponsored by the Ministry of Social Welfare, brought out the changes taking place in the family, the long period of care because of increase in life expectancy and the growing inability to cope with the problems of aged persons without supportive programmes and services by the state and other agencies. The studies strongly advocated that the needs of the elderly must be incorporated in the development plans.

The United Nations continued to pursue its advocacy functions. It came out with the United Nations Principles for Older Persons, which was adopted by the General Assembly in 1991. It also declared the Proclamation on Aging and Global Targets, 1992. It organized meetings, both regional and international, to keep the interest alive. Subsequent Declarations, Conferences and Summits of the United Nations have reiterated the rights of older persons to have a fair share of development. Included among them are the Copenhagen Declaration and Programme of Action of the World Summit on Social Development, 1995, Beijing Declaration and Platform for Action of the Fourth World Conference on Women, 1995, and several United Nations Resolutions. The International Labour Organization adopted Conventions and made recommendation for promoting social security of the economically active population. Observance of 1999 as the International Year of Older Persons, with the theme of society for all ages, gave a further fillip to the efforts. The Second World Assembly on Ageing in Madrid in 2002 adopted the

International Plan of Action on Ageing giving detailed guidelines and principles that could be followed.

A change in perception of the role of the central government to ageing issues was becoming evident. The Ministry of Social Welfare introduced for the first time in 1983–84, soon after the World Assembly of Ageing, a general grant-in-aid programme to voluntary organizations working for the welfare of the aged. In the other ministries, however, ageing issues were not specifically mentioned, nor any specific programmes framed for them except for the scheme of the Ministry of Health to control blindness through cataract operations which had been in existence for a long time. Policy statements, formulated by different Ministries in the 1980s and 1990s, did not show cognizance of the problems faced by older persons as, for instance, the National Health Policy (1983), the National Nutrition Policy 1993), and the National Housing Policy (1988, 1999).

A big programme to provide public assistance to the destitute elderly came into existence when the Prime Minister announced, in his address to the nation on 30 July 1995, a new centrally sponsored scheme of national old age pension at Rs.75 per month for persons aged 65 years and above, who were below the poverty line and were facing near destitution as they did not have the means to support them in old age. The scheme provided that states would be reimbursed for implementing the scheme. It would be in addition to their own budgetary provisions on state old age pensions. States would thus be enabled, as a result of the scheme, to provide a higher rate of pension and increase the coverage. The scheme on old age pension was announced by the Prime Minister in 1995, even though it was not included in the Ninth Five Year Plan. It showed that the chief political executive ultimately decided on welfare matters where large expenditures were involved. Later, again in 2000, the central government announced a programme under the plan budget to give 10 kg. of foodgrains free of cost to persons aged 65 years and above who were below the poverty line but were not getting old age pension. Here, too, the scheme had not been included in the Tenth Plan document. It may be recalled that when old age pensions were started in the states from the 1950s, it was at the initiative of Chief Ministers, aware as they were of the ground reality facing the old in disadvantaged circumstances.

National Policy on Older Persons

As people became more aware of ageing issues through dissemination of research studies, media reports, conferences and discussions, voluntary organizations for advocacy and welfare were being formed, specially in states which were at the forefront of non-government initiative on social issues. They began to urge the government for a national policy on ageing. A decision was taken to formulate it after several meetings and conferences had been held, a process which was spread over almost eight years. Finally, the National Policy on Older Persons (NPOP) was framed in 1998, and was adopted in January 1999. The policy provides a policy framework for action A ten to fifteen year perspective has been kept in view. Action by the state has been emphasized, whether as provider, promoter, supporter, facilitator or a watchdog. The role of *panchayati raj* institutions has been outlined. NPOP also recognizes the role of the individual, the not-for-profit sector, the private sector, non-governmental organizations and other institutions of civil society in providing services. NPOP serves as an enabling statement which gives the broad areas of action and the strategies so that within the framework, central as well as state governments and other agencies, can prepare their own action plans, and work out the targets, the schemes and the funding requirements within a timeframe. The policy has taken a realistic view on what was feasible even though it fell short of what was desirable. Definitive statements and targets to be achieved within a timeframe have been left out, keeping in view past experiences in implementation. It would also have meant, at the national level, an exercise in abstraction. NPOP is not to be considered as a document which limits action to areas mentioned in it, nor does it set boundaries. It is to be viewed as a stepping store for multi-sectoral action, with such additions as may be necessary, depending on local and regional circumstances.

NPOP has stated the basic assumption on which it has been formulated. It declares that older persons must get an equitable share in development benefits. It observes that the concerns of older persons are national concerns and their interests will not be 'unprotected, ignored or marginalized'. It calls for affirmative action so that older persons can be assured of a dignified existence, and a meaningful purpose in the last phase of their life. NPOP recognizes that older persons are a heterogeneous group and that strategies and services need to be developed accordingly. It is based on the principle of equity so that all categories of senior citizens benefit. It recognizes the importance of strengthening inter-generation bonds. NPOP seeks active and productive involvement of older persons, and not just their care as they, too, have to be viewed as a resource. It endeavours to empower older persons in decision making on matters concerning them. NPOP urges larger budgetary allocations and special programmes for the rural and urban poor. It calls for special schemes for women, so that they do not become victims of neglect and discrimination on account of gender, illiteracy, assetlessness, widowhood and age. It views the life cycle as a continuum. It emphasizes strengthening of the capacity of families to cope with caring responsibilities. It acknowledges the urgent need to expand social and community services for older persons from all segments, including the poor and the vulnerable and to remove socio-cultural, economic and physical barriers. It recognizes integration of the roles of the individual, the family, the community, the market, institutions of civil society and the State for promoting the well being of the old, and securing them a dignified placed in society.

The principal areas of intervention and action identified by NPOP are:

Financial Security

Non-contributory old age pensions for those below the poverty line; better returns from provident funds; better administration of retirement benefits: pension schemes for employees in the private sector and for those in self-employment; tax relief to older persons and families supporting older persons; promoting long-term saving instruments; organizing pre-retirement counselling programmes; promoting income generation opportunities; making legislative provisions to protect the right of parents without any means to be supported by their children.

Healthcare and Nutrition

Affordable health services, very heavily subsidized for the poor and a graded system of user charges for others; facilitating a judicious mix of health service providers comprising the state, non-governmental organizations, and private medical care; assisting trusts, charitable societies and voluntary agencies to provide health service, free for the very poor, and reasonable user charges for others; promoting health insurance schemes with the provision of state subsidy for packages which cater to lower income groups; strengthening of the public health structure at primary, secondary and tertiary level; expanding geriatric care facilities; facilitating access and utilization of health services by older persons; making much larger public sector allocations in healthcare streamlining the healthcare delivery system, particularly in rural areas; training and orientation of medical personnel in geriatric care; encouraging hospitals to set up Welfare Funds for poor patients; setting up hospices for the chronically ill without any family or financial support; developing educational material on healthcare and nutritional needs in old age and disseminating them among all segments of the population, particularly women; promoting the concept of healthy aging; expanding mental health services; assisting non-governmental organizations; strengthening health education programmes.

Shelter

Increasing the stock of housing for different income segments: earmarking 10 per cent housing/house sites for allotment to older persons; providing easy access to loans for purchase of housing and for major repairs; promoting layouts in residential areas which are sensitive to the requirements of the elderly and facilitate their mobility, accessibility, recreation and safety; earmarking sites for multi-purpose centres for older persons; promoting group housing arrangements with common facilities for meals, laundry, recreation and other services; orienting town planners, architects and housing administrators on the life styles and the needs of older persons; controlling pollution.

Education

Meeting the education, information and training needs of older persons and removing age related discriminations, which hinder access; developing educational material relevant to the lives of older persons and disseminating the same; encouraging and supporting continuing education programmes covering a wide spectrum ranging from career development to skills in community work and welfare activities; including in the curriculum at all stages of formal education material about old age to help strengthen inter-generation bonds; promoting interaction of schools with older persons; disseminating information about the aging process and the contribution of older persons inside the household and outside, and dispelling negative images on ageing.

Welfare

Giving higher priority in welfare services to vulnerable sections such as the poor, the disabled, the infirm, the chronically sick and those without family support; promoting, assisting and supporting institutional and non-institutional services; including old age homes, day care centres, community centres, home visits, counselling services, training and orientation of personnel employed in welfare institutions; setting up Welfare Funds for older persons.

Protection of Life and Property

Ensuring the safety of life and property of older persons through better policing and other measures; protection from fraudulent dealings; protection from physical and emotional abuses within the household and outside.

Other Areas of Action

Concessions to old persons in travel, etc; earmarking seats in public transport and making entry and exit easy for older persons in public transport vehicles; regulating the flow of traffic to facilitate safe movement of older persons when crossing streets or in public places; priority in gas and telephone connections and in fault repair; speedy disposal of complaints; collecting and disseminating information on facilities, concessions and relief given by government and other bodies.

Strengthening the Coping and Caring Capacities of the Family

Promoting and reinforcing family values, promoting and assisting voluntary organizations to provide services to strengthen the coping capacity of families to provide support and care to older persons in the family setting; sensitizing society to accept the role of married daughters in sharing caring responsibilities towards older parents; promoting policies which encourage children to co-reside with parents by allowing tax relief, rebates for medical expenses etc.; promoting short-term stay facilities for older parents so that children can get some relief when they go out on a short vacation or are required to attend to urgent personal matters at other places.

Strengthening Non-governmental Effort

Promoting and strengthening voluntary effort; facilitating networking and exchange of information; streamlining the grant-in-aid policy; supporting initiatives of older persons for advocacy, mobilization of public opinion; supporting the setting up of volunteer programmes.

Media

Involving mass media as well as traditional and non-formal communication channels on ageing issues to sensitize society; promote the concept of active ageing, and to identify emerging issues and areas of action.

For implementing the National Policy, a series of measures have been indicated in the policy statement. These are:

- Widely disseminating the National Policy on Older Persons.
- Setting up collaborative arrangements between different agencies.
- Setting up a separate Bureau of Older Persons in the nodal Ministry of Social Justice & Empowerment to promote and coordinate action.
- Constituting an inter-ministerial Committee to coordinate matters relating to implementation of the national policy and monitor its progress.
- Setting up an autonomous National Council of Older Persons headed by the Minister of Social Justice & Empowerment to promote and coordinate action .
- Urging apex level organizations of older persons to mobilize public opinion, generate pressures, and function as a watchdog.
- Preparation of five year plans and annual action plans for older persons by each ministry indicating the schemes, the targets and the funds needed.
- Making budgetary allocations every year.
- Preparation of a detailed review of progress every three years which will be a public document to be discussed in a national convention to be convened for the purpose.
- Establishing an autonomous National Association of

Older Persons to mobilize senior citizens, articulate their concerns, promote their programmes and advise the government on policy matters relating to older persons. The Association will have national, state and district level offices.

- Involving *panchayati raj* institutions in the implementation of the national policy.
- Seeking collaboration with institutions of civil society.
- Urging state governments to take action to implement the national policy.
- Take assistance from experts on implementation of the policy.

Follow Up Action on the National Policy

As a follow up of the National Policy of Older Persons, a National Council of Older Persons (NCOP) was constituted on 10 May 1999, with the Minister of Social Justice and Empowerment as the Chairperson, and representatives from Central and State ministries, National Human Rights Commission, National Commission for Women, non-governmental organizations, and experts as members. The Council is expected to advise the government on policies and programmes for older persons, organize consultations, and prepare and release to the public at the end of every year a report on the status of older persons. It was also expected to lobby with the government for concessions, rebates and discounts.

The composition of NCOP constituted in 1999 shows that some important Ministries have been left unrepresented as, for instance, the Ministry of Finance, Ministry of Health and Family Welfare, Ministry of Human Resource Development, Ministry of Labour, and the Planning Commission, all of which have a very vital role to play in the implementation of the policy.

Based on the suggestions of NPOP, the Ministry of Social Justice and Empowerment prepared a programme of action indicating the steps that each ministry/department should

undertake. Letters were addressed to central ministries and
state governments for implementing programmes concerning
them. The slow pace of implementation of the policy has been
a matter of concern.

Meetings of the National Council of Older Persons have
been very infrequent. Its first meeting was held in June 2000,
more than 16 months after its constitution. The second meeting
was held in October 2002, twenty-seven months after the first
meeting. The agenda in the meeting did not have specific policy
issues. There was no reference to inter-sectoral concerns and
policy issues, particularly from the main ministries which
impinge on the lives of the elderly, namely, Ministry of
Health and Family Welfare, Ministry of Rural Development,
Ministry of Finance, Ministry of Labour, Ministry of Housing
and Ministry of Home Affairs. The third meeting was on
7 February 2003. The Council hardly performed the intended
functions. The term of the Council ended on May 13, 2004. A
new Council has since been constituted.

The Ministry of Social Justice and Empowerment
functions as the nodal Ministry of NPOP. Yet national policy
statements on several other sectors such as the National Health
Policy (2002) and the National Policy on the Empowerment of
Women (2002), which were introduced by the Government of
India subsequent to NPOP, do not reflect the concerns of older
persons. These documents could have been placed before
NCOP to elicit its views and suggestions for incorporation into
these policy statements.

NPOP is inter-sectoral in character and draws strength
when implemented as an inter-departmental endeavour. Yet
no inputs were prepared by the respective ministries for
incorporation into the Tenth Plan proposals of different
ministries to reflect the needs of older persons. The nodal
ministry, apparently, did not interact with the other ministries,
voicing the need for coordinated action. Similarly, the
legislation on domestic violence against women placed in
Parliament was not taken up for discussion by NCOP. The
Council must play a more inter-active role with other ministries
and voluntary organizations so that the interests of older
persons are adequately reflected.

There are some areas which NPOP has not adequately touched. It has not adequately discussed issues pertaining to old age income security of different segments of the population, particularly workers in the informal sector, and the institutional arrangements that need to be framed so that persons in their working life can save for meeting their needs in old age. Specific directions are needed for health security needs of older persons, particularly in rural areas and urban slums. NPOP has not elaborated on the programmes to be adopted for vulnerable categories such as the chronically sick, the abandoned, the disabled, the deserted and the widowed.

The appointment of the Minister of Social Justice and Empowerment as the Chairperson of NCOP tends to restrict the effectiveness of its recommendations. It would have been much better if the Minister was made the Vice-Chairperson, while the Deputy Chairman of Planning Commission was made the Chairperson so that the multi-sectoral character of interventions could be better discussed, articulated and directions given. To give teeth to NPOP, it would be necessary to set up a National Commission on Older Persons through a statute. While NCOP will look at policy issues and review the same, the Commission will oversee the implementation aspects and ensure that the old persons are not subject to discrimination, and their rights are duly enforced. It could investigate specific complaints of old persons when the normal administrative machinery fails to deliver justice. The monitoring arrangement for NPOP must vest with the Planning Commission. A separate Ministry of Older Persons has to be set up to push the programmes for this segment.

Some constitutional amendments would be necessary to incorporate more specifically the concerns of older persons. Article 15 of the Constitution, which guarantees the right to equality as a Fundamental Right, states in Section (3): "nothing in this Article shall prevent the State from making any special provision for women and children". It would be necessary to include old persons and the disabled in this Section through an amendment in the Constitution. The amended entry would then read as follows: "nothing in this Article shall prevent the

State from making any special provision for women, children, the disabled and the old". Another amendment to the Constitution should be to incorporate under Fundamental Duties a separate clause indicating the duty of every citizen to look after the parents in their old age and not to neglect them in any form. Such a provision will help the centre and the states to have a separate Act on maintenance of parents by children. A third amendment that needs to be introduced is to delete reference to old age in Article 41, a Directive Principle of State Policy, and introduce a new Article (Article 41 A) stating specifically that "The State shall make effective provision for right to social security in old age".

In the coming years, the profile of older persons will undergo changes. There will be a larger percentage of persons with higher education, income levels and professional qualifications. Aspirations of older persons will be different. A large number of persons would view at least the first ten years after 60 years of age as a period where they would be reasonably healthy and can pursue their interests. Grand parenting, religious pursuits and *sanyas* may not be the only options for them. They may have a desire for various other roles which can give them identity and purpose in life. It should be left to older persons to decide whether they wish to rest and relax, to foster relationships with members of the extended family or friends, engage in community work as volunteers, seek creative and productive pursuits, enter into full time or part time work, and/or engage themselves in learning experiences.

Old age is not a crisis. Elderly persons should never be treated only as a liability, or as a burden on the family, the community and the State. Society must consciously inculcate the values of integration between generations. The old have contributed to the nation, the family and community in their prime days. Active ageing for older persons below 75 years of age has to be promoted. They have to be considered as a human resource. Their learning, experience and maturity have to be put to use. A separate human resource development plan for older persons must be prepared which will give them an opportunity to take advantage of new educational and technological advancements and embark on a separate career after retirement. Facilties for education, training and entrepreneurship development have to be promoted. Financial institutions and academic bodies must modify their policy and tailor their programmes to suit the needs of old persons, viewing them as a resource. Discrimination on the bases of age must end. Stereotypes against older persons have to be dispelled as these are not linked to their capacity to contribute. Older persons must themselves collectively seek an identity for themselves as equal partners.

NPOP assured older persons in January 1999, when the statement was adopted by the government, that "their concerns are national concerns, and they will not live unprotected, ignored or marginalized". It added: "the State will extend support for financial security, healthcare, shelter, welfare and other needs of older persons, provide protection against abuse and exploitation, make available opportunities for development of the potential of older persons, seek their participation and provide services so that they can improve the quality of their lives." Unfortunately, these have not been translated into programmes. The State has only acted in providing better deals to its own employees, ignoring the social security needs of ninety-five per cent of the population. This has been one of the most blatant cases of inequalities perpetuated by the government which has acted to benefit only the bureaucracy, indicating that the state's resources are meant primarily for their well-being. The national programme of action of the coalition government voted to power in 2004 has not thought it fit to mention the goals it wishes to achieve for 13 per cent of the electorate. The previous government, too, ignored the concerns, except that the national policy was formulated during its tenure.

Non-governmental organizations must take the initiative to keep NPOP alive and active. They should also prepare a Charter of Rights of Senior Citizens covering health, income maintenance, shelter, care, protection of life and property, leisure and recreation and welfare. They should press upon the central and state governments to adopt the Charter and to implement it. It is tragic that though 13 per cent of the country's electorate comprises persons aged 60 years and above (76.6 million voters, as per the 2001 census, growing annually at the rate of about 3 per cent), the election manifestos make a casual mention of the concerns of older persons. Some do not even mention the subject. The old do not find a place in the agenda of action, when a party is voted to power.

Older persons in India are not organized as a pressure group. The bulk are illiterate, unorganized, dispersed, largely poor, live in backward areas, and have virtually no voice. The organizational and managerial problems of how to organize older persons need to be addressed by non-governmental bodies. They have to mobilize and assert aggressively the concerns of older persons and interact with political parties so that the latter include concerns for the old in their agenda. A fair deal for older persons will be feasible if there is collaborative participation by the legislature and the executive, and also by the individual, the family, the community, the market, non-governmental organizations, and other institutions of civil society.

References

Ahuja, Rajeev (2004): "New pension system: ensuring safeguards", *Economic and Political Weekly*, 12 June, pp. 2429–31.

Anand, Mukesh and Rejeev Ahuja (2004): "Government Pensions: Liability and Assumptions", *Economic and Political Weekly*, 19 June, pp. 2569–76.

Angra, S.K. G.V.S. Murthy, S.K. Gupta and Vivek Angra (1997): 'Cataract related blindness in India, and its social implications', *Indian Journal of Medical Research*, Vol. I, October, pp. 312–324.

Anklesaria, P.S., S.M. Pohujani, V.J. Ashar, K.N. Joshi and K.C. Gupta, (1996): "Demographic and clinical characteristics of the urban elderly people", In Vinod Kumar ed., *Ageing; Indian Perspective and Global Scenario.* New Delhi: Proceedings of the International Symposium on Gerontology and Seventh Conference of the Association of Gerontology, India.

Bachani, D., G.V.S. Murthy and K.S. Gupta (2000): "Rapid assessment of cataract blindness in India", *Indian Journal of Pediatrics*, Vol, 34, no. 3, pp. 82–89.

Bahl, V.K., D. Prabhakaran and G. Karthikeyan (2001): "Coronary artery disease in Indian", *Indian Heart Journal*, Vol. 53, November-December, pp. 707–13.

Bahl, V.K., D. Prabhakaran and G. Kartikeyan (2001): "Coronary artery disease in Indians", *Indian Heart Journal*, Vol. 53, pp. 707–13.

Bhat, P.N. Mari (1998): "Widowhood and mortality in India" in Martha Alter Chen ed. *Widows in India: Social Neglect and Public Action*, New Delhi: Sage Publication.

Bose, A.B. (1982): "Social Welfare Services for the Aged in India". In K.G. Desai, ed. *Ageing in India*, Bombay: Tata Institute of Social Sciences.

Bose, A.B. and K.D. Gangrade (1988): *The Ageing in India*, New Delhi: Abhinav Publications.

Bose, A.B. (1996): "Caring for the aged: programmes and services", In *Added Years of Life*, Bangkok: UN ESCAP.

Chadha, S.L., S.Radhakrishnan, K. Ramachandran, Ukaul and N. Gopinath (1990): "Epidemiological study of coronary heart disease in urban population of Delhi", *Indian Journal of Medical Research*, December, pp. 424-30.

Common Cause (1987): *Common Cause*, Vol. 6, No. 1.

Dalal, P.M. (1997): "Strokes in the elderly: prevalence, risk factors and the strategies for prevention," *Indian Journal of Medical Research*, Vol. 106, October, pp. 325-332.

Dandekar, Kumudini (1996): *The Elderly in India*, New Delhi: Sage Publications.

Dandona, Lalit, Rakhi Dandona and Rakesh K. John (2001): "Estimation of blindness in India from 2000 through 2020: Implications of the blindness control policy", *The National Medical Journal of India*, Vol. 14, No. 6, pp. 327-334.

De, Shobhaa, (2005): "Insurance or Con-game", *Times of India*, 4 September, New Delhi.

Department of Food and Public Distribution (2003, 2004, 2005): *Annual Reports*, New Delhi.

Department of Posts, (2005): *Annual Report* 2004-2005, New Delhi: Government of India.

Dey, A.B. and D. Chaudhary (1997): Infections in the elderly", *Indian Journal of Medical Research* , Vol. 106, October, pp. 273-282.

Dhoot, Vikas, (2005): "EPFO to zero in on 8 per cent at today's meet", *Indian Express*, 7 December, New Delhi.

Duggal, Ravi and Sucheta Amin (1997): "Morbidity, healthcare utilization and expenditure: Maharashtra 1987", in *Household Health Expenditure in Two States*, Mumbai/Pune Foundation for Research in Community Health.

Employees' Provident Fund Organization (1997 to 2002): *Annual Reports*, New Delhi.

Employees' State Insurance Corporation (2002): *Annual Report*, New Delhi.

Enas, A.E., A. Garg, M. Davidson, V.M. Nair, B.A. Huet, Salim

Yusuf (1996): "Coronary heart disease and its risk factors in first generation immigrant Asian Indians to the United States of America, *Indian Heart Journal*, July-August, pp. 343-353.

George, Alex, Ila Shah and Sunil Nandraj (1997): Morbidity, healthcare utilization and expenditure: Madhya Pradesh 1990-91 in *Household Health Expenditure in Two States*, Mumbai/Pune: Foundation for Research in Community Health.

Government of India (1984): Against Undeserved Want, *Report of the Working Group on Social Security*, Economic Administration Reforms Commission, New Delhi.

Gulati, Leela and Mitu Gulati (1997): "Female labour in the unorganized sector: the brick worker revisited", *Economic and Political Weekly*, 3 May, pp. 68-71.

Gulati, Leela, (1998): "The Poor Widows of Kootam: A study of widows in a squatter settlement". In Maratha Alter Chan ed *Widows in India: Social Neglect and Public Action*, New Delhi: Sage Publishers.

Gupta, Sanjeev K., G.V.S. Murthy and S.K. Angra (1996): "Social implications of cataract related blindness in rural India". In *Ageing: Indian Perspective and Global Scenario*, New Delhi: All India Institute of Medical Sciences.

Gurumurthy, K. G. (1998): *The Aged in India*, New Delhi: Reliance Publishing House.

Harmony (2004): "Rest assured", August, pp. 6-7.

Hasan, Saiyid Zafar (1963): *Federal Grants and Public Assistance*, Allahabad: Kitab Mahal.

HelpAge India (2003): "Non-contributory pensions in India: A case study of Uttar Pradesh", paper presented at the *Seminar on Social Assistance for the Elderly*, 1-20 January.

HelpAge. India (2004): Twenty-five Years, New Delhi.

Indian Council of Medical Research (1983): *Collaborative Study in Prevalence and Aetiology of Hearing Impairment*, New Delhi.

Indian Council of Medical Research (1991): *Evaluation of Quality of Family Welfare Services at Primary Health Centre Level*, New Delhi.

International Institute of Population Sciences (2000): *National Family Health Survey*, 1998–99, Mumbai.

Jesani, Amar, Ravi Duggal and Manisha Gupta (1996): *NGOs in Rural Health Care*, Mumbai/Pune: Foundation for Research in Community Health.

Kacker, S.K. (1997) "Hearing impairment in the aged", *Indian Journal of Medical Research*, Vol. 106, October, pp. 333–37.

Khetarpal, K., S. Soneja and Vinod Kumar (1996): "Physical and neuro-psychiatric impairments amongst the aged and their relationship to socio-economic status". In *Ageing: Indian Perspective and Global Scenario*, New Delhi: All India Institute of Medical Sciences.

Malaker, C.R. and S. Guha Roy (1990): "Reconstruction of Indian life table for 1901–81 and projections for 1981–2001, *Sankhya*, Vol. 52, Series B, Pt.3.

Ministry of Finance (2000): *Report of the Eleventh Finance Commission*, New Delhi.

Ministry of Finance (2002, 2003, 2004): *Economic Survey 2001–02, 2002–03, 2003–04*, New Delhi.

Ministry of Health and Family Welfare (2004): *Annual Report: 2003–04*, New Delhi. Government of India.

Ministry of Home Affairs (2004): *Annual Report, 2003–04*, New Delhi.

Ministry of Labour (2004): *Annual Report, 2003–04*, New Delhi.

Ministry of Labour (2004): *Report of the National Commission on Labour*, New Delhi.

Ministry of Social Justice and Empowerment (1999): *National Policy on Older Persons*, New Delhi.

Mohan, Madan (1989): *National Survey of Blindness, India*, New Delhi: All India Institute of Medical Sciences.

Nair, Jyotsna (2001): "The economic aspects of diabetes in India", *The Social Researcher*, 1 June, pp 121–14 (newsletter).

Nair, T. Krishnan (1980): *Older People in Tamil Nadu, Madras*: Madras School of Social Work.

National Sample Survey Organization (1998): *Morbidity and Treatment of Ailments*, NSS Fifty-second Round, July 1995–June 1996, New Delhi : Department of Statistics.

National Sample Survey Organization (1998): *The Aged in India: A Socio-Economic Profile*, NSS, Fifty-second Round. July 1995–June 1996, New Delhi : Department of Statistics.

Natrajan, V.S. (1997): "Common geriatric problems", *Research and Development Journal*, Vol. 3, No. 2, pp. 3–11.

Panda, Pradeep Kumar, (1998): "The Elderly in Rural Orissa: Alone in Distress", *Economic and Political Weekly*, 20 June, pp. 1545–1550.

Planning Commission (2001): *Report of the Task Force on Employment Opportunities*, New Delhi.

Pradeepa, R and V. Mohan (2002): "The changing scenario of the diabetics epidemic: Implications for India", *Indian Journal of Medical Research*, Vol. 116, October, pp. 121–132.

Prasad, K.V. Eswara (1998): "The pension scheme for widows in Tamil Nadu". In *Widows in India: Social Neglect and Public Action*, New Delhi. Sage Publications.

Programme Evaluation Organization (1999): *Evaluation Study on Functioning of Community Health Centres*, New Delhi.

Rajan, Irudaya, U.S. Mishra and P.S. Sarma (1999): *India's Elderly: Burden or Challenge*, New Delhi: Sage.

Rao, A. Venkoba (1990): *Health Care of the Rural Aged*, New Delhi: Indian Council of Medical Research.

Rao, Venkoba (1997): "Psychiatric morbidity in the aged", *Indian Journal of Medical Research*, Vol. 106, October, pp. 361–369.

Registrar General (1990 to 2001): *Annual Statistical Reports of Sample Registration System*, New Delhi.

Registrar General of India (1961, 1971, 1981, 1991, 2000, 2001): *Census Reports.*

Registrar General (1996): *Population Projections for India and States, 1996–2016*, New Delhi.

Registrar General (1999): *Ageing Population in India: An Analysis of the 1991 Census Data*, New Delhi.

Registrar General (2000, 2002): *Survey of Causes of Death, Rural*, New Delhi.

Registrar General (2000): *SRS Abridged Life Tables*, New Delhi.

Reserve Bank of India (2003): *State Finances: A Study of Budgets 2002–03*, Bombay.

Shah, Bela and A.K. Prabhakar (1997): "Chronic morbidity profile among elderly", *Indian Journal of Medical Research,* Vol. 106, October, pp. 265–272.

Sharma, K.L. and B.G. Prasad (1962): "An epidemiological study of blindness in Banki Block of Barabanki district, Uttar Pradesh", *Indian Journal of Medical Research,* Vol. 50, No. 6, November, pp. 842–863.

Society for Development Studies (1999): *Evaluation of NSAP in Uttar Pradesh,* New Delhi (cyclostyled).

Srivastava, Mamta, Umesh Kapil, Vinod Kumar, A.B. Dey, K.M. Nagarkar and G. Sekaran (1996): "Knowledge, attitude and practices regarding nutrition in patients attending geriatric clinic at AIIMS", in Vinod Kumar ed, *Ageing: Indian Perspective and Global Scenario,* New Delhi: All India Institute of Medical Sciences.

Statesman, (2001): "Even dead are eligible for Delhi govt's pension", 6 April, New Delhi.

Swain, Sibani and Pronab Sen (2004): *Pension Liabilities of the Central Government: Projections and Implications,* New Delhi: Planning Commission.

Times of India, (2005): "Courtesy Left, it's curtains for Pension Bill", 27 July, New Delhi.

United Nations (1994): *Ageing and the Family,* New York.

United Nations (2003): *World Population Prospects: The 2002 Revision,* Vol. 1 & 2, New York.

Vijaya Kumar, S. (1998): "Health services for the rural elderly", *Social Change,* Vol. 28, No. 4, pp. 71–76.

Wadhwa, Arvind, M. Sabharwal and Sushma Sharma (1997): "National Status of the Elderly", *Journal of Medical Research,* 106, October, pp. 340–48.

Index

Abuse: concept, 226-27, 232; forms, 227-28; perpetrators, 229, abandonment, 229, widows, 229-30; role of NGOs, 230-31
Accidental deaths, 224-25, 232
Age distribution, broad age groups: more developed regions, 8; less developed regions, 8; India, 24-25
Age distribution, older persons, more developed regions, 10-12, 46; less developed regions, 10-12, 46; India, 27-28
Ageing, India, 17-18, 46
Ageing, selected countries, 15-17, 46
Age and sex pyramid, India, 21, 23
Aged population, more developed regions, 2-4; less developed regions, 2-4
Aged population in electorate, India, 43-44, 47, 252
Annapurna scheme, 83-84, 137
Antodaya Anna Yojana, 84-85, 137
Article 41, Directive Principle, 233, 237, 250

Beijing Declaration and Platform for Action, 239

Central Government Health Scheme, 182-86, 200
Changing family environment and care, 48-50, 202-07
Charter of Rights, 251

Community based universal health insurance, 197-98
Concurrent List, 233, 236
Contributory Provident Fund, 109-10, 112
Cooperatives in health care, 179-81
Criminal Procedure Code, 234-35
Critical illness insurance, 191-93, 195-96, 200

Day care centres, 220
Decadal increase in age segments, more developed regions, 9-10; less developed regions 9-10; India, 26, 46
Demographic projections on ageing: world 3, more developed regions, 3, 9-10, 45; less developed regions, 3, 9-10, 45, India, 46
Dependency ratio: more developed regions, 12-13; less developed regions 13; India, 29, 46, 48-49
Directive Principle, 233, 250
Domestic violence, 230, 248
Disability: types, 164-68; inter state variation, 165-66

Employees' Deposit Linked Insurance Scheme, 94, 96
Employees' Pension Scheme, 94, 97, 102-05, 135
Employees' Provident Fund, 94-102, 134-35
Employees' State Insurance Scheme, 186-87, 200

Employment in organized sector, 63-64

Employment status, 61-62, 134-35

Expectation of life at birth; world, 1, 4-5, more developed regions, 5-6, less developed regions 4-6, India, 19-20, 138-39

Expectation of life at age 60 years: India, 139-40; rural urban, 140-41, 146; states, 142-46

Expectation of life at age 70 years: India, 139-40; rural urban, 140-41, 145-46

Family environment and care, 48-50, 202-08

Fifth Central Pay Commission, 113-15, 117, 120, 135

Finance Commission, 73-74, 117, 135

Food rations, 83-84, 137

Fundamental Duty, 250

Fundamental Right, 249

General Provident Fund, 110-11

Gratuity, 108-09

Health care providers: public sector, 170-74, 199, 201; private sector, 174-76, 199, non-governmental, 176-79, 199

Health cooperatives, 179-81

Health insurance, 181-98, 200

Himachal Pradesh Maintenance of Parents and Dependents' Act, 235

Hindu Adoptions and Maintenance Act, 234

Human resource development for older persons, 250

Insurance, 125-28, 136

International Covenant on Economic, Social and Cultural Rights, 238

International Labour Organization, 238-39

International Plan of Action on Ageing, 239

International Year of Older Persons, 239

Jan Arogya Bima Policy, 192

Krishi Shramik Samaj Suraksha Yojana, 88

Leave encashment, 108

Legal responsibility of children, 234-36

Legislations, 234-36

Literacy status, 38-40, 47

Living arrangements, 207-11, 231

LIC, 129, 193-94, 217-18

Malnutrition, 169-70

Marital status of older persons, India, 31-37

Median age: world, 7: more developed regions, 6-7, 44-45, less developed regions, 6-7, 44-45; India and states, 20-21, 22, 47

Mediclaim, 187-91

Morbidity, 156-63

Mortality: age distribution, India, 147, states, 148, age specific death rate,India, 150-51, 198; rural urban, 151-53; sex, 151-52; states, 151-53

Mutual Funds, 131-33

National Commission on Labour, 85, 100

National Commission on Older Persons, 249

National Commission on Rural Labour, 85
National Commission on Self Employed Women and Women in Informal Sector, 85
National Council of Older Persons, 247-49
National Health Policy, 197, 240, 248
National Housing Policy, 240
National Nutrition Policy, 240
National Old Age Pension Scheme, 74-77, 240
National Policy on Empowerment of Women, 248
National Policy on Older Persons: legislation provisions, 233-36; evolution, 236-41; principles, 241-42; areas of intervention, 242-46; implementation, 246-47; follow up action 247-48, 251; critique, 249-50
National Social Assistance Programme, 74

OASIS, 90-93, 134
Old age homes, 137, 218-22, 233
, Old age pensions: evolution, 66-69, 73-74, 136, 236; criteria, 69-72; quantum 72-73; budgetary provisions 73-74; national old age pension scheme, 74-77, 240; implementation problems, 77-79; norms, 79-81; state schemes, 81-82; freedom fighters, 82-83, 187

Pension: from government, 111-25; insurance companies and mutual funds, 127
Pension Fund Regulatory and Development Authority, 123-24

Planning for old age, 50-51
Planning Commission, 73-74, 237
Post Office Savings Schemes, 130-31
Poverty line, India and states, 64-66
Proclamation on Ageing and Global Targets, 239
Protection of life, 222-24, 232
Public Provident Fund, 105-07, 135

Reserve Bank of India, 121
Role of central and state governments, 236-41
Rural urban distribution, 31

Savings schemes, 128-31
Second World Assembly of Ageing, 239
Sex ratio among older persons: more developed regions, 14-15, 46; less developed regions, 14-15, 46, India, 30
Senior Citizens' Savings Schemes, 129
Shelter: ownership, 212-13; rooms, 214, 231; facilities, 215-16, 231; market, 216-18, 232
Singapore Maintenance of Parents' Act, 235
Suicides, 225-26
Supreme Court, 111, 113-14

Unemployment, 66

Unit Trust of India Senior Citizens Unit Plan, 194-95
Universal Declaration of Human Rights, 238
United Nations Principles for Older Persons, 239
Unorganized sector workers: financial insecurity, 85-88; OASIS, 90-93, 133

Unorganized sector social security schemes, 88-89; state schemes, 89-90

Varistha Pension Bima Yojana Scheme, 129
Victims of crime, 222-24

Widowed old, 31-37, 46, 229-30

Work category, 59-61
Work participation: age and sex, 51-54, 57-59, 134; states, 54-56; rural urban, 51-54
World Assembly on Ageing, 238-39
World Summit on Social Development, 239